Minnesota's State Parks
By Anne Arthur

Adventure Publications, Inc.
Cambridge, Minnesota

The following is take from the Minnesota Department of Natural Resources. Although not stated in the following rules, collecting, or even hunting for Indian artifacts on public land is against state law.

So Everyone Can Enjoy the Park

The Park Belongs to all Minnesotans. Please treat it with respect and help us to protect it by following the rules.

The park is open year-round. On a daily basis, the park gate is closed from 10:00 PM to 8:00 AM the following morning except to registered campers.

Camp in designated locations.

The use of firearms, explosives, air guns, slingshots, traps, seines, nets, bows and arrows, and all other weapons is prohibited in state parks.

Pets must be restrained on a leash no longer than six feet. Pets are not allowed in park buildings.

Park in designated areas only.

Motor bikes and other licensed vehicles are allowed only on park roads, not on trails.

Enjoy park wildlife and plants but please respect them. Do not pick or dig up plants, disturb or feed animals, or scavenge dead wood.

Build fires only in designated locations – fire rings or fireplaces. Wood is available for purchase from park staff. Portable stoves or grills are permitted.

Daily or annual permits are required for all vehicles entering a state park. The may be purchased at the park headquarters or the Information Center in St. Paul.

Copyright 1998 by Anne Arthur
Published by Adventure Publications
PO Box 269
Cambridge, MN 55008
1-800-678-7006
All Rights Reserved
Printed in the United States of America
ISBN 1-885061-51-X
Book design by Paula Roth and Jonathan A. Norberg

Special Thanks to The Minnesota Department of Natural Resources, the Adventure Staff, Gene Colan, Stuart Immonen, Joe R. Landsdale, and Charles Beaumont.

INTRODUCTION

As a native Minnesotan and avid camper, I've always felt blessed by all of the amazing places in my home state. For several years I've wanted to check out Minnesota's various state parks, but wasn't sure that they would be to my liking. "Too many people," I thought, "too much noise and 'civilization.'" But I finally decided to give them a try, and with at least one of my two children in tow, I went to check out the parks. I was amazed at all the things to explore and learn. Today, I think I could spend the rest of my life in these parks and still not see it all.

My goal in writing this book was to gather the essential information about Minnesota's State Parks, and assemble it all into an easy-to-use package. I tried to be as non-judgmental as possible, allowing others to find the parks that fit their needs.

As I worked on the project, I discovered that there was no one place to find all the information I wanted to include in my book. I also discovered that the information I found in one source often conflicted with the information given in another! So others can avoid this confusion, I've pulled together the most accurate data available.

For additional information on the establishment of the state park system, read "Everyone's Country Estate" by Roy Meyer, Published in 1991 by the Minnesota Historical Society Press.

MINNESOTA'S STATE PARKS

Minnesota's first state park, Itasca, was established in 1891. This foresight has enabled pieces of land rich in beauty, history, and resources to be protected for future generations.

Many of the early state parks were established around historical sites. As Minnesota's population began to grow, some parks were also established to provide recreation near large population sources.

At the time of this writing, there are 68 established State Parks in Minnesota. They encompass the full-range of Minnesota's environment, offering lush woodlands, prairies, river blufflands, rivers, and lake shores. Each of these parks also offers plenty of places to relax, explore, and enjoy the outdoors.

With hundreds of miles of scenic foot-trails, hiking is one of the most popular park activities. Many parks also offer interpretative trails, with signs or brochures that offer information about the flora, fauna, and history of the park. In the winter, many of these trails are transformed into cross-country ski trails.

Biking is another popular park activity, park roads are always available for bicyclists and several parks offer paved off-road bike trails. In addition to these trails, 14 parks offer mountain bike trails (usually following snowmobile trails).

Many parks offer pleasant places for picnicking for an afternoon getaway, Some of the parks have large shelters which can be reserved for group use.

Swimming facilities can be found in 33 State Parks, varying from sandy lake shores to man-made, sand-bottomed swimming pools. The rivers, streams, and lakes found in many parks provide wonderful fishing and boating.

Many parks offer interpretative programs, which include hikes, slide shows, films, bird watching, collecting maple syrup, and other learning opportunities, Some of the programs are only offered at certain times of the year, so be sure to check with the park office for the schedule. School groups or organizations can contact the park naturalists to arrange special programs.

Camping is offered at most of the parks. The camping facilities vary widely, from the ultra-primitive to the ultra-modern. No matter what type of camping you desire, a park can be found that will meet your needs. Campsites designated as walk-in sites are generally more rustic, and located less than a quarter mile from a parking area. Backpack sites are typically more than a quarter mile from the parking areas, and water may not be readily available in the area. Canoe sites are accessible from lakes or rivers. Eighteen parks offer horse campsites, which provide hitching posts, water, and room for horse-trailers.

GENERAL PARK INFORMATION

State parks are open to the public from 8:00 AM to 10:00PM daily.

State Park Permits are required on all vehicles. Daily and annual passes may be purchased at any state park or from the Department of Natural Resources Building, 500 Lafayette Road, St. Paul, MN.

Campsites can be reserved from 3 to 90 days in advance. (This is recommended for the more popular parks.) Parks that offer camping cabins and modern or group campsites require reservations in advance. Reservations can be made 24 hours a day, seven days a week by calling 1-800-246-CAMP, or 612-922-9000 in the metro area. There is a non-refundable fee for site reservation. Each park also has sites available on a "first come, first serve" basis.

Permits and camping fees may be paid for by cash, check, Visa, or Mastercard.

Some parks offer accommodations other than campgrounds. These facilities can be rented, and reservations are required.

GUEST HOUSES

Bear Head Lake, Scenic, St. Croix, and Wild River State Parks offer guest houses for smaller groups. The houses are accessible by car, and available on a year round basis. Guest houses include multiple bedrooms, bathrooms, and fully equipped kitchens. Visitors are required to bring their own linens. Check the individual park listings for further information.

MODERN GROUP CENTERS

Modern Group Centers are available in six state parks: Flandreau, Lake Carlos, Lake Shetek, St. Croix, Sibley, and Whitewater. These centers are the perfect place for large gatherings, offering a great wilderness experience with modern facilities. These centers have dining areas, kitchens, lodging areas, and bathrooms. Visitors must bring their own linens and food to the otherwise equipped centers. Whitewater's group center is the only one that is winterized. Check the individual park listings for further information.

SEMI-MODERN GROUP CENTERS

Myre-Big Island and Itasca have semi-modern group centers available, offering a dining hall, kitchen, and bathrooms only. Visitors must have their own tents or RVs for sleeping. Check the individual park listings for further information.

CAMPING CABINS

Some state parks have camping cabins available for rent. They are generally small cabins with bunks but no water or electricity – perfect for people who wish to enjoy the parks but don't have the equipment for camping. Check the individual park listings for further information.

CLUBS

The Minnesota State Parks system runs two "clubs" – the Passport Club and the Hiking Club.

Passport Club. After paying a small membership fee, members receive a passport, tote bag, journal, and map of the state. Each time they visit a park they have their passport stamped at the park office, with the goal of fulling their passport. After 8, 16, 32, 48, and 68 parks have been visited, members receive patches. A certificate for a free night of camping is awarded after visiting 32 and 68 parks.

Hiking Club. After paying the membership fee, members receive a fanny pack and a booklet allowing them to keep track of their hikes. Sixty-two parks have trails designated as part of the hiking club. Awards patches are given after hiking 25, 50, 75, and 100 miles, and certificates for a free night of camping are awarded after 75 and 100 miles.

Photo by author

MINNESOTA STATE PARKS

1. Afton State Park
2. Banning State Park
3. Bear Head State Park
4. Beaver Creek Valley State Park
5. Big Stone Lake State Park
6. Blue Mounds State Park
7. Buffalo River State Park
8. Camden State Park
9. Carley State Park
10. Cascade River State Park
11. Charles A. Lindberg State Park
12. Crow Wing State Park
13. Father Hennepin State Park
14. Flandreau State Park
15. Forestville/Mystery Cave State Park
16. Fort Ridgely State Park
17. Fort Snelling State Park
18. Franz Jevene State Park
19. Frontenac State Park
20. George H. Crosby-Manitou State Park
21. Glacial Lakes State Park
22. Glendalough State Park
23. Gooseberry Falls State Park
24. Grand Portage State Park
25. Great River Bluffs State Park
26. Hayes Lake State Park
27. Hill Annex State Park
28. Interstate State Park
29. Itasca State Park
30. Jay Cooke State Park
31. John A. Latsch State Park
32. Judge C.R. Magney State Park
33. Kilen Woods State Park
34. Lac Qui Parle State Park
35. Lake Bemidji State Park
36. Lake Bronson State Park
37. Lake Carlos State Park
38. Lake Louise State Park
39. Lake Maria State Park
40. Lake Shetek State Park
41. McCarthy Beach State Park
42. Maplewood State Park
43. Mille Lacs Kathio State Park
44. Minneopa State Park
45. Minnesota Valley Trail State Park
46. Monson Lake State Park
47. Moose Lake State Park
48. Myre-Big Island State Park
49. Nerstrand Big Woods State Park
50. Old Mill State Park
51. Rice Lake State Park
52. St. Croix State Park
53. Sakatah Lake State Park
54. Savanna Portage State Park
55. Scenic State Park
56. Schoolcraft State Park
57. Sibley State Park
58. Soudan Underground Mine State Park
59. Split Rock Creek State Park
60. Split Rock Lighthouse State Park
61. Temperance River State Park
62. Tettegouche State Park
63. Upper Sioux Agency State Park
64. Whitewater State Park
65. Wild River State Park
66. William O'Brien State Park
67. Zippel Bay State Park

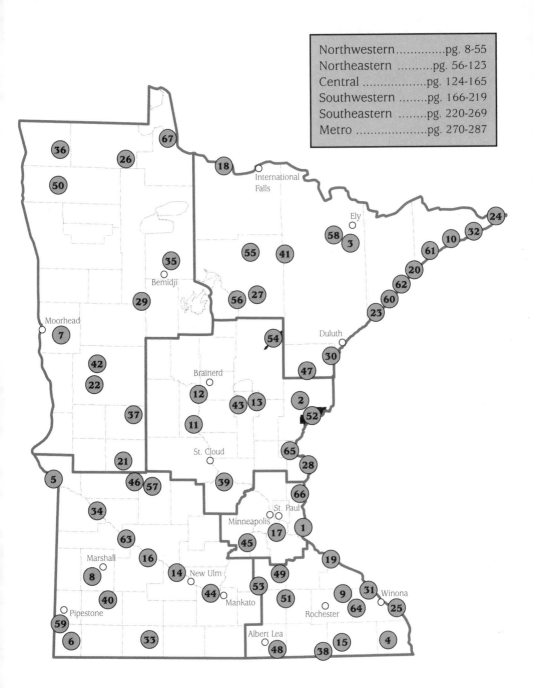

PARK	ACREAGE
Buffalo River State Park	1,367 acres
Glacial Lakes State Park	1,755 acres
Glendalough State Park	1,924 acres
Hayes Lake State Park	2,950 acres
Itasca State Park	32,690 acres
Lake Bemidji State Park	1,688 acres
Lake Bronson State Park	2,983 acres
Lake Carlos State Park	1,174 acres
Maplewood State Park	9,250 acres
Old Mill State Park	287 acres
Zippel Bay State Park	2,906 acres

NORTHWESTERN REGION

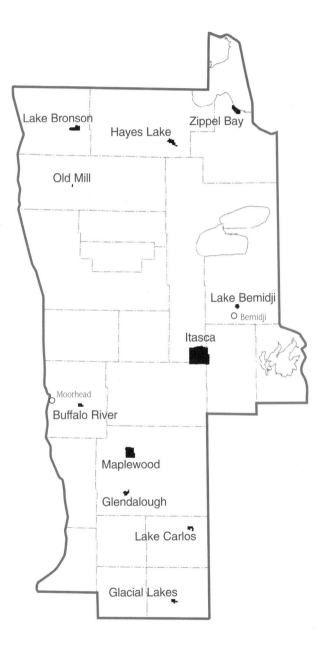

Lake Bronson

Hayes Lake

Zippel Bay

Old Mill

Lake Bemidji

O Bemidji

Itasca

Moorhead
O

Buffalo River

Maplewood

Glendalough

Lake Carlos

Glacial Lakes

Buffalo River State Park
RR 2 Box 256
Glyndon, MN 56542
218-498-2124

DIRECTIONS

The park is located just off Highway 10 west of Moorhead.

ABOUT THE PARK

Buffalo River State Park, which covers 1,367 acres, was created in 1937. The Works Progress Administration (WPA) came to the park during the late 1930s to construct the park's roads, toilets, swimming area, and two small dams. The park preserves a remnant of what people would have encountered when they first traveled to this area. It offers a large undisturbed prairie, and the woods along the river must have been an oasis for early travelers.

The recreational facilities make the park very popular for the local residents, and visitors can see up to 250 species of wild flowers and native grasses.

IF YOU GO . . .

Bring you hiking shoes and binoculars! Try the trail through the woods and prairie that border the Buffalo River. Keep an eye out along the banks of the river for birds, wildflowers, and old buffalo bones.

BUFFALO RIVER STATE PARK

FACILITIES

Visitor Center:	seasonal Visitor Center
Picnic Area:	picnic area with an enclosed shelter

RECREATION

Children's play area:	no
Horseshoe pits:	yes
Volleyball courts:	no
Swimming:	swimming beach
Fishing:	river fishing
Boating:	no

CAMPGROUND

Campsites:	44 drive-in campsites
Electric:	8 electric campsites
Hike or carry-in:	no
Canoe campsites:	no
Dump station:	yes
Toilets:	flush toilets
Showers:	yes
Group Campground:	primitive group campground

TRAILS

Hiking Trails:	12 miles
Hiking Club Trail:	4.4 miles, starting at the Savanna Cut Off self-guided trail
Biking Trails:	no
Cross-country Ski:	8 miles
Warming house:	yes
Snowmobile Trails:	no
Horse Trails:	no
Horse Campsites:	no

INTERPRETIVE PROGRAMS

Seasonal interpretive programs are available in the park, including a one-mile self-guided nature trail. The Visitor Center is also seasonal, and offers interpretive exhibits.

BUFFALO RIVER STATE PARK

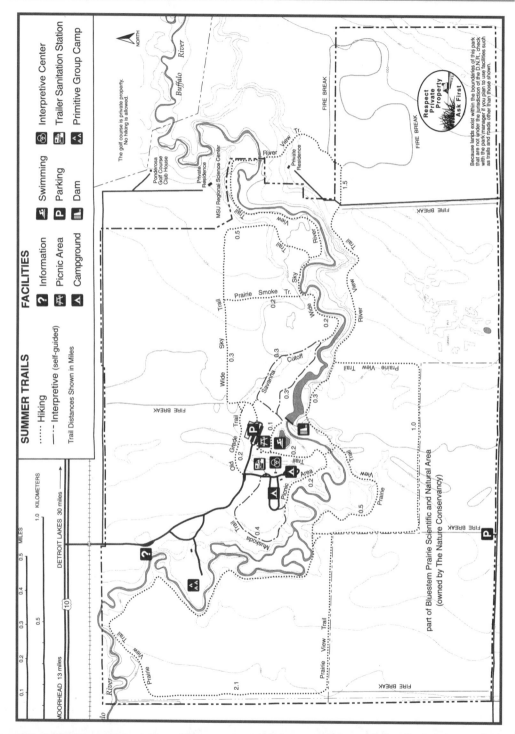

SUMMER TRAILS

- ...... Hiking
- – – – Interpretive (self-guided)

Trail Distances Shown in Miles

FACILITIES

? Information	🏊 Swimming	ⓘ Interpretive Center
🏕 Picnic Area	P Parking	🚽 Trailer Sanitation Station
⛺ Campground	🏚 Dam	⛺⛺ Primitive Group Camp

Buffalo River

Ponderosa Golf Course Club House

The golf course is private property. No hiking is allowed.

Private Residence

MSU Regional Science Center

River View Tr.

Private Residence

River View Trail

Sky Trail

Prairie Smoke Tr.

Wide View Trail

Wide Sky Trail

Savanna Cutoff

River View Trail

Prairie View Trail

Old Grade Trail

Muskoda Trail

Picnic Area

Prairie View Trail

Prairie View Trail

FIRE BREAK

FIRE BREAK

FIRE BREAK

FIRE BREAK

Respect Private Property Ask First

Because lands exist within the boundaries of this park that are not under the jurisdiction of the D.N.R., check with the park manager if you plan to use facilities such as trails and roads other than those shown.

part of Bluestem Prairie Scientific and Natural Area (owned by The Nature Conservancy)

NORTH

MOORHEAD 13 miles

DETROIT LAKES 30 miles

10

MILES

KILOMETERS

0.1 0.2 0.3 0.4 0.5 1.0

American Robin Photo by Dudley Edmondson

NEARBY PLACES TO VISIT

Clay County Museum and Archives - Moorhead, 218-233-4604
Comstock House - Moorhead, 218-233-0848, 218-291-4211
Heritage-Hjemkomst Interpretive Center - Moorhead, 218-233-5604
Moorhead/Fargo Convention and Visitor's Bureau - Fargo, 800-235-7654, 701-282-3653
MSU Regional Science Center - Moorhead, 218-236-2904

OUR NOTES

Date visited   What we liked

T R I V I A

*Check out the virgin prairie at Buffalo River State Park
and Blue Mounds State Park.*

GLACIAL LAKES STATE PARK

Glacial Lakes State Park
RR 2 Box 126
Starbuck, MN 56381
320-239-2860

DIRECTIONS

The park is located 5 miles south of Starbuck on County Road 41.

ABOUT THE PARK

Glacial Lakes State Park encompasses about 1,880 acres of hills and valleys, created by glaciers that moved through the area more than 10,000 years ago. The park was created in 1963, and features several lakes and marshes. Mountain Lake, the largest in the park, is spring fed and makes for excellent swimming. There are hiking trails along the ridges, offering many enjoyable views. Many trails also feature interpretive signs which explain the park's wildlife, flora, and fauna. For more information, the park office offers brochures on the prarieland and wildflowers.

IF YOU GO . . .

Bring your horse! Glacial Lakes offers miles of horseback riding trails. Start at the trail center and ride the trails along the ridges for some scenic panoramas. If horses aren't your thing, you can hike the trail, starting from any of the parking lots. This trail heads around Mountain Lake, so stops can be made at any of the four fishing piers or the swimming beach.

GLACIAL LAKES STATE PARK

FACILITIES

Visitor Center: no
Picnic Area: 2 picnic areas with an open shelter along Mountain Lake

RECREATION

Children's play area: yes
Horseshoe pit: no
Volleyball courts: yes
Swimming: swimming beach on Mountain Lake
Fishing: lake fishing
                       fishing pier on Mountain Lake
Boating: boating on Mountain Lake with launch access
                       boat and canoe rental

CAMPGROUND

Campsites: 2 campgrounds
                       total of 42 drive-in campsites
Electric: 14 electric campsites
Hike or carry-in: 4 backpack campsites
Canoe campsites: no
Dump station: yes
Toilets: flush toilets
Showers: yes
Group Campground: yes

TRAILS

Hiking Trails: 16 miles
Hiking Club Trail: 4.7 miles, starting at the southeast picnic area
Biking Trails: 4 miles of bike trails are nearby
Cross-country Ski: 6 miles
Snowmobile Trails: 11 miles
Horse Trails: 11 miles
Horse Campsites: 3 horse campsites

INTERPRETIVE PROGRAMS

Although there are no established interpretive programs at the park, the park staff occasionally offers programs, so visitors are encouraged to check in at the office for their availability. There are interpretive signs posted all along the trails, and brochures are available in the park office.

GLACIAL LAKES STATE PARK

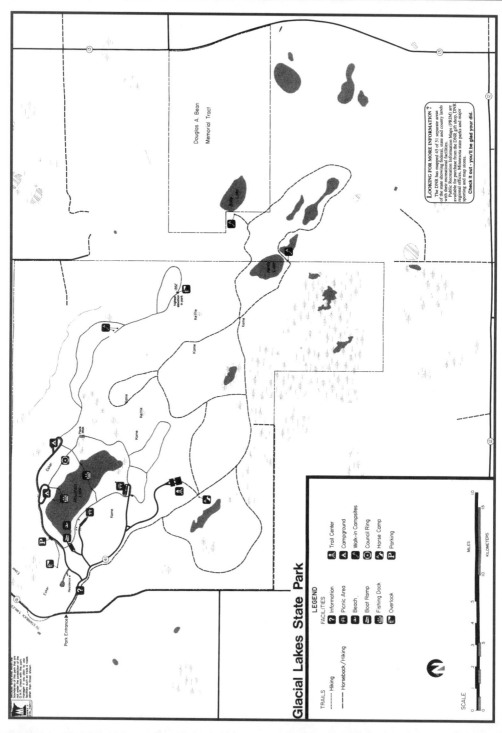

Glacial Lakes State Park

LEGEND

TRAILS

······· Hiking

——— Horseback / Hiking

FACILITIES

🅰	Trail Center
2	Information
🚻	Picnic Area
🛥	Boat Ramp
🎣	Fishing Dock
🔭	Overlook

🏕	Campground
🥾	Walk-in Campsites
⊙	Council Ring
🐎	Horse Camp
🅿	Parking

SCALE

Douglas A. Bean Memorial Tract

LOOKING FOR MORE INFORMATION ?
The DNR has mapped 45 of 51 separate areas of the state showing federal, state and county lands with their recreational facilities.
Public Recreation Information Maps (PRIM) are available for purchase from the DNR gift shop, DNR regional offices, Minnesota state parks and major sporting and map stores.
Check it out - you'll be glad you did.

Black-Capped Chickadee   Photo by Dudley Edmondson

NEARBY PLACES TO VISIT

Glacial Ridge Trail Association - Glenwood, 800-782-9937
Glenwood Area Chamber - Glenwood, 800-304-5666
Pope County Historical Museum - Glenwood, 320-634-3293
Stevens County Historical Museum - Morris, 320-589-1719

OUR NOTES

Date visited   What we liked

T R I V I A

Minnesota has....
over 12,500 miles of snowmobile trails,
over 4200 miles of hiking trails, and
over 2,000 miles of cross country ski trails.

Glendalough State Park
PO Box 358
Battle Lake, MN 56515
218-864-5403

DIRECTIONS

To find the park entrance, follow Highway 78 north from Battle Lake to County Road 16 east.

ABOUT THE PARK

Glendalough State Park's 1,924 acres were donated by the Nature Conservancy to the state in 1992, making this the newest park in the system. At this point the park is open to the public, but it remains undeveloped, with no facilities available.

Glendalough, which was originally developed as a summer retreat, was sold to W. J. Murphy, the owner of the Minneapolis Tribune, in 1920. During the depression, Murphy bought the farms surrounding the retreat and added them to Glendalough, in the hopes of developing a game farm. When the Minneapolis Tribune was sold to John Cowles, Glendalough was included in the sale. Cowles preserved the game farm, and played host to many dignitaries, including President Eisenhower. The Cowles family donated Glendalough to the Nature Conservancy.

Development plans for the park have been finalized, but the work will not proceed until funding is available. Plans include a campground overlooking Annie Battle Lake along with some canoe campsites, a picnic area and swimming beach on Molly Stark Lake, a boat access to both Molly Stark and Annie Battle Lake, and an interpretive center near Annie Battle Lake.

IF YOU GO . . .

Plan to hike! Since the park is in development, hiking is the only activity available. To obtain a passport stamp look for a significant aspect of the park. Then go to Lake Carlos State Park and describe the aspect to get the stamp.

GLENDALOUGH STATE PARK

FACILITIES

Visitor Center:	no
Picnic Area:	no

RECREATION

Children's play area:	no
Volleyball courts:	no
Horseshoe pits:	no
Swimming:	no
Fishing:	check with park officials for fishing regulations
Boating:	boat access to Molly Stark Lake

CAMPGROUND

Campsites:	no
Electric:	no
Hike or carry-in:	no
Canoe campsites:	no
Dump station:	no
Toilets:	no
Showers:	no
Group Campground:	no

TRAILS

Hiking Trails:	4 miles
Biking Trails:	no
Cross-country Ski:	no
Snowmobile Trails:	no
Horse Trails:	no
Horse Campsites:	no

INTERPRETIVE PROGRAMS

There are no interpretive programs available in the park.

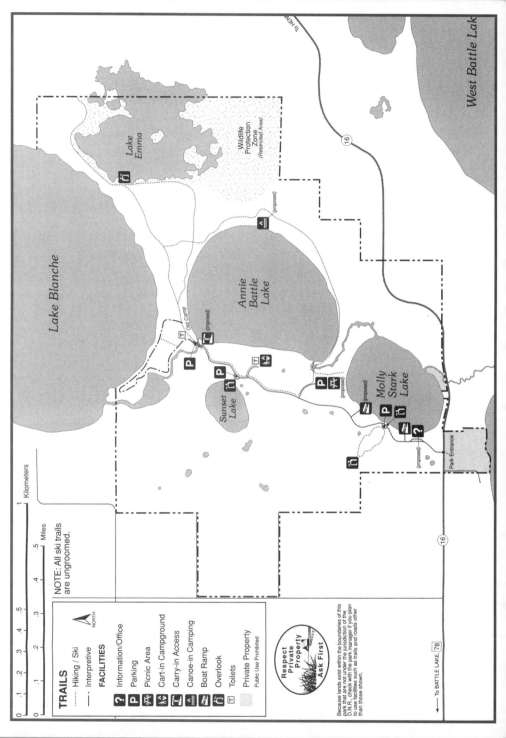

TRAILS

..... Hiking / Ski
— · — Interpretive

FACILITIES

? Information/Office
P Parking
Picnic Area
Cart-in Campground
Carry-in Access
Canoe-in Camping
Boat Ramp
Overlook
T Toilets
Private Property
Public Use Prohibited

NORTH

NOTE: All ski trails are ungroomed.

Kilometers

Miles

Respect
Private
Property
Ask First

Because lands exist within the boundaries of this park that are not under the jurisdiction of the D.N.R., check with the park manager if you plan to use facilities such as trails and roads other than those shown.

→ To BATTLE LAKE 78

Lake Emma

Wildlife Protection Zone *(Restricted Area)*

Lake Blanche

Annie Battle Lake

Sunset Lake

Molly Stark Lake

West Battle Lake

16

Old Camp

Park Entrance

Canada Goose   Photo by Dudley Edmondson

NEARBY PLACES TO VISIT

Battle Lake Civic & Commerce - Battle Lake, 218-864-5236, 800-634-6112
Glacial Ridge Trail Association - Glenwood, 800-782-9937
Maplewood State Park - Pelican Rapids, 218-863-8383
Otter Tail County Historical Museum - Fergus Falls, 218-736-6038
Otter Trail Scenic Byway - Fergus Falls, 218-739-0125
Pope County Historical Museum - Glenwood, 320-634-3293

OUR NOTES

Date visited   What we liked

T R I V I A

There are more than 14 species of toads and frogs found in Minnesota.

Hayes Lake State Park
Star Rt 4 Box 84
Roseau, MN 56751
218-425-7504

DIRECTIONS

The park is located 22 miles southeast of Roseau with access from County Road Highway 4.

ABOUT THE PARK

The 2,950 acres of Hayes Lake State Park border the western edge of Beltrami Island State Forest. The park is located where the transition from farmlands to forest occurs, so it is very surprising to reach the wooded terrain after a long drive through the farms. Because of its remoteness, one can truly experience solitude in this park.

This area was settled during the early 1900s, and the remains of the original settler's homestead and family cemetery can still be seen on the western edge of the park. The park was established in 1967, and named for A. F. Hayes, one of the area's early settlers. Hayes Lake was created by a dam built on the North Fork Roseau River in 1971.

IF YOU GO . . .

Plan for a hike! Head northwest from the dam and follow the River Tower Trail until it meets up with the Homestead Interpretive trail. This trail leads past the remains of the original homestead and the family graves. There are also some scenic views of the North Fork Roseau River along the trail, which eventually circles back to the River Tower Trail.

HAYES LAKE STATE PARK

FACILITIES

Visitor Center: no
Picnic Area: 2 picnic areas:
      1 on Hayes Lake
      1 at the dam on the North Fork Roseau River

RECREATION

Children's play area: yes
Horseshoe pits: yes
Volleyball courts: no
Swimming: swimming beach on Hayes Lake
Fishing: fishing in Hayes Lake
      fishing on the North Fork of the Roseau River
      fishing pier
Boating: boat access on Hayes Lake

CAMPGROUND

Campsites: 35 drive-in campsites
Electric: 9 electric campsites
Hike or carry-in: 2 hike-in campsites
Canoe campsites: no
Dump station: yes
Toilets: flush toilets
Showers: yes
Group Campground: 1 group campsite
Camping Cabins: 2

TRAILS

Hiking Trails: 12 miles
Hiking Club Trail: 2 miles, starting at the Pine Ridge
      Interpretive Trail at the picnic area
Biking Trails: 5 miles
Cross-country Ski: 6 miles
Snowmobile Trails: 6 miles
Horse Trails: 3 miles
Horse Campsites: no

INTERPRETIVE PROGRAMS

There are no interpretive programs available in the park.

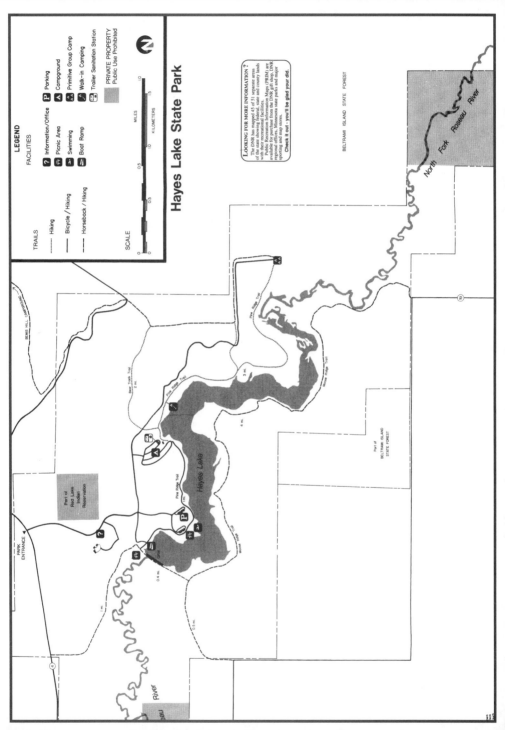

Hayes Lake State Park

LEGEND

FACILITIES

- 2 Information/Office
- P Parking
- Picnic Area
- Compound
- Swimming
- Primitive Group Camp
- Boat Ramp
- Walk-in Camping
- Trailer Sanitation Station

PRIVATE PROPERTY
Public Use Prohibited

TRAILS

- Hiking
- Bicycle / Hiking
- Horseback / Hiking

SCALE

MILES

KILOMETERS

LOOKING FOR MORE INFORMATION?

The DNR has mapped 45 of 51 separate areas of the state showing federal, state and county lands with their own recreational facilities.

Public Recreation Information Maps (PRIM) are available for purchase from the DNR gift shop, DNR regional offices, Minnesota state parks and major sporting and map stores.

Check it out - you'll be glad your did.

BELTRAMI ISLAND STATE FOREST

North Fork Roseau River

Part of
Beltrami Island
State Forest

Hayes Lake

Pine Ridge Trail

Moose Ridge Trail

Bear Track Trail
2 mi.

Moose Loop Trail

Part of
Red Lake
Indian
Reservation

PARK
ENTRANCE

Roseau River

Dark-eyed Junco (female)   Photo by Dudley Edmondson

NEARBY PLACES TO VISIT

Lake Bronson State Park - Lake Bronson, 218-754-2200
Lake of the Woods Cty History Museum - Baudette, 218-634-1200
Lake of the Woods Area Tourism - Baudette, 800-382-3474, 218-634-1174
Pioneer Farm and Village - Roseau, 218-463-2187, 218-463-3052
Roseau Civic & Commerce - Roseau, 218-463-1542
Roseau County Historical Museum - Roseau, 218-463-1918
Warroad Museum - Warroad, 218-386-1283
Zippel Bay State Park - Williams, 218-783-6252

OUR NOTES

Date visited   What we liked

T R I V I A

Showy Ladyslipper is Minnesota's state flower.
It can require up to 16 years to produce a flower.
Minnesota is home to 43 different orchids including the Ladyslipper.

Itasca State Park
HCO 5 Box 4
Lake Itasca, MN 56460
218-266-3654

DIRECTIONS

The park is located 21 miles north of Park Rapids on Highway 71.

ABOUT THE PARK

Itasca State Park is the oldest, most popular, and most developed park in the system. The park was founded in 1891 to protect and celebrate the headwaters of the Mississippi River, and has now grown to include 32,000 acres that offer something for any and all visitors.

IF YOU GO . . .

There is much to see and do at Itasca, but try the following:

It is possible to "circle" drive around the park to explore different areas. On the Main Park Drive visitors can see:

- The Mississippi Headwaters: take a picture stepping over the Mississippi River. There is a Headwaters History Center and museum, with exhibits and videos. There is also a gift shop at the headwaters.

- Preachers Grove is a stand of red pines which began growing after a forest fire in 1714. There was once a religious convention held here.

- Peace Pipe Vista is a scenic overlook of Lake Itasca.

- Pioneer Cemetery is the final resting place for many of the early settlers of the area. A sign provides information about these pioneers.

- Wegmann Cabin Site contains the ruins of the store run by Theodore Wegmann. He was also the first game warden for the park.

- Indian Cemetery is the site of burial mounds which are more than 500 years old . There are interpretive signs about this area.

Wilderness Drive, a one-way 10 mile long drive, connects with the main park drive on the western side of the park. Here are some of the sites along the drive:

Lake Itasca Wilderness Sanctuary is a 2,000 acre virgin forest designated as a Registered Natural Landmark.

Landmark Interpretive Trail is a short self-guided trail.

Blowdown Trail is a short, newly developed trail showing the effects of windstorms.

Bohall Trail is a short trail going into the center of the National Natural Landmark.

Forestry Demonstration Area shows forest management methods.

Minnesota's Big Pines are 300 year old white and red pines, accessible by a short trail.

Bison Kill Site, which archeologists have dated back to 7,000 years, reveals that prehistoric peoples hunted bison in the area.

Nicollet Cabin is accessible by a 1 mile trail. It was built in 1917 and used by the foresters who patrolled the area.

Alton Heights Fire Tower is a tower you can climb for a spectacular view.

One area of the park, known as the Douglas Lodge Area, contains many historic log structures. A free booklet is available at the Douglas Lodge or the Forest Inn.

Historic Douglas Lodge was built between 1904 and 1906 and is located on Lake Itasca

Itasca Clubhouse was constructed in 1911.

Forest Inn is a stone and log structure built by the Veteran Conservation Corps during 1939 and 1941.

Dr. Roberts self-guided Trail begins at the Douglas Lodge where trail guides can be found.

Old Timer's Cabin is located on the Dr. Roberts Trail. It was the first building constructed by the Civilian Conservation Corps (CCC) at the park in 1934.

ITASCA STATE PARK

FACILITIES

Visitor Center:	seasonal Visitor Center
Picnic Area:	2 picnic areas, 1 with a shelter

RECREATION

Children's play area:	no
Horseshoe pit:	no
Volleyball courts:	yes
Swimming:	swimming beach on Lake Itasca
Fishing:	both lake and river fishing
	fishing pier near Douglas Lodge on Lake Itasca
Boating:	access on Lake Itasca
	boat and canoe rentals
	boat excursions on Lake Itasca

CAMPGROUND

Campsites:	Pine Ridge Campground has 150 campsites
	Bear Paw Campground has 80 campsites
Electric:	Pine Ridge has 65 electric campsites
	Bear Paw has 34 electric campsites
Hike or carry-in:	Bear Paw campground has 11 cart-in campsites
	11 backpack campsites on southern end of park
Canoe campsites:	no
Dump station:	yes, at Bear Paw campground
Toilets:	flush toilets
Showers:	yes
Group Campground:	Elk Lake group campground is a primitive camp
Semi modern Group Center:	Lake Ozawindib group camp
	staff cabin with 2 bedrooms
	dining hall, kitchen, toilets, and tenting area
Accommodations:	Douglas Lodge:
	2 dining rooms, suites, and guest rooms
	Douglas Lodge Cabins:
	12 cabins and 1 fourplex unit
	Nicollet Court Motel:
	18 units with showers and heat
	Clubhouse:
	2 story log building with 10 rooms
	and lobby, rented as a unit
	Housekeeping Units:
	6 located in Bear Paw Campground

Mississippi Headwaters Hostel:
    6 rooms with 4 to 6 bunks and kitchen
Squaw Lake Wilderness Cabin:
    located on Squaw Lake
    2 bedrooms, living room with fireplace
    Pit toilets and a well are located nearby

TRAILS

iking Trails:	33 miles
iking Club Trail:	3 miles, start south of the south Itasca Center parking lot
iking Trails:	17 miles bike rentals
ross-country Ski:	31 miles
arming house:	yes
nowmobile Trails:	31 miles
nowshoe rentals:	yes
orse Trails:	no
orse Campsites:	no

INTERPRETIVE PROGRAMS

he park's Visitor Center offers interpretive displays, and various naturalist pro-
ams that are available from Memorial Day to Labor Day. Visitors should check
e various bulletin boards around the park for schedules.

HERE 1475 FT
ABOVE
THE OCEAN
THE MIGHTY
MISSISSIPPI
BEGINS
TO FLOW
ON ITS
WINDING WAY
2552 MILES
TO THE
GULF OF
MEXICO

Photo by author

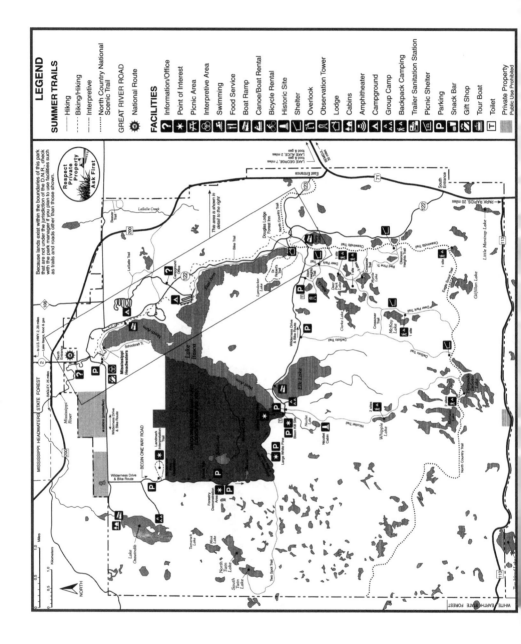

Itasca State Park   Photo by author

NEARBY PLACES TO VISIT

Cass County & Walker Museum Historical Society's - Walker, 218-547-7251
Bagley Wildlife Museum - Bagley, 218-694-2491
Bemidji Convention/Visitor's Bureau - Bemidji, 800-458-2223, 218-751-3540
Fireplace of States and Tourist Info Center - Bemidji, 800-458-2223
Goose Lake Recreation Area - Walker, 218-547-1044
Heartland State Trail - Park Rapids, 612-296-6157, 800-766-6000
Lake Bemidji State Park - Bemidji, 218-755-3843, 218-755-3844 INFO
Lake George Association - Lake George, 218-266-3347
Leech Lake Area Chamber - Walker, 800-833-1118, 218-547-1313
Leech Lake Area Tourism Bureau - Walker, 218-654-3150
North Country Scenic Trail - Walker, 218-755-3969
Shingobee Recreation Area Trail System - Walker, 218-755-3969

OUR NOTES

Date visited   What we liked

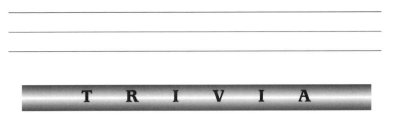

TRIVIA

Minnesota's state tree is the Norway Pine. Itasca State Park is home to the oldest and tallest at 300 years and 120 feet.

LAKE BEMIDJI STATE PARK

Lake Bemidji State Park
3401 State Park Road NE
Bemidji, MN 56601
218-755-3843

DIRECTIONS

The park is located 7 miles north of Bemidji off County Road 21.

ABOUT THE PARK

Lake Bemidji State Park was established in 1923, and has grown to cover 1,600 acres. The Dakota Indians hunted and fished the area until the 18th century, when they were forced out by the Anishinabe. The Anishinabe called the lake "Pemidjigumaug," which was unpronounceable by the white settlers, who simply called the lake "Bemidji." Several sawmills were operated in the area, with the foundation of one still visible near the beach. Much of the park area was logged, but several virgin pine areas survived in the park.

The Civilian Conservation Corps (CCC) was employed in the park, and the park offers some fine examples of their work.

IF YOU GO . . .

Bring your walking shoes! Head north out of the campground, and cross the highway. Follow the Old Logging Trail to the right until you reach the Bog Trail. This trail is a boardwalk that wanders through marshland until it gets to Big Bog Lake.

LAKE BEMIDJI STATE PARK

FACILITIES

Visitor Center: yes
Picnic Area: on Lake Bemidji with enclosed shelter

RECREATION

Children's play area: no
Horseshoe pit: no
Volleyball courts: yes
Swimming: swimming beach on Lake Bemidji
Fishing: lake fishing on Lake Bemidji
Boating: drive-in boat access to Lake Bemidji
      boat rental

CAMPGROUND

Campsites: 100 drive-in campsites
Electric: 43 electric campsites
Hike or carry-in: no
Canoe campsites: no
Dump station: yes
Toilets: flush toilets
Showers: yes
Group Campground: 2 group campsites

TRAILS

Hiking Trails: 14 miles
Hiking Club Trail: 2 miles, start at the Visitor Center and follow
      the Bog Trail
Biking Trails: 1 paved mile
      5 miles of mountain bike trails
Cross-country Ski: 9 miles
Warming house: yes
Snowshoe rental: yes
Snowmobile Trails: 3 miles
Horse Trails: no
Horse Campsites: no

INTERPRETIVE PROGRAMS

Interpretive programs are available throughout the year. From Memorial Day to Labor Day programs are offered almost daily, including snowshoeing, skiing, and enjoying winter wildlife. The park has a trail center that is open year round as a gathering place.

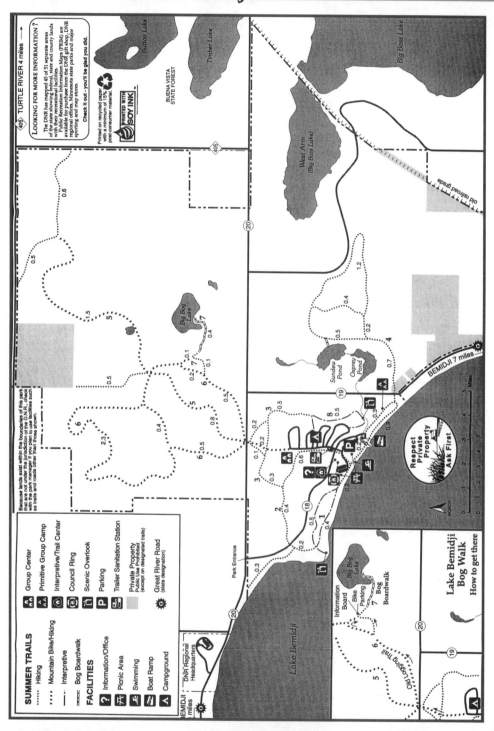

SUMMER TRAILS

- ····· Hiking
- •••• Mountain Bike/Hiking
- —·— Interpretive
- ===== Bog Boardwalk

FACILITIES

- ? Information/Office
- 🚻 Picnic Area
- 🏊 Swimming
- 🚤 Boat Ramp
- ⛺ Campground
- 👥 Group Center
- 👥 Primitive Group Camp
- Interpretive/Trail Center
- ⊗ Council Ring
- 🏠 Scenic Overlook
- P Parking
- Trailer Sanitation Station
- Private Property Public Use Prohibited (except on designated trails)
- ✻ Great River Road (state designation)

LOOKING FOR MORE INFORMATION?

The DNR has mapped 45 of 51 separate areas of the state showing federal, state and county lands with their recreational facilities. Public Recreation Information Maps (PRIM) are available for purchase from the DNR gift shop, DNR regional offices, Minnesota state parks and major sporting and map stores.

Check it out - you'll be glad you did.

Printed on recycled paper with a minimum of 15% post-consumer material.

BUENA VISTA STATE FOREST

TURTLE RIVER 4 miles

BEMIDJI 7 miles

Respect Private Property Ask First

Lake Bemidji Bog Walk How to get there

Lake Bemidji State Park   Photo by author

NEARBY PLACES TO VISIT

Bemidji Convention/Visitor's Bureau - Bemidji, 800-458-2223, 218-751-3540
Clearwater County Historical Museum - Shevlin, 218-785-2000
Fireplace of States and Tourist Info Center - Bemidji, 800-458-2223
Heartland State Trail - Park Rapids, 612-296-6157, 800-766-6000
Itasca State Park - Lake Itasca, 218-266-2100
Lake George Association - Lake George, 218-266-3347
Leech Lake Hunting Area - Federal Dam, 218-654-3998
Lyle's Logging Camp and Museum - Cass Lake, 218-335-6723, 800-356-8615
Paul Bunyan State Trail - Baxter, 218-828-2561

OUR NOTES

Date visited   What we liked

T R I V I A

Leech Lake is Minnesota's 3rd largest lake. It was named by the Ojibway for a giant leech that was swimming across the lake.

Lake Bronson State Park
Box 9
Lake Bronson, MN 56734
218-754-2200

DIRECTIONS

The park is located 1 mile east of Lake Bronson on County Road Highway 28.

ABOUT THE PARK

Lake Bronson State Park covers 2,983 acres, and was created in 1937 as Two Rivers Sate Park.

Lake Bronson was created during the 1930s when local wells dried up, and the residents wanted to avoid future problems. To do this, they dammed the South Fork River to create an artificial lake. Dam construction began in 1936, but there was a slight delay when quicksand was discovered at the dam site.

Since the lake is the only sizable body of water for many miles around, it offers tremendous water recreational opportunities that otherwise would not exist.

IF YOU GO . . .

Bring you bike! Lake Bronson State Park has several miles of bike trails. The trails start at the picnic area parking lot, and hook up with county roads to circle around the lake. Upon returning to the picnic area, head to the swimming beach for a dip.

LAKE BRONSON STATE PARK

FACILITIES

Visitor Center: no
Picnic Area: picnic area with open shelter

RECREATION

Children's play area: yes
Horseshoe pit: no
Volleyball courts: yes
Swimming: swimming beach on Lake Bronson
Fishing: both lake and river fishing
Boating: drive-in boat access to Lake Bronson
                           boat rental

CAMPGROUND

Campsites: 190 drive-in campsites
Electric: 35 electric campsites
Hike or carry-in: no
Canoe campsites: no
Dump station: yes
Toilets: flush toilets
Showers: yes
Group Campground: primitive group campsite and enclosed shelter

TRAILS

Hiking Trails: 14 miles
Hiking Club Trail: 3.4 miles, starting at the swimming area
                           parking lot
Biking Trails: 5 miles of mountain bike trails
Cross-country Ski: 6 miles
Warming house: yes
Snowmobile Trails: 10 miles
Horse Trails: no
Horse Campsites: no

INTERPRETIVE PROGRAMS

In addition to the 1 mile self-guided nature trail, the park offers Interpretive programs during the summer months. For more information, check bulletin boards for schedules.

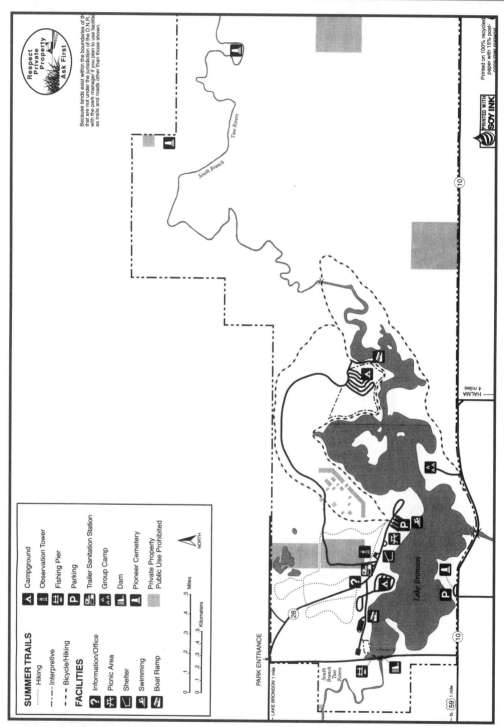

Respect Private Property
Ask First

Because lands exist within the boundaries of the park that are not under the jurisdiction of the D.N.R., check with the park manager if you plan to use facilities, such as trails and roads other than those shown.

SUMMER TRAILS

...... Hiking
–·– Interpretive
–·–·– Bicycle/Hiking

FACILITIES

?	Information/Office	△	Campground
⚊	Picnic Area	⛫	Observation Tower
⚊	Shelter	⚊	Fishing Pier
⚊	Swimming	P	Parking
⚊	Boat Ramp	⚊	Trailer Sanitation Station
		⚍	Group Camp
		⚊	Dam
		⚊	Pioneer Cemetery
			Private Property Public Use Prohibited

NORTH

0 .1 .2 .3 .4 .5 Miles
0 .1 .2 .3 .4 .5 Kilometers

PARK ENTRANCE

LAKE BRONSON 1 mile

to 59 1 mile

South Branch Two Rivers

Lake Bronson

South Branch Two Rivers

HALMA 4 miles

PRINTED WITH SOY INK

Printed on 100% recycled paper with 15% post-consumer material

Gray Wolf (black morph)   Photo by Dudley Edmondson

NEARBY PLACES TO VISIT

Hayes Lake State Park - Roseau, 218-425-7504
Lake of the Woods Cty Historical Museum - Baudette, 218-634-1200
Lake of the Woods Area Tourism - Baudette, 800-382-3474, 218-634-1174
Warroad Museum - Warroad, 218-386-1283
Zippel Bay State Park - Williams, 218-783-6252

OUR NOTES

Date visited   What we liked

Minnesota is home to more wolves than any other state except Alaska.

Lake Carlos State Park
RR 2 Box 240
Carlos, MN 56319
320-852-7200

DIRECTIONS

The park is located 10 miles north of Alexandria on Highway 29.

ABOUT THE PARK

Lake Carlos State Park was established in 1936, and covers 1,174 acres.

The Carlos area is known to have been home to prehistoric peoples and, later, the Dakota Indians. After the treaty of Traverse de Sioux, the area was opened to white settlers, many of whom temporarily fled the area during the Dakota Uprising of 1862.

During the late 1930s the Works Progress Administration (WPA) came to the park and created the roads, buildings, and campground. The park is located in a heavily visited area of the state, with a large number of lakes and tourist activities, making Lake Carlos State Park one of the more heavily used parks in the system.

IF YOU GO . . .

Come for a hike! From the parking area at the swimming beach, look for the self-guided interpretive trail. This trail follows Hidden Lake as it swings through a maple and basswood forest, and ends at the lower campground. The western edge of the campground offers a trail along Lake Carlos back to the swimming beach. For the horse lover, there is a trail that goes through a forestry demonstration area as it heads to the Prairie Pothole Trail.

LAKE CARLOS STATE PARK

FACILITIES

Visitor Center: seasonal
Picnic Area: 2 picnic areas with an open shelter

RECREATION

Children's play area: no
Horseshoe pits: yes
Volleyball courts: no
Swimming: swimming beach and bath house at
Lake Carlos
Fishing: fishing and fish cleaning house on Lake Carlos
Boating: drive-in boat access to Lake Carlos
carry-in boat access to Hidden Lake

CAMPGROUND

Campsites: 2 campgrounds
total of 126 drive-in campsites
Electric: 68 electric campsites
Hike or carry-in: 2 walk-in campsites
Canoe campsites: no
Dump station: yes
Toilets: flush toilets
Showers: yes
Group Campground: primitive group campsite
Modern Group Camp: 2 barracks that sleep 24 people each
staff quarters for 12, dining hall, kitchen,
classroom, and sanitation building
minimum of 40 people
available from Memorial Day to Labor Day

TRAILS

Hiking Trails: 12 miles
2.8 miles of self-guided interpretive trail
Hiking Club Trail: 2.9 miles, starting at the beach area parking lot
Biking Trails: no
Cross-country Ski: 5 miles
Warming house: yes
Snowmobile Trails: 9 miles
Horse Trails: 8 miles
Horse Campsites: 6 horse campsites

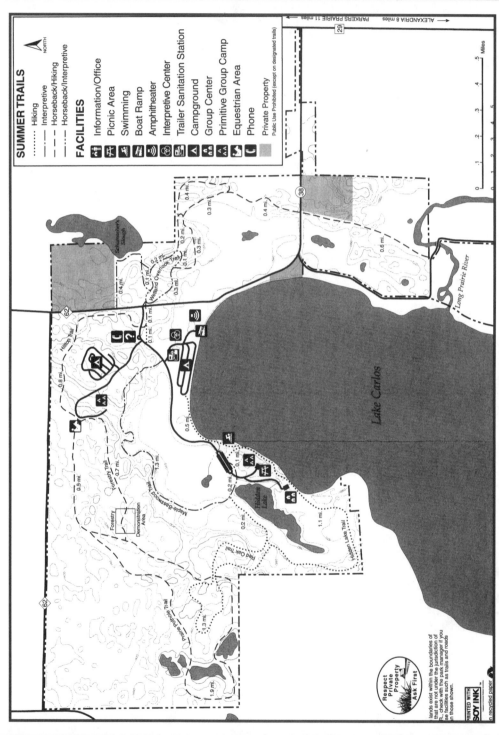

SUMMER TRAILS

- Hiking
- Interpretive
- Horseback/Hiking
- Horseback/Interpretive

FACILITIES

- Information/Office
- Picnic Area
- Swimming
- Boat Ramp
- Amphitheater
- Interpretive Center
- Trailer Sanitation Station
- Campground
- Group Center
- Primitive Group Camp
- Equestrian Area
- Phone
- Private Property
  Public Use Prohibited (except on designated trails)

Schumacher's Slough

Wetland Overlook Trail

Long Prairie River

Hilltop Trail

Lake Carlos

Forestry Trail

Forestry Demonstration Area

Maple-Basswood Trail

Hidden Lake

Hidden Lake Trail

Red Oak Trail

Red Oak Trail

ALEXANDRIA 8 miles
PARKERS PRAIRIE 11 miles

Miles

Respect Private Property Ask First

Lands exist within the boundaries of that are not under the jurisdiction of R., check with the park manager if you use facilities such as trails and roads in those shown.

PRINTED WITH SOY INK

In recycled paper

American Coot   Photo by Dudley Edmondson

NEARBY PLACES TO VISIT

Alexandria Lakes Area Chamber - Alexandria, 800-235-9441, 320-763-3161
Cyclone House - Osakis, 320-859-4283
Knute Nelson House/Douglas County Historical Society
    Alexandria, 320-762-0382
Runestone Museum - Alexandria, 320-763-3160

OUR NOTES

Date visited   What we liked

T R I V I A

Minnesota is the northernmost state in the lower 48 states.

Maplewood State Park
RR 3 Box 422
Pelican Rapids, MN 56572
218-863-8383

DIRECTIONS

The park is located 7 miles east of Pelican Rapids on Highway 108.

ABOUT THE PARK

Maplewood State Park was established in 1963 and currently covers 9,250 acres. The park was created to protect the wooded hills and valleys from developers, and offers interesting hiking, beautiful vistas, with many lakes for swimming, fishing, and other water activities.

Archeological evidence indicates that people, most likely hunters, inhabited the area approximately 1300 years ago. Recent settlements did not begin until the 1880s.

IF YOU GO . . .

Plan on a winter weekend getaway! Reserve the Wilson Lake Cabin, which is available on a year-round basis. The park also offers 17 miles of cross-country ski trails, which visit many of the lakes within the park boundaries. There are also 14 miles of snowmobile trails.

MAPLEWOOD STATE PARK

FACILITIES

Visitor Center: no
Picnic Area: 2 picnic areas on Lake Lida

RECREATION

Children's play area: no
Volleyball courts: no
Horseshoe pits: no
Swimming: swimming beach on Lake Lida
Fishing: lake fishing on the many lakes within the park
Boating: drive-in boat access on both Lake Lida and Beers Lake
boat and canoe rentals

CAMPGROUND

Campsites: 61 drive-in campsites
Electric: no
Hike or carry-in: 3 backpack campsites
Canoe campsites: 2 canoe campsites which can also be hiked to
Dump station: yes
Toilets: flush toilets
Showers: yes
Group Campground: primitive group campsite
Guest House: Lake Wilson Modern Cabin is an A-frame cabin
sleeps up to 14 people
heated with electricity
1 bedroom and a loft, 2 bathrooms, a living room, dining room, kitchen and a garage

TRAILS

Hiking Trails: 25 miles
Hiking Club Trail: 6.2 miles, starting at the trail access parking lot
Biking Trails: no
Cross-country Ski: 17 miles
Snowmobile Trails: 14 miles
Horse Trails: 15 miles
Horse Campsites: 20 horse campsites

INTERPRETIVE PROGRAMS

Self guided trails are available, as is a demonstration forest showing different types of forest management.

MAPLEWOOD STATE PARK

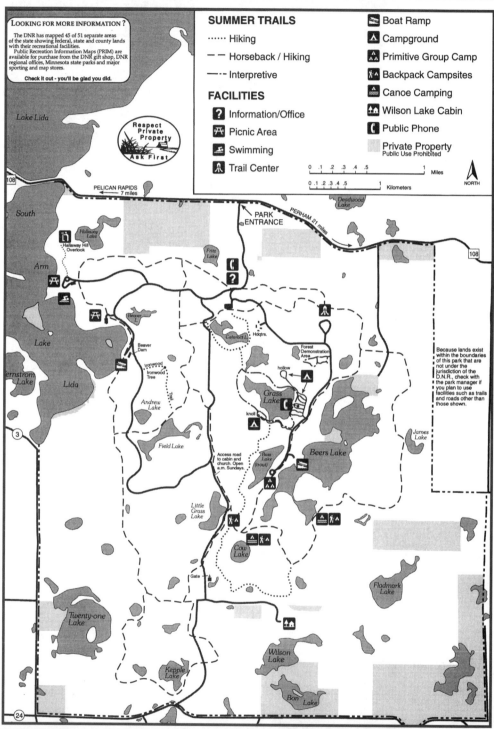

LOOKING FOR MORE INFORMATION ?

The DNR has mapped 45 of 51 separate areas of the state showing federal, state and county lands with their recreational facilities.

Public Recreation Information Maps (PRIM) are available for purchase from the DNR gift shop, DNR regional offices, Minnesota state parks and major sporting and map stores.

Check it out - you'll be glad you did.

Respect Private Property Ask First

SUMMER TRAILS

...... Hiking

– – – Horseback / Hiking

—·— Interpretive

FACILITIES

? Information/Office

A Picnic Area

S Swimming

A Trail Center

S Boat Ramp

A Campground

AA Primitive Group Camp

A Backpack Campsites

C Canoe Camping

AA Wilson Lake Cabin

C Public Phone

Private Property
Public Use Prohibited

0 .1 .2 .3 .4 .5 — 1 Miles

0 .1 .2 .3 .4 .5 — 1 Kilometers

NORTH

Lake Lida

108

South

Arm

Lake

Lida

ernstrom Lake

PELICAN RAPIDS 7 miles

PARK ENTRANCE

PERHAM 21 miles

108

Deadwood Lake

Hallaway Lake

Hallaway Hill Overlook

Fritz Lake

Beaver L.

Beaver Dam

Ironwood Tree

Ironwood Trail

Andrew Lake

Field Lake

Cataract L.

Hdqtrs.

Forest Demonstration Area

hollow

Grass Lake

knoll

Access road to cabin and church. Open a.m. Sundays.

Bass Lake (trout)

Beers Lake

James Lake

Little Grass Lake

Cow Lake

Gate

Twenty-one Lake

Fladmark Lake

Kepple Lake

Wilson Lake

Bon Lake

3

24

Because lands exist within the boundaries of this park that are not under the jurisdiction of the D.N.R., check with the park manager if you plan to use facilities such as trails and roads other than those shown.

American White Pelican   Photo by Dudley Edmondson

NEARBY PLACES TO VISIT

Detroit Lakes Regional Chamber - Detroit Lakes, 800-542-3992 x104, 218-847-9202
Heartland State Trail - Park Rapids, 612-296-6157, 800-766-6000
Otter Tail County Historical Museum - Fergus Falls, 218-736-6038
Otter Trail Scenic Byway - Fergus Falls, 218-739-0125
Park Rapids Area Chamber - Park Rapids, 800-247-0054, 218-732-4111
Pelican Rapids Area Chamber - Pelican Rapids, 800-545-3711, 218-863-6571

OUR NOTES

Date visited   What we liked

T R I V I A

A fossilized skeleton, probably 20,000 years old,
was discovered near Pelican Rapids.

Old Mill State Park
RR 1 Box 42
Argyle, MN 56713
218-473-8174

DIRECTIONS

The park is located 13 miles east of Argyle off County Road 4.

ABOUT THE PARK

Old Mill State Park was established in 1937, and covers 287 acres. It was originally called the Middle River State Park, but the name was changed to Old Mill in 1951. This area was first settled in the 1880s by the Larson family. The family built a water mill first, which was destroyed by flooding. Next they built a windmill, which was destroyed by a wind storm. Finally, they built another water mill, which lasted until 1897, when it was moved next to a steam-powered mill at its present site. Volunteers demonstrate grinding on Labor Day weekend and a few other times during the summer. Check with the park office for dates. There is also an old farmhouse located on the site.

IF YOU GO . . .

Plan to tour! Old Mill State Park is a small oasis in the middle of farmlands. Park at the Old Mill site, and check out the old cabin and mill site. If possible, find out when there are grinding days so the mill will be in operation. From the mill site, cross the Middle River and hike down the west side of it. Just beyond the dam there is a bridge to cross back over to the east side of the river. Then, back by the swimming pond, there is a picnic area and group campsite before the mill site.

OLD MILL STATE PARK

FACILITIES

Visitor Center:	no
Picnic Area:	picnic area with a shelter are located on the Middle River

RECREATION

Children's play area:	yes
Horseshoe pits:	yes
Volleyball courts:	yes
Swimming:	swimming pond
Fishing:	fishing on the Middle River
Boating:	no

CAMPGROUND

Campsites:	26 drive campsites
Electric:	10 electric campsites
Hike or carry-in:	no
Canoe campsites:	no
Dump station:	no
Toilets:	flush toilets
Showers:	yes
Group Campground:	primitive group campground

TRAILS

Hiking Trails:	7 miles
Hiking Club Trail:	3 miles, starting at southwest end of the main parking lot
Biking Trails:	no
Cross-country Ski:	9 miles
Sliding Hill:	yes
Warming house:	yes
Snowshoe rental:	yes
Snowmobile Trails:	no
Horse Trails:	no
Horse Campsites:	no

INTERPRETIVE PROGRAMS

There is a self-guiding trail in the park known as the Agassiz Trail, and park naturalists lead programs on Sundays during the summer. Check with the park office for a schedule.

OLD MILL STATE PARK

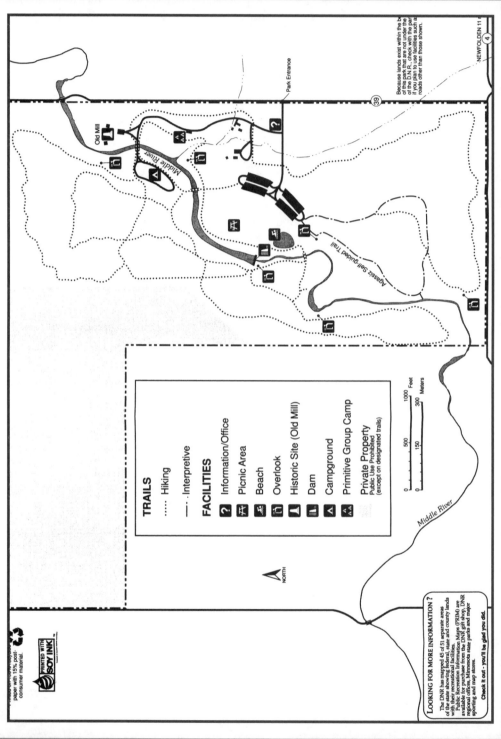

Old Mill

Middle River

Agassiz Self-guided Trail

Park Entrance

NEWFOLDEN 11 mi

Because lands exist within the boundary of this park that are not under the control of the D.N.R., check with the park if you plan to use facilities such as roads other than those shown.

TRAILS

..... Hiking

—∙— Interpretive

FACILITIES

? Information/Office

🔳 Picnic Area

🔳 Beach

🔳 Overlook

🔳 Historic Site (Old Mill)

🔳 Dam

🔳 Campground

🔳 Primitive Group Camp

Private Property
Public Use Prohibited
(except on designated trails)

0   500   1000 Feet
0   150   300 Meters

Middle River

NORTH

LOOKING FOR MORE INFORMATION ?

The DNR has mapped 45 of 51 separate areas of the state showing federal, state and county lands with their recreational facilities.

Public Recreation Information Maps (PRIM) are available for purchase from the DNR gift shop, DNR regional offices, Minnesota state parks and major sporting and map stores.

Check it out - you'll be glad you did.

Old Mill State Park   Photo by author

NEARBY PLACES TO VISIT

Marshall County Historical Museum - Warren, 218-745-4803
Riverland Tourism Assoc - Thief River Falls, 218-681-3720
Peder Engelstad Pioneer Village - Thief River Falls, 218-681-5767, 218-681-4931
Thief River Falls Area Chamber/CVB - Thief River Falls, 800-827-1629, 218-681-3720

OUR NOTES

Date visited   What we liked
_____
_____
_____
_____
_____

Old Mill State Park is home to Old Mill built in 1896.

Zippel Bay State Park
HC 2, Box 25
Williams, MN 56686
218-783-6252

DIRECTIONS

The park is located 10 miles northeast of Williams on County Road 8.

ABOUT THE PARK

Zippel Bay State Park is located on the shores of Lake of the Woods, an amazing lake with 65,000 miles of shore line and 14,000 islands. The park was established in 1959 and has about 2,900 acres along the lake and the Zippel Bay.

Archaeological surveys of Lake of the Woods and Rainy River, just to the east of the park, have produced evidence of prehistoric peoples. More recently the Cree, Monsonis, Assinboine, Dakota, and Ojibway Indians have inhabited the area. The first Europeans came to the area In the mid 1700s for trading. In 1887 William Zippel came to the area and built his home on the land at the entrance to Zippel Bay. By the early 1900s a small hamlet, the remains of which can still be seen, had developed around the area's fishing opportunities.

IF YOU GO . . .

Bring your water toys! Head over to Zippel Bay, where there is a boat launch, and try your luck at fishing in Lake of the Woods or along either branch of Zippel Creek. Next, head over to the picnic area on Lake of the Woods, which offers a wonderful sand beach with great swimming. Follow the trail along the lake which circles back to the picnic area, and walk the beaches of the park — they always provide new sights.

ZIPPEL BAY STATE PARK

FACILITIES

Visitor Center: no
Picnic Area: picnic areas on Lake of the Woods and
                           Zippel Bay

RECREATION

Children's play area: no
Horseshoe pit: no
Volleyball courts: yes
Swimming: swimming beach on Lake of the Woods
Fishing: fishing on Lake of the Woods
                           fishing pier on Zippel Bay
                           fish cleaning house
Boating: drive-in boat access to Zippel Bay and into Lake of
                           the Woods
                           carry-in boat access to Lake of the Woods
                           Lake of the Woods boat sight-seeing at the
                           harbor by arrangement

CAMPGROUND

Campsites: Lady's Slipper Campground has 11 drive-in
                           campsites
                           Birch Campground has 15 drive-in campsites
                           Ridge Campground has 13 drive-in campsites
                           Angler's Campground has 15 drive-in campsites
Electric: no
Hike or carry-in: no
Canoe campsites: no
Dump station: yes
Toilets: pit toilets
Showers: no
Group Campground: primitive group campsite

TRAILS

Hiking Trails: 6 miles
Hiking Club Trail: 2 miles, long starting near the park office
Biking Trails: no
Cross-country Ski: 5 miles
Snowmobile Trails: 4 miles
Horse Trails: no
Horse Campsites: no

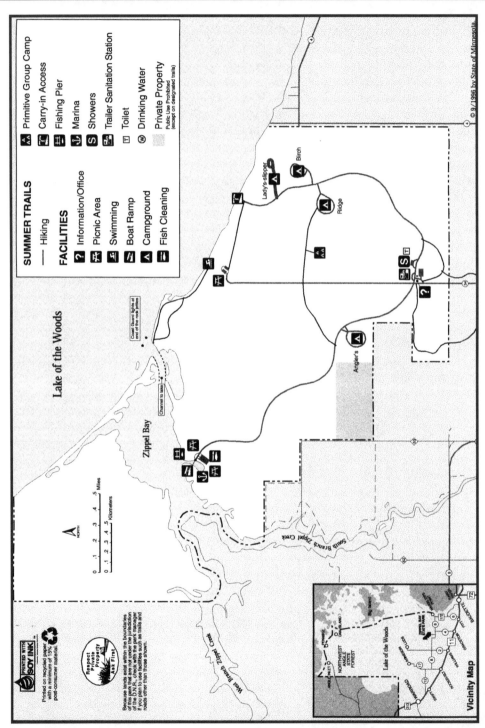

Lake of the Woods

Zippel Bay

SUMMER TRAILS

— Hiking

FACILITIES

- ? Information/Office
- 🏞 Picnic Area
- 🏊 Swimming
- 🚤 Boat Ramp
- ▲ Campground
- 🐟 Fish Cleaning

- ▲ Primitive Group Camp
- 🅿 Carry-in Access
- 🎣 Fishing Pier
- ⚓ Marina
- S Showers
- 🚻 Trailer Sanitation Station
- 🚽 Toilet
- ⊗ Drinking Water
- Private Property
  Public Use Prohibited
  (except on designated trails)

Birch

Ladys-slipper

Ridge

Anglers

Coast Guard lights at end of the rock jetties

Channel to lake

West Branch Zippel Creek

South Branch Zippel Creek

NORTH

0 .1 .2 .3 .4 .5 Miles
0 .1 .2 .3 .4 .5 Kilometers

Printed on recycled paper with a minimum of 15% post-consumer material.

Because lands exist within the boundaries of this park that are not under the jurisdiction of the DNR, check with the park manager if you plan to use facilities such as trails and roads other than those shown.

© 9/1996 by State of Minnesota

Vicinity Map

Zippel Bay State Park   Photo by author

NEARBY PLACES TO VISIT

Lake of the Woods Cty Historical Museum - Baudette, 218-634-1200
Lake of the Woods Area Tourism - Baudette, 800-382-3474, 218-634-1174
Warroad Museum - Warroad, 218-386-1283

OUR NOTES

Date visited   What we liked

_____

_____

_____

_____

_____

_____

T R I V I A

Lake of the Woods covers 2,000 square miles and contains 14,000 islands.

PARK	ACREAGE
Bear Head State Park	4,375 acres
Cascade River State Park	2,813 acres
Franz Jevene State Park	118 acres
George H. Crosby-Manitou State Park	5,259 acres
Gooseberry Falls State Park	1,662 acres
Grand Portage State Park	300 acres
Hill Annex State Park	635 acres
Jay Cooke State Park	8,818 acres
Judge C.R. Magney State Park	4,514 acres
McCarthy Beach State Park	2,311 acres
Moose Lake State Park	1,194 acres
Scenic State Park	2,649 acres
Schoolcraft State Park	295 acres
Soudan Underground Mine State Park	1,300 acres
Split Rock Lighthouse State Park	1,987 acres
Temperance River State Park	534 acres
Tettegouche State Park	8,468 acres

NORTHEASTERN REGION

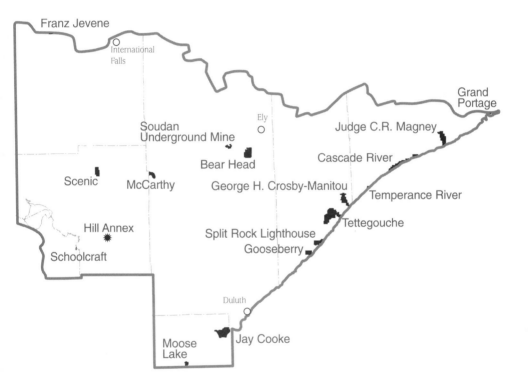

Franz Jevene

International Falls ○

Soudan Underground Mine

Ely ○

Judge C.R. Magney

Grand Portage

Bear Head

Cascade River

Scenic

McCarthy

George H. Crosby-Manitou

Temperance River

Hill Annex ✳

Tettegouche

Split Rock Lighthouse

Schoolcraft

Gooseberry

Duluth ○

Moose Lake

Jay Cooke

✳ Boundries not available

Bear Head Lake State Park
9301 Bear Head State Park Road
Ely, MN 55731
218-365-7229

DIRECTIONS

Take US Highway 169 18 miles east of Tower to County Road 128, then go south 6 miles to the park entrance.

ABOUT THE PARK

Bear Head Lake State Park contains about 4,300 acres, and was established in 1961. This popular park is situated near the Boundary Waters Canoe Area, and offers great outdoor activities such as canoeing, boating, fishing, camping, and hiking. The park protects miles of beautiful land, including a small stand of virgin pines.

Logging was the major industry of northern Minnesota In the mid-1890s, and from 1907-1909 the Allen and Whittenburg Company logged the area around Bear Head Lake, after which the local mill was shipped back to Tower. Forest fires swept through the area in 1911 and 1913, leaving the charred stumps that can be still be seen along the hiking trails.

IF YOU GO . . .

Plan to spend some time on the lake! Put your boat into Bear Head Lake for a relaxing day of fishing. After feasting on the day's catch, follow the beach path from the campground over to the picnic area, and see if any of the park's Bald Eagles are around. After exploring Bear Head Lake, try a hike to Blueberry or Norberg Lake, and finish the day with a swim.

FACILITIES

isitor Center:	no
icnic Area:	picnic area and shelter on Bear Head L

RECREATION

hildren's play area:	no
olleyball courts:	no
orseshoe pits:	no
wimming:	swimming beach on Bear Head Lake
ishing:	fishing dock
	lake and stream fishing
oating:	boat access on Bear Head and Eagles Nest Lake
	boat and canoe rentals

CAMPGROUND

ampsites:	73 drive-in campsites
lectric:	no electric campsites
ike or carry-in:	4 backpack campsites
	1 on Becky Lake
	3 on Blueberry Lake
anoe campsites:	1 canoe/boat campsite on Bear Head Lake
ump station:	yes
oilets:	flush toilets
howers:	yes
roup Campground:	yes
uest House:	located on a bay of Bear Head Lake
	split level, winterized
	sleeps up to 10 people, they supply linens
	3 bedrooms, 2 baths, kitchen, and deck

TRAILS

iking Trails:	17 miles
iking Club Trail:	3 miles, starting at the picnic area
iking Trails:	no
ross-country Ski:	6 miles
nowmobile Trails:	1 mile, connects to the Taconite Trail
orse Trails:	no
orse Campsites:	no

INTERPRETIVE PROGRAMS

here are no specific interpretive programs offered in the park.

BEAR HEAD LAKE STATE PARK

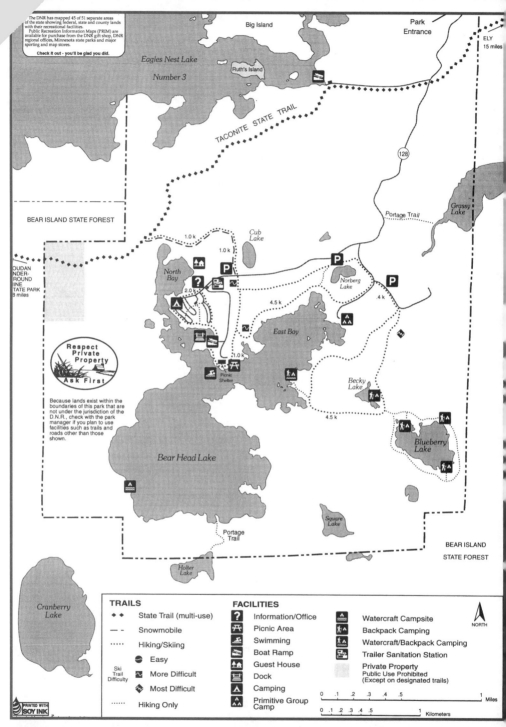

The DNR has mapped 45 of 51 separate areas of the state showing federal, state and county lands with their recreational facilities.
Public Recreation Information Maps (PRIM) are available for purchase from the DNR gift shop, DNR regional offices, Minnesota state parks and major sporting and map stores.

Check it out - you'll be glad you did.

Big Island

Park Entrance

ELY 15 miles

Eagles Nest Lake

Number 3

Ruth's Island

TACONITE STATE TRAIL

128

BEAR ISLAND STATE FOREST

Grassy Lake

Portage Trail

OUDAN
NDER-
ROUND
INE
TATE PARK
5 miles

1.0 k

Cub Lake

1.0 k

North Bay

?

2.0 k

P

P

Norberg Lake

.4 k

4.5 k

East Bay

Respect
Private
Property
Ask First

Because lands exist within the boundaries of this park that are not under the jurisdiction of the D.N.R., check with the park manager if you plan to use facilities such as trails and roads other than those shown.

1.0 k

Picnic Shelter

Becky Lake

4.5 k

Bear Head Lake

Blueberry Lake

Square Lake

Portage Trail

BEAR ISLAND

STATE FOREST

Holter Lake

Cranberry Lake

TRAILS

- ◆ ◆ State Trail (multi-use)
- — — Snowmobile
- ····· Hiking/Skiing

Ski Trail Difficulty
- ⬤ Easy
- ∿ More Difficult
- ❀ Most Difficult

- ······ Hiking Only

FACILITIES

- ? Information/Office
- 🛆 Picnic Area
- 🏊 Swimming
- 🚤 Boat Ramp
- 🏠 Guest House
- 🛏 Dock
- 🛆 Camping
- 🛆🛆 Primitive Group Camp

- Watercraft Campsite
- Backpack Camping
- Watercraft/Backpack Camping
- Trailer Sanitation Station
- Private Property
  Public Use Prohibited
  (Except on designated trails)

NORTH

0 .1 .2 .3 .4 .5   1 Miles

0 .1 .2 .3 .4 .5   1 Kilometers

PRINTED WITH SOY INK

Gray Wolf   Photo by Dudley Edmondson

NEARBY PLACES TO VISIT

Arrowhead State Trail - Tower, 612-296-6699, 218-753-6256
Dorothy Molter Museum - Ely, 218-365-4451, 218-365-4058
Ely Chamber - Ely, 218-365-6123, 800-777-7281
International Wolf Center - Ely, 218-365-4695, 800-359-9653
Manitou Falls - Finland, 218-226-3539 (in George Crosby Park)
Minntac Taconite Plant - Mountain Iron, 218-749-7470
Tower City Trail - Tower, 218-753-4070
Tower-Soudan Chamber - Tower, 800-648-5897, 218-753-2301
Tower-Soudan Historical Museum - Tower, 218-753-3041
Vermilion Interpretive Center History Museum - Ely, 218-365-3226

OUR NOTES

Date visited   What we liked

TRIVIA

Voyageurs National Park is the only national park that contains more water than land surface.

Cascade River State Park
HCR 3, Box 450
Lutsen, MN 55612
218-387-1543
218-387-3053

DIRECTIONS

The park is located on US Highway 61, 21 miles northeast of Tofte or 9 miles southwest of Grand Marais.

ABOUT THE PARK

Cascade River State Park was created in 1934. Its 2,813 acres encompass several creeks, the Cascade River, and 5 miles of Lake Superior shoreline. The park was developed after the completion of Highway 61, when the highway department created a picnic area and some trails in an attempt to erase some of the scars from the construction. The park changed hands from the highway department to the park system in 1957.

IF YOU GO . . .

Put on your hiking shoes or cross-country skis! For a scenic hike, start at the campground and head up the trail towards the series of waterfalls referred to as the Cascades. The trail crosses a bridge, which provides a nice view of the river and Cascades. Follow the trail along the river until it splits, and take the fork to the east to part of the Superior Hiking Trail. Head towards Lookout Mountain for a spectacular view of Lake Superior. From there follow one of the trails back to the Cascade Lodge Restaurant. The campground is a short hike from the lodge.

CASCADE RIVER STATE PARK

FACILITIES

Visitor Center:	no
Picnic Area:	many campsites along Lake Superior

RECREATION

Children's play area:	no
Volleyball courts:	no
Horseshoe pits:	no
Swimming:	no
Fishing:	Lake Superior and Cascade River trout fishing
Boating:	no

CAMPGROUND

Campsites:	40 drive-in campsites
Electric:	no
Bike or carry-in:	5 backpack campsites
Canoe campsites:	no
Dump station:	yes
Toilets:	flush toilets
Showers:	yes
Group Campground:	2 group camp campsites

TRAILS

Hiking Trails:	18 miles access to the Superior Hiking Trail
Hiking Club Trail:	4 miles, starting at the picnic shelter
Biking Trails:	no
Cross-country Ski:	17 miles
Warming house:	yes
Snowmobile Trails:	2 miles access to the North Shore State Trail
Horse Trails:	no
Horse Campsites:	no

INTERPRETIVE PROGRAMS

There are no interpretive programs available in the park.

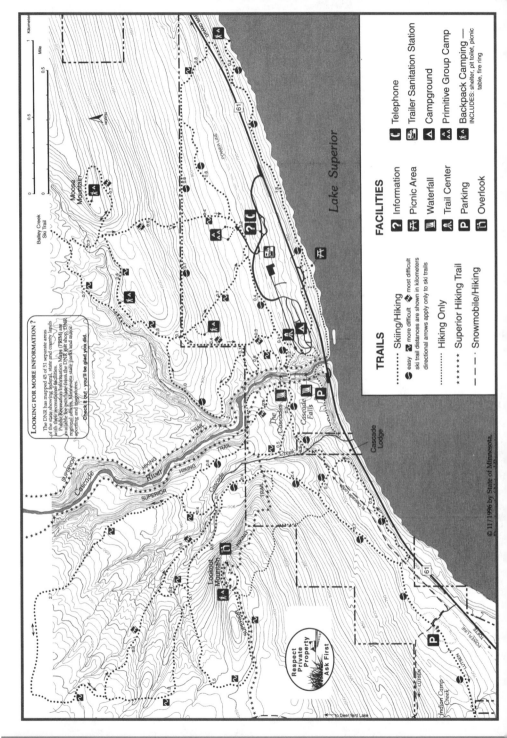

FACILITIES

- ? Information
- ⛏ Picnic Area
- 🏞 Waterfall
- 🏠 Trail Center
- P Parking
- 🔭 Overlook
- ☎ Telephone
- 🚽 Trailer Sanitation Station
- ⛺ Campground
- 🏕 Primitive Group Camp
- 🥾 Backpack Camping — INCLUDES: shelter, pit toilet, picnic table, fire ring

TRAILS

- ········· Skiing/Hiking
- ⚲ easy ◼ more difficult ◼ most difficult
  ski trail distances are shown in kilometers
  directional arrows apply only to ski trails
- ·········· Hiking Only
- ✶✶✶✶✶✶ Superior Hiking Trail
- — — — Snowmobile/Hiking

LOOKING FOR MORE INFORMATION?

The DNR has mapped 45 of 51 separate areas of the state showing federal, state and county lands with their recreational facilities.

Public Recreation Information Maps (PRIM) are available for purchase from the DNR gift shop, DNR regional offices, Minnesota state parks and major sporting and superstores.

Check it out - you'll be glad you did.

Lake Superior

Moose Mountain

Bailey Creek Ski Trail

Cascade River

Superior Hiking Trail

The Cascades

Cascade Falls

Cascade Creek

Cascade Lodge

Lookout Mountain

Respect Private Property — Ask First

← to Deer Yard Lake

Indian Camp Creek

© 11/1996 by State of Minnesota.

Near Grand Portage State Park   Photo by Dudley Edmondson

NEARBY PLACES TO VISIT

Cook County His. Society/Johnson Heritage Post - Grand Marais, 218-387-2314
Devil's Kettle Falls - Grand Marais, 218-387-2929, 218-226-3539
Grand Portage National Monument - Grand Marais, 218-387-2788, 218-475-2202
Lutsen-Tofte Tourism Assoc - Tofte, 218-663-7804, 888-616-6784
Superior National at Lutsen - Lutsen, 218-663-7195, 218-387-2314

OUR NOTES

Date visited   What we liked

Eagle Mountain is the highest point in Minnesota at 2,301 feet.

Franz Jevene State Park
RR 3 Box 230
Birchdale, MN 56629

DIRECTIONS

The park is located 41 miles west of International Falls or 29 miles east of Baudette on Highway 11.

ABOUT THE PARK

Franz Jevene is a 118 acre park, situated on the Rainy River. The park was created in 1969 when the land was donated by the family of Franz Jevene, an early resident of the area. This is the only State Park in the system that is free, since it is supported by private funding. Development of the park is proceeding slowly, but with much thought toward the future. Passport Club members need to visit Zippel Bay State Park to get their stamp.

The good spring fishing is the major draw of the park. The Sault Rapid is one of only two rapids on the river. The terrain is rough and beautiful, and the park is so remote that many of the visitors are local. As a result, the campsites are rarely full.

There are several remote sites available by boat or hiking. Many of the campsites are on the Rainy River, and offer a view of Canada. Across the river to the Canadian side, seven Indian burial mounds are visible.

IF YOU GO . . .

Bring your fishing pole! There is a boat launch onto the Rainy River, or you can follow the trail through the park for several incredibly scenic and peaceful spots where you can try to catch your dinner.

FRANZ JEVENE STATE PARK

FACILITIES

Visitor Center:	no
Picnic Area:	picnic area with shelter

RECREATION

Children's play area:	no
Volleyball courts:	no
Horseshoe pits:	no
Swimming:	no
Fishing:	fishing on the Rainy River
Boating:	boating on the Rainy River
	drive-in boat access

CAMPGROUND

Campsites:	15 drive-in campsites
Electric:	no
Hike or carry-in:	2 campsites
Canoe campsites:	1 canoe campsite
Dump station:	no
Toilets:	pit toilets
Showers:	no
Group Campground:	no

TRAILS

Hiking Trails:	2 mile
Hiking Club Trail:	no
Biking Trails:	no
Cross-country Ski:	5 kilometers
Snowmobile Trails:	no
Horse Trails:	no
Horse Campsites:	no

INTERPRETIVE PROGRAMS

There are no interpretive programs available in the park.

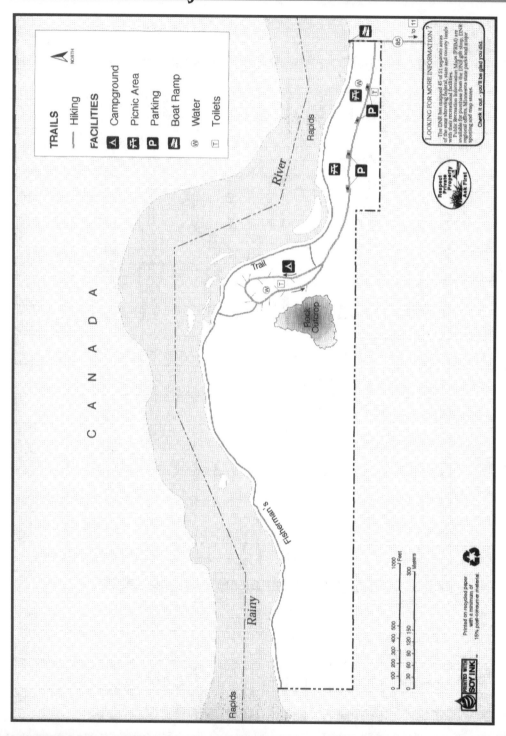

TRAILS

—— Hiking

FACILITIES

▲ Campground

🏕 Picnic Area

🅿 Parking

🚤 Boat Ramp

Ⓦ Water

🅣 Toilets

NORTH

C A N A D A

River

Rapids

Trail

Rock Outcrop

Fisherman's

Rainy

Rapids

LOOKING FOR MORE INFORMATION?

The DNR has mapped 45 of 51 separate areas of their coming federal, state and county lands with their recreational facilities.

Public Recreation Information Maps (PRIM) are available for purchase from the DNR gift shop, DNR regional offices, Minnesota state parks and major sporting and map stores.

Check it out - you'll be glad you did.

Respect Property Ask First

to 11

85

0 100 200 300 400 500 Feet 1000
0 30 60 90 120 150 Meters 300

PRINTED WITH SOY INK

Printed on recycled paper with a minimum of 15% post-consumer material.

Snowshoe Hare   Photo by Dudley Edmondson

NEARBY PLACES TO VISIT

Grand Mound History Center - International Falls, 218-285-3332
International Falls Chamber - International Falls, 800-325-5766, 218-283-9400
International Falls Travel Information Center - International Falls, 218-285-7623
Koochiching County Historical & Bronco Nagurski Museums
    International Falls, 218-283-4316
Lake of the Woods Cty Historical Museum - Baudette, 218-634-1200
Lake of the Woods Area Tourism - Baudette, 800-382-3474, 218-634-1174

OUR NOTES

Date visited   What we liked

TRIVIA

Franz Jevene is the only free park in the state park system.

George H. Crosby-Manitou State Park
474 Highway 61 E
Silver Bay, MN 55614
218-226-3539

DIRECTIONS

To find the park entrance, take Highway 1 to Finland, MN, then County Road 7 for 7 miles.

ABOUT THE PARK

George H. Crosby-Manitou State consists of 5,259 acres located along the Manitou River. George H. Crosby was a mining magnate who donated the land for the park in order that it remain a "wilderness." In keeping with his wishes, this is a park where visitors can get away from the crowds. The only campsites are primitive, and accessible only through rugged trails. Any water taken from the river must be treated, or fresh water carried from the office. The picnic area, located alongside Benson Lake, is small and peaceful.

The area around the park was logged over and cleared for farming earlier in the century. As the land was changed, so did the wildlife, with the white-tail deer and wolf increasing. The Moose population has waxed and waned throughout the years.

IF YOU GO . . .

Bring your backpack and your hiking boots! If a day hike is in the offering, start at the parking lot and head up the middle trail, being sure to stop at the overlooks. The trail connects to the West Manitou River Trail, which heads north to the Cascades. Just past campsite two, the Humpback Trail goes off to the west, and circles back to the parking lot.

GEORGE H. CROSBY-MANITOU STATE PARK

FACILITIES

Visitor Center: no
Picnic Area: picnic area on Bensen Lake

RECREATION

Children's play area: no
Volleyball courts: no
Horseshoe pits: no
Swimming: no
Fishing: fishing on Bensen Lake and the Manitou River
Boating: no

CAMPGROUND

Campsites: there are no drive-in campsites
Electric: no
Hike or carry-in: 21 carry-in campsites
Canoe campsites: no
Dump station: no
Toilets: pit toilets
Showers: no
Group Campground: no

TRAILS

Hiking Trails: 24 miles
Hiking Club Trail: 4.2 miles, starting at the parking lot
Biking Trails: no
Cross-country Ski: 11 miles
Snowmobile Trails: no
Horse Trails: no
Horse Campsites: no

INTERPRETIVE PROGRAMS

There are no interpretive programs available in the park.

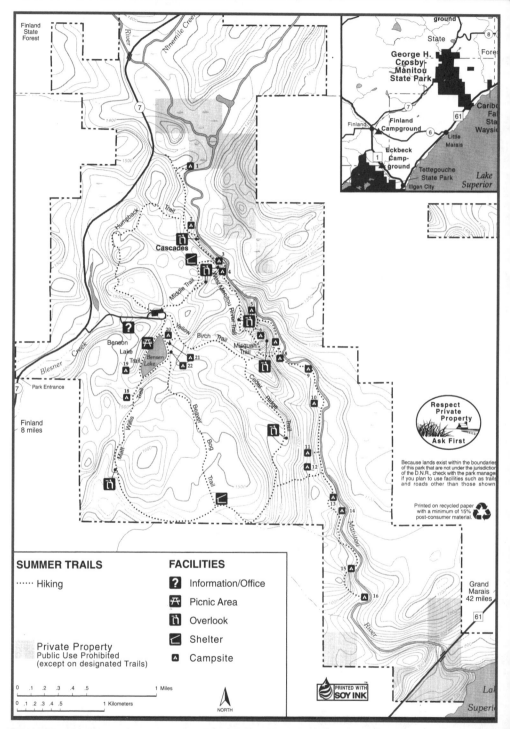

Finland State Forest

ground

State

Fore

George H. Crosby-Manitou State Park

Carib Fa Sta Waysi

Finland

Finland Campground

Little Marais

Eckbeck Camp-ground

Tettegouche State Park

Lake Superior

Illgen City

Ninemile Creek

River

Humback Trail

Cascades

Middle Trail

West Manitou River Trail

Benson Lake Trail

Benson Lake

Blesner Creek

Finland 8 miles

Park Entrance

Yellow Birch Trail

Misquah Trail

Matt Willis Trail

Beaver Bog Trail

Cedar Ridge Trail

Manitou River

Respect Private Property
Ask First

Because lands exist within the boundaries of this park that are not under the jurisdiction of the D.N.R., check with the park manage if you plan to use facilities such as trails and roads other than those shown

Printed on recycled paper with a minimum of 15% post-consumer material.

Grand Marais 42 miles

Lake Superio

SUMMER TRAILS

⋯⋯ Hiking

Private Property
Public Use Prohibited
(except on designated Trails)

FACILITIES

❓ Information/Office

🅰 Picnic Area

📷 Overlook

◰ Shelter

🅰 Campsite

0 .1 .2 .3 .4 .5   1 Miles

0 .1 .2 .3 .4 .5   1 Kilometers

NORTH

PRINTED WITH SOY INK

George H. Crosby-Manitou State Park
Photo by author

NEARBY PLACES TO VISIT

Baptism River High Falls - Silver Bay, 218-226-3539
Silver Bay Chamber - Silver Bay, 218-226-4870
Tettegouche State Park - Silver Bay, 218-226-6365

OUR NOTES

Date visited   What we liked

T R I V I A

Crosby-Manitou was Minnesota's first "backpack only" park.

Gooseberry Falls State Park
1300 Highway 61 E
Two Harbors, MN 55616
218-834-3855

DIRECTIONS

The park is located on Highway 61, 12 miles northeast of Two Harbors.

ABOUT THE PARK

Gooseberry Falls State Park covers 1,662 acres, preserving the Gooseberry River as it flows into Lake Superior. The park's beautiful lake frontage features five waterfalls, including the spectacular Upper and Lower Falls.

Gooseberry Falls State Park was the first park created on the north shore of Lake Superior, and it receives a million visitors during the year. The original Visitor Center and rest area, located next to Highway 61, were built by the Civilian Conservation Corps (CCC) during the late 1930s. The CCC also created roads, buildings, and the fresh water supply. The proximity of the falls to the highway have helped its popularity and created dangerous traffic situations. To relieve the congestion, a new Visitor Center was built on the lake side of the highway. The new Visitor Center does not require a permit, and includes a rest stop, gift shop, Interpretive Center, plenty of parking, and easy access to the river or lake.

The trail system features a hike along the river to the Fifth Falls and connects to the Lake Superior Hiking Trail. The trails also include some incredible views of Lake Superior and several interior trails, one of which features several spectacular foot bridges across the Gooseberry River.

IF YOU GO . . .

Plan to hike! For the visitor who has some time to spend there are many scenic spots to explore. Here is one route to try: Go down to the picnic area and hike along the rocks on the shore of Lake Superior until you find the Lower Rim Trail. Follow the trail up the river to the lower falls and cross the highway to the Upper Falls. Continue on past a scenic overlook to the Fifth Falls, where the trail joins up with the Superior Hiking Trail. Cross the river and explore! These trails make for some wonderful cross-country skiing.

GOOSEBERRY FALLS STATE PARK

FACILITIES

Visitor Center:	yes
Picnic Area:	3 picnic areas along Lake Superior
	enclosed shelter

RECREATION

Children's play area:	no
Volleyball courts:	no
Horseshoe pits:	no
Swimming:	no
Fishing:	river fishing in Gooseberry River
	lake fishing in Lake Superior
Boating:	no

CAMPGROUND

Campsites:	70 drive-in campsites
Electric:	no
Hike or carry-in:	no
Canoe campsites:	no
	kayak campsite as part of the Lake Superior Water Trail
Dump station:	yes
Toilets:	flush toilets
Showers:	yes
Group Campground:	3 group campsites

TRAILS

Hiking Trails:	18 miles
	access to the Superior Hiking Trail
Hiking Club Trail:	2.2 miles, starting at the Interpretive Center
Biking Trails:	10 miles
Cross-country Ski:	15 miles
Warming house:	yes
Snowmobile Trails:	3 miles
Horse Trails:	no
Horse Campsites:	no

INTERPRETIVE PROGRAMS

The park offers seasonal interpretive programs. Check the Visitor Center for a schedule of events.

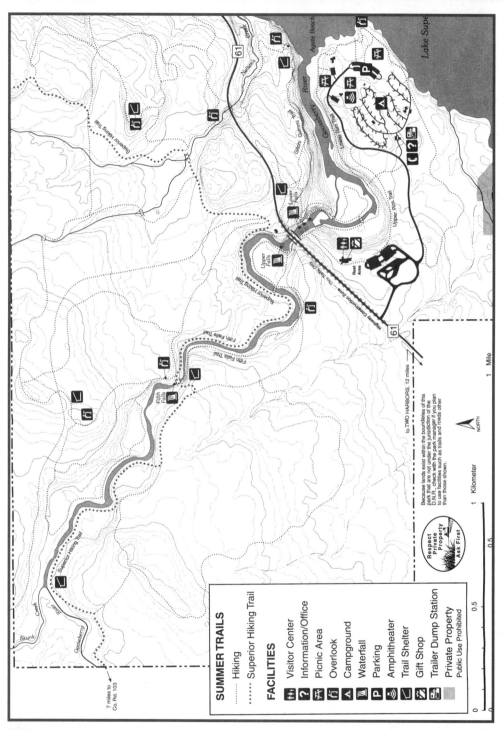

SUMMER TRAILS
- .... Hiking
- •••••••• Superior Hiking Trail

FACILITIES
- Visitor Center
- Information/Office
- Picnic Area
- Overlook
- Campground
- Waterfall
- Parking
- Amphitheater
- Trail Shelter
- Gift Shop
- Trailer Dump Station
- Private Property
  Public Use Prohibited

Because lands exist within the boundaries of this park that are not under the jurisdiction of the D.N.R., check with the park manager if you plan to use facilities such as trails and roads other than those shown.

Respect Private Property
Ask First

to TWO HARBORS, 12 miles

7 miles to Co. Rd. 103

Gooseberry Falls State Park
Photo by Dudley Edmondson

NEARBY PLACES TO VISIT

3M/Dwan Museum - Two Harbors, 218-834-4898
Great Lakes Fur Trade Museum & Shop - Two Harbors, 218-834-3323
Lake County Historical Museum - Two Harbors, 218-834-4898
Lighthouse Point & Harbor Museum - Two Harbors, 218-834-4898
Split Rock Lighthouse Historic Site - Two Harbors, 218-226-6372, 218-834-4898
Superior Hiking Trail - Two Harbors, 218-834-4436, 218-834-2700

OUR NOTES

Date visited   What we liked

Two Civilian Conservation Corps (CCC) camps were established
at Gooseberry Falls State Park. There were 200 men there working.
Gooseberry Falls State Park has five waterfalls in the park.

GRAND PORTAGE STATE PARK

Grand Portage State Park
HCR 1, Box 7
Grand Portage, MN 55605
218-475-2360

DIRECTIONS

The park is located 8 miles northeast of Grand Portage, on Highway 61.

ABOUT THE PARK

Grand Portage State Park is relatively new, having been established in 1989. This park is not owned by the state, but is leased from the Bureau of Indian Affairs for the Grand Portage Band. The park is still under development, with plans to develop a picnic area and to enhance the trail system.

The park's 300 acres preserve the beauty and history of the Pigeon River, the longest river along the north shore of Lake Superior. This area was long used for hunting and fishing by the Indians, since it provides access from Lake Superior to the inland waterways. Unfortunately, the lower Pigeon River has 20 miles of rapids, making it unnavigable. To bypass the rapids, the native Indians created the Grand Portage, a nine mile trail that starts at Lake Superior and bypasses the rapids to Fort Charlotte. During the fur trade, voyageurs would traverse the portage carrying several 90 pound "bales!"

IF YOU GO . . .

Plan to see the falls! One of the highlights of the park is the one mile round trip trail that leads to the incredible High Falls. The trail is handicapped accessible via a boardwalk that covers the last part of the trail.

GRAND PORTAGE STATE PARK

FACILITIES

Visitor Center:	no
Picnic Area:	picnic area along the Pigeon River

RECREATION

Children's play area:	no
Volleyball courts:	no
Horseshoe pits:	no
Swimming:	no
Fishing:	no
Boating:	no

CAMPGROUND

Campsites:	no
Electric:	no
Hike or carry-in:	no
Canoe campsites:	no
Dump station:	no
Toilets:	no
Showers:	no
Group Campground:	no

TRAILS

Hiking Trails:	5 miles
Hiking Club Trail:	no
Biking Trails:	no
Cross-country Ski:	no
Snowmobile Trails:	no
Horse Trails:	no
Horse Campsites:	no

INTERPRETIVE PROGRAMS

There are no interpretive programs available in the park.

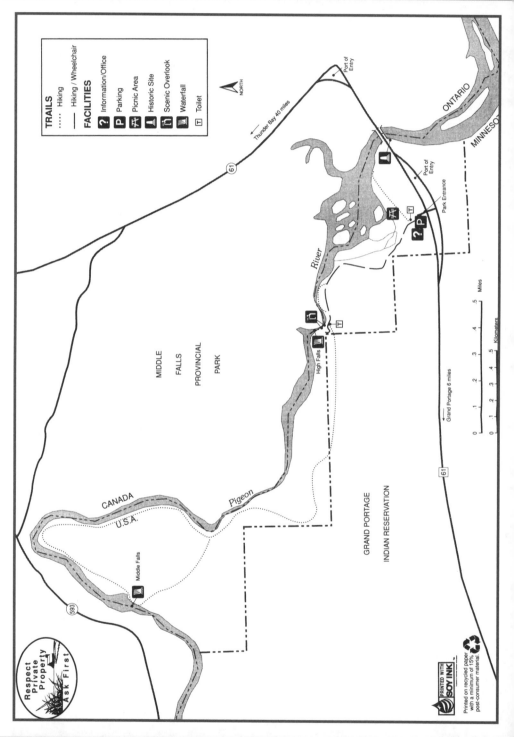

Grand Portage State Park   Photo by author

NEARBY PLACES TO VISIT

Grand Portage Tourist Assoc - Grand Portage, 218-475-2401, 800-232-1384
Grand Portage Travel Information Center - Grand Portage, 218-475-2592

OUR NOTES

Date visited   What we liked

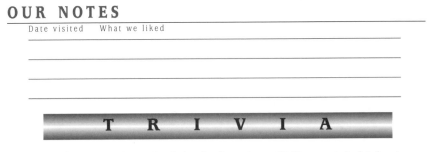

T R I V I A

Grand Portage State Park is the location of Minnesota's highest waterfall (between Minnesota and Canada) at 120 feet.

Grand Portage State Park is home to a "grand portage" trail going nine miles around 20 miles of rapids on the Pigeon River. Where the trail connects with Lake Superior, a reconstructed fort from the early part of the 19th century can be toured.

HILL ANNEX MINE STATE PARK

Hill Annex Mine State Park
Box 376
Calumet, MN 55716
218-247-7215

DIRECTIONS

The park is located north of Calumet on Highway 169.

ABOUT THE PARK

Hill Annex Mine State Park is an intact open pit iron ore mine that operated from 1914 to 1978. The park consists of 635 acres, and was created in 1988 when its ownership was transferred from the Iron Range Resources and Rehabilitation Board.

The highlight of the park is the tour of the mine, which lasts 1.5 hours. As visitors are led into the mine, they can view the historic buildings and equipment.

IF YOU GO . . .

Tour the mine! Mine tours are available to the general public Memorial Day weekend through Labor Day weekend. School and senior citizen groups can call for information on group tours during the spring and fall months.

NEARBY PLACES TO VISIT

Carey Lake Regional Park - Hibbing, 218-263-8851
Edge of the Wilderness Scenic Byway - Grand Rapids, 218-326-9607
Forest History Center - Grand Rapids, 218-327-4482
Grand Rapids Visitor/Convention Bureau
    Grand Rapids, 800-472-6366, 218-326-9607
Greyhound Bus Origin Center - Hibbing, 218-263-5814 218-263-6485
Hibbing Chamber - Hibbing, 800-444-2246, 218-262-3895
Hibbing Historical Society Museum - Hibbing, 218-263-8522
Hull Rust Mahoning Mine - Hibbing, 218-262-4166 218-262-4900
Judy Garland Birthplace Museum - Grand Rapids, 800-664-5839, 218-327-9276
Mahoning Mine Hull Rust - Hibbing, 218-262-4166, 218-262-4900
Taconite State Trail - Grand Rapids, 612-296-6699, 218-327-4408

HILL ANNEX MINE STATE PARK

FACILITIES

Visitor Center: seasonal
Picnic Area: no

RECREATION

Children's play area: no
Volleyball courts: no
Horseshoe pits: no
Swimming: no
Fishing: no
Boating: no

CAMPGROUND

Campsites: no
Electric: no
Hike or carry-in: no
Canoe campsites: no
Dump station: no
Toilets: no
Showers: no
Group Campground: no

TRAILS

Hiking Trails: no
Hiking Club Trail: no
Biking Trails: no
Cross-country Ski: no
Snowmobile Trails: no
Horse Trails: no
Horse Campsites: no

INTERPRETIVE PROGRAMS

The Visitor Center, where visitors meet for the tours, offers exhibits about mine life.

TRIVIA

Hill Annex Mine is on the National Register of Historic Places.

Jay Cooke State Park
500 E Highway 210
Carlton, MN 55718
218-384-4610

DIRECTIONS

The park is located 3 miles east of Carlton on Highway 210.

ABOUT THE PARK

Jay Cooke State Park was established in 1915 and currently contains 8,818 acres. The initial acreage was a donation by the heirs of Jay Cooke, a local financier.

This area was inhabited by the Dakota Indians until the Ojibway forced them to move west. When fur trading developed in the area the rapids and rugged terrain of the St. Louis River forced the creation of another "grand portage" to bypass that section of the river. The 7 mile portage trail connected the Savanna Portage, Big Sandy Lake, and the Mississippi River. Eventually the railroads made it to northern Minnesota and Duluth, which brought in many settlers. The land surrounding the river was purchased for the city of Duluth, in anticipation of the need for power, and was never farmed.

IF YOU GO . . .

Bring your bike! Jay Cooke State Park intersects the Willard Munger State Trail, and also offers 8 miles of mountain bike trails. Check out the Visitor Center, a beautiful building built during the depression by the Civilian Conservation Corps (CCC). From there, walk across the St. Louis River on the swinging bridge, which was remodeled in 1940. Once across the river, do some hiking and relaxing along the rock formations.

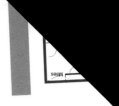

FACILITIES

sitor Center:	yes
	2 shelters with fireplaces
cnic Area:	2 picnic areas, Oldenburg Point and Louis River

RECREATION

hildren's play area:	yes
olleyball court:	yes
orseshoe pits:	yes
wimming:	no
shing:	river fishing
oating:	no

CAMPGROUND

ampsites:	80 drive-in campsite
ectric:	21 electric campsites
ike or carry-in:	4 backpack campsites
	3 walk-in campsites
anoe campsites:	no
ump station:	yes
oilets:	flush toilets
nowers:	yes
roup Campground:	2 group campsites

TRAILS

iking Trails:	50 miles
iking Club Trail:	3.5 miles, starting at the River Inn area and crossing the swinging bridge
king Trails:	5 miles of paved trails
	9 miles of paved trails are part of the Willard Munger State Trail
	8 miles of Mountain Bike trails
oss-country Ski:	32 miles
	8 miles of skate/ski trails
arming house:	yes
nowmobile Trails:	12 miles
orse Trails:	no
orse Campsites:	no

INTERPRETIVE PROGRAMS

park naturalist conducts programs during the summer months. Check the bul-
tin boards at the contact station for schedules.

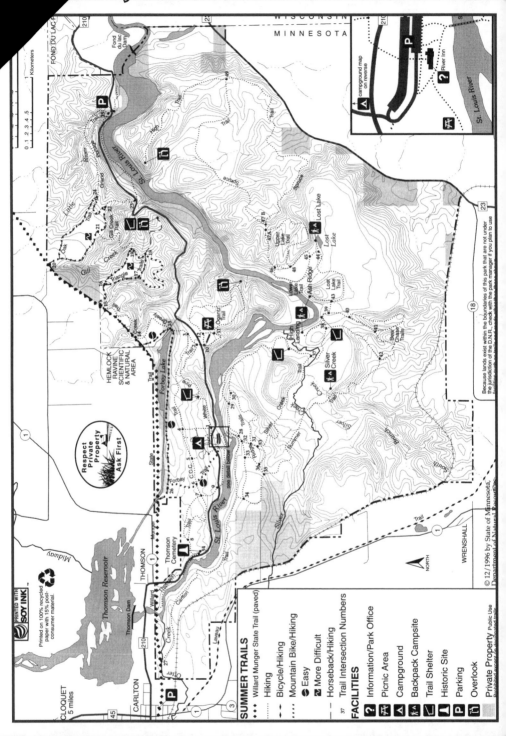

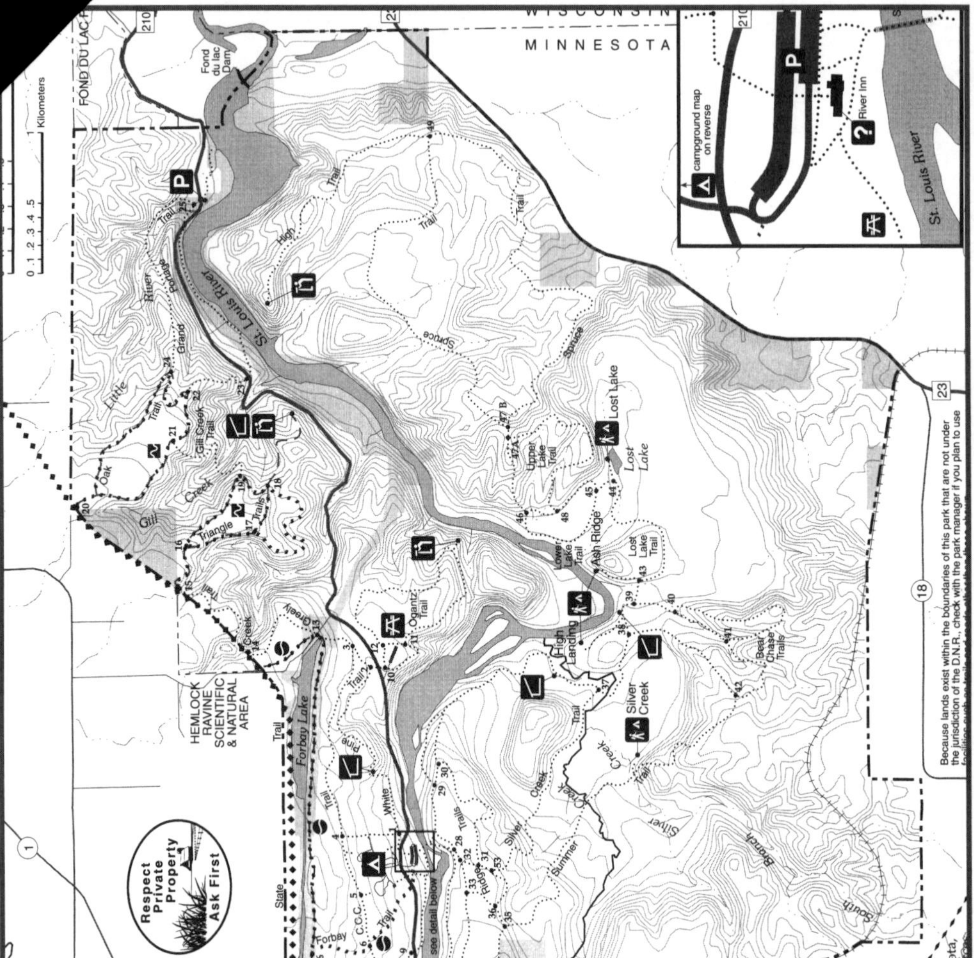
SUMMER TRAILS
Willard Munger State Trail (paved)
Hiking
Bicycle/Hiking
Mountain Bike/Hiking
Easy
More Difficult
Horseback/Hiking
37 Trail Intersection Numbers
FACILITIES
Information/Park Office
Picnic Area
Campground
Backpack Campsite
Trail Shelter
Historic Site
Parking
Overlook
Private Property Public Use
Printed on 100% recycled paper with 15% post-consumer material.
PRINTED WITH SOY INK
Respect Private Property Ask First
© 12/1996 by State of Minnesota, Department of Natural Resources
Because lands exist within the boundaries of this park that are not under the jurisdiction of the D.N.R., check with the park manager if you plan to use
WISCONSIN
MINNESOTA
FOND DU LAC
Fond du lac Dam
Kilometers
St. Louis River
Thomson Reservoir
Thomson Dam
THOMSON
CARLTON
CLOQUET 5 miles
WRENSHALL
NORTH
HEMLOCK RAVINE SCIENTIFIC & NATURAL AREA
Forbay Lake
Thomson Cemetery
Lost Lake
Ash Ridge
High Landing
Silver Creek
River Inn
campground map on reverse
see detail below

Jay Cooke State Park   Photo by Dudley Edmondson

NEARBY PLACES TO VISIT

Carlton Area Chamber - Carlton, 218-384-4281
Carlton County Historical Society Museum - Cloquet, 218-879-1938
Duluth Children's Museum - Duluth, 218-733-7543, 218-733-7548
Glensheen Mansion - Duluth, 218-724-8864, 888-454-4536
Highway 210 - Scenic Byway - Carlton, 218-384-4610
Karpeles Manuscript Library Museum - Duluth, 218-728-0630
Lake Superior Museum of Transportation - Duluth, 218-733-7590
Marine Museum - Duluth, 218-727-2497, 218-720-5271
St Louis County Heritage & Arts Center - Duluth, 218-727-8025
St Louis County Historical Society - Duluth, 218-733-7580
William A. Irvin Ore Boat Tour - Duluth, 218-722-7876, 800-628-8385
Willard Munger State Trail - Moose Lake, 612-296-6699, 800-263-0586

OUR NOTES

Date visited   What we liked

_____

_____

_____

T R I V I A

At Jay Cook State park there is a "grand portage" 7 miles in length bypassing the rapids of the St. Louis River. Using this portage, it took early travelers 3-5 days to complete their journey from the Lake Superior watershed to the upper Mississippi watershed.

Judge C. R. Magney State Park
Box 500 East Star Rt
Grand Marais, MN 55604
218-387-2929

DIRECTIONS

The park is located 14 miles northeast of Grand Marais on Highway 61.

ABOUT THE PARK

Judge C. R. Magney State Park was established in 1957. The original name of the 4,514 acre park was Bois Brule State Park, but the legislature later changed the name to honor Judge Magney, an important advocate of the state parks who was instrumental to the creation of parks along the north shore of Lake Superior.

The Civilian Conservation Corps (CCC) had a camp based here, and the foundations of their buildings can still be seen. They farmed their own food, built fire trails, logged, and carried out many other public service projects, including the building of a small tourist camp next to the Brule River. The men helped to fight a forest fire near the camp during the summer of 1936, and afterwards built a sawmill to salvage the leftover wood.

IF YOU GO . . .

Check out the waterfalls! The Brule River cascades through the park just before it flows into Lake Superior. There are three waterfalls on this portion of the river, all of which are accessible to visitors. Upper and Lower Falls are a short hike from the parking area, and further up the trail is Devil's Kettle, where the rocks divide the river into two segments. One segment falls 50 feet into a pool below, while the other one plunges into a pothole "never to be seen again," according to local legend.

JUDGE C. R. MAGNEY STATE PARK

FACILITIES

Visitor Center: no
Picnic Area: 3 picnic areas

RECREATION

Children's play area: no
Volleyball courts: no
Horseshoe pits: no
Swimming: no
Fishing: seasonal river fishing
Boating: no

CAMPGROUND

Campsites: 36 drive-in campsites
Electric: no
Hike or carry-in: 1 backpack campsite
Canoe campsites: no
Dump station: no
Toilets: pit toilets
Showers: no
Group Campground: no

TRAILS

Hiking Trails: 9 miles
Hiking Club Trail: 2.5 miles, starting at the trail head parking lot
Biking Trails: no
Cross-country Ski: 5 miles
Snowmobile Trails: no
Horse Trails: no
Horse Campsites: no

INTERPRETIVE PROGRAMS

There are no interpretive programs available in the park.

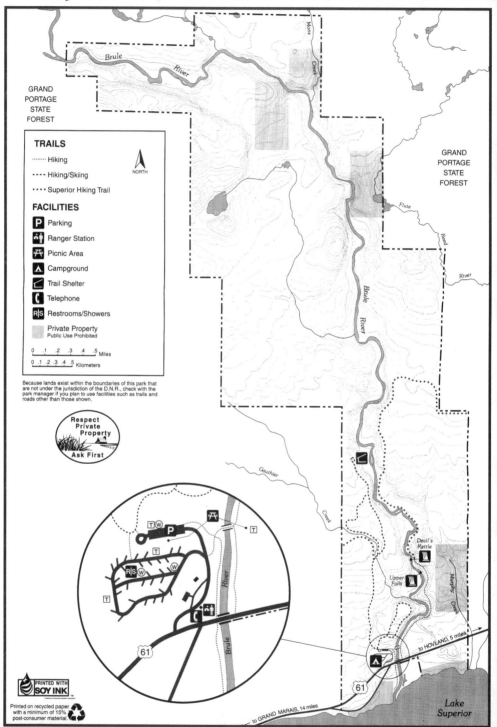

GRAND
PORTAGE
STATE
FOREST

GRAND
PORTAGE
STATE
FOREST

TRAILS

······· Hiking

···· Hiking/Skiing

•••• Superior Hiking Trail

NORTH

FACILITIES

🅿 Parking

🛉 Ranger Station

🎋 Picnic Area

🛆 Campground

◪ Trail Shelter

☎ Telephone

R|S Restrooms/Showers

Private Property
Public Use Prohibited

0 .1 .2 .3 .4 .5 Miles
0 .1 .2 .3 .4 .5 Kilometers

Because lands exist within the boundaries of this park that
are not under the jurisdiction of the D.N.R., check with the
park manager if you plan to use facilities such as trails and
roads other than those shown.

Respect
Private
Property
Ask First

Brule River

Mons Creek

Flute

Reed River

Brule River

Gauthier Creek

Devil's Kettle

Upper Falls

Murphy Creek

to HOVLAND, 5 miles

61

to GRAND MARAIS, 14 miles

Lake Superior

PRINTED WITH
SOY INK

Printed on recycled paper
with a minimum of 15%
post-consumer material.

Great Gray Owl
Photo by Dudley Edmondson

NEARBY PLACES TO VISIT

Cook County Historical Society/Johnson Heritage Post - Grand Marais, 218-387-2314
Grand Marais Chamber - Grand Marais, 888-922-5000, 218-387-2524
Grand Portage National Monument - Grand Marais, 218-387-2788, 218-475-2202

OUR NOTES

Date visited   What we liked

_____

_____

_____

_____

_____

T R I V I A

Water from Minnesota feeds 3 separate watersheds.
Water from the Red River flows to Hudson Bay.
Water from Lake Superior flows to the Atlantic Ocean.
Water from the Mississippi flows to the Gulf of Mexico.

McCarthy Beach State Park
7622 McCarthy Beach Road
Side Lake, MN 55781
218-254-2411

DIRECTIONS

From Hibbing, take 169 north to County Road 5. It is 15 miles to the park entrance.

ABOUT THE PARK

McCarthy Beach State Park was established in 1945, and has grown to contain 2,566 acres. offers an abundance of lakes for water sports and hilly terrain for hiking. Sturgeon and Side Lakes are the two major lakes in the area, with only a narrow strip of land separating them.

During the late 1890s, this heavily wooded area was logged when a railroad was built to Sturgeon Lake from Hibbing. The giant red and white pine logs were then transported down the Mississippi to the sawmills in Minneapolis. Local settlers made use of the area, once homesteaded by John McCarthy, for picnics and water recreation. The original park consisted of 135 acres, and most of the development has occurred there. The bathhouse and other buildings were created from left over Civilian Conservation Corps (CCC) materials from Jay Cooke State Park.

IF YOU GO . . .

Bring you swimming suit, fishing pole, and water craft! This park has seven lakes for fishing, two of which have boat landings. After an early morning fishing excursion, take a hike through the red and white pines, and then back to Sturgeon Lake for a swim.

McCARTHY BEACH STATE PARK

FACILITIES

Visitor Center:	no
Picnic Area:	picnic area with shelter on Sturgeon Lake

RECREATION

Children's play area:	no
Horseshoe pits:	yes
Volleyball courts:	no
Swimming:	swimming beach on Sturgeon Lake
Fishing:	fishing on 7 lakes
Boating:	drive-in boat access to Sturgeon Lake, Side Lake and Beatrice Lake
	boat rentals

CAMPGROUND

Campsites:	59 drive-in campsites on Side Lake
	32 rustic drive-in campsites on Beatrice Lake
Electric:	no
Bike or carry-in:	3 campsites
Canoe campsites:	no
Dump station:	yes
Toilets:	flush toilets
Showers:	yes
Group Campground:	yes

TRAILS

Hiking Trails:	18 miles
Biking Club Trail:	3.4 miles, starting at the parking lot
Biking Trails:	17 miles
Cross-country Ski:	9 miles
Warming house:	yes
Snowmobile Trails:	12 miles
Horse Trails:	12 miles
Horse Campsites:	no

INTERPRETIVE PROGRAMS

During the summer months a park naturalist provides a variety of programs. Bulletin boards should be checked for the schedule of activities.

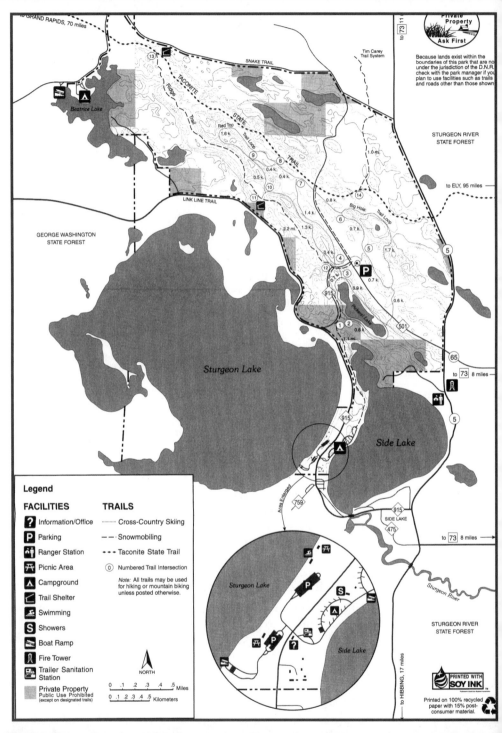

Legend

FACILITIES

?	Information/Office
P	Parking
🚶	Ranger Station
🏓	Picnic Area
▲	Campground
🏕	Trail Shelter
🏊	Swimming
S	Showers
🚤	Boat Ramp
🔦	Fire Tower
🚽	Trailer Sanitation Station
	Private Property

Public Use Prohibited
(except on designated trails)

TRAILS

.... Cross-Country Skiing

– – · Snowmobiling

–·–· Taconite State Trail

(0) Numbered Trail Intersection

Note: All trails may be used for hiking or mountain biking unless posted otherwise.

NORTH

0 .1 .2 .3 .4 .5 Miles

0 .1 .2 .3 .4 .5 Kilometers

GEORGE WASHINGTON STATE FOREST

STURGEON RIVER STATE FOREST

Sturgeon Lake

Side Lake

Sturgeon River

Beatrice Lake

TACONITE

Ridge Trail

SNAKE TRAIL

STATE

Trail Loop

Red Top
1.6 k.

TRAIL

LINK LINE TRAIL

Big Hole Trail Loop

Pickerel Lake

Tim Carey Trail System

Private Property Ask First

Because lands exist within the boundaries of this park that are not under the jurisdiction of the D.N.R., check with the park manager if you plan to use facilities such as trails and roads other than those shown.

to GRAND RAPIDS, 70 miles

to ELY, 95 miles

to HIBBING, 17 miles

to 73 8 miles

to 73 8 miles

SIDE LAKE

Area Enlarged

PRINTED WITH SOY INK

Printed on 100% recycled paper with 15% post-consumer material.

Yellow-rumped Warbler (female)   Photo by Dudley Edmondson

NEARBY PLACES TO VISIT

Carey Lake Regional Park - Hibbing, 218-263-8851
Greyhound Bus Origin Center - Hibbing, 218-263-5814, 218-263-6485
Hibbing Chamber - Hibbing, 800-444-2246, 218-262-3895
Hibbing Historical Society Museum - Hibbing, 218-263-8522
Hull Rust Mahoning Mine - Hibbing, 218-262-4166, 218-262-4900
Ironworld Discovery Center - Chisholm, 800-372-6437, 218-254-3321
Minnesota Museum of Mining - Chisholm, 218-254-5543, 218-254-7158
Olcott Heritage Museum - Virginia, 218-741-1136

OUR NOTES

Date visited   What we liked

TRIVIA

Need information about Minnesota Tourism, just call 800-657-3700 or 612-296-5029.
The phone is answered 24 hours a day for the caller to leave a message
requesting information free of charge.

Moose Lake State Park
RR 2 1000 Co. 137
Moose Lake, MN 55767
218-485-5420

DIRECTIONS

The park is located 1 mile east of Interstate 35 at the Moose Lake exit.

ABOUT THE PARK

Moose Lake State Park was established in 1971, and contains about 1,200 acres. The original forest that once blanketed the area was logged, so the park's fields (originally from the Moose Lake State Hospital) are slowly being restored back to their original forested condition.

The settlement of Moose Lake was a stop on the 1860s stagecoach run from St. Paul to Duluth. The town moved to its present location to be on the railroad.

The sandy beach and good fishing make this park very popular, especially with the local population. The campground overlooks Echo Lake.

IF YOU GO . . .

Plan on some fishing and swimming on Echo Lake. There is a boat launch on the east side of the lake. Northern and walleye are found in the lake. Take a break on the drive to Lake Superior for a swim at the sandy beach.

MOOSE LAKE STATE PARK

FACILITIES

Visitor Center:	no
Picnic Area:	2 picnic areas on Echo Lake

RECREATION

Children's play area:	no
Volleyball courts:	no
Horseshoe pits:	no
Swimming:	swimming beach on Echo Lake
Fishing:	fishing on Echo Lake
Boating:	drive-in boat access to Echo Lake
	boat rental

CAMPGROUND

Campsites:	18 drive-in campsites
Electric:	no
Hike or carry-in:	no
Canoe campsites:	no
Dump station:	no
Toilets:	pit toilets
Showers:	no
Group Campground:	no

TRAILS

Hiking Trails:	4 miles
Hiking Club Trail:	2 miles, starting just east of the park office
Biking Trails:	no
Cross-country Ski:	7 miles
Snowmobile Trails:	2 miles
Horse Trails:	no
Horse Campsites:	no

INTERPRETIVE PROGRAMS

There are no interpretive programs available in the park.

MOOSE LAKE STATE PARK

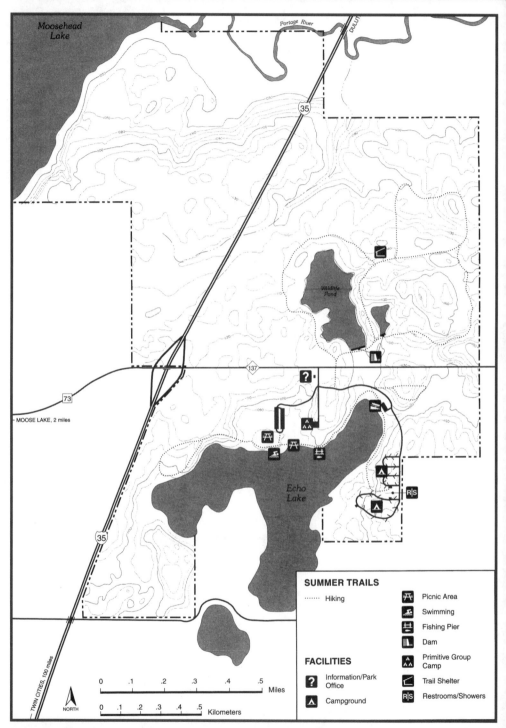

Moosehead Lake

Portage River

DULUTH

35

Wildlife Pond

73

MOOSE LAKE, 2 miles

137

Echo Lake

35

R|S

TWIN CITIES, 100 miles

SUMMER TRAILS

...... Hiking

🎋 Picnic Area

🏊 Swimming

🎣 Fishing Pier

Dam

⛺ Primitive Group Camp

Trail Shelter

R|S Restrooms/Showers

FACILITIES

? Information/Park Office

🅰 Campground

| 0 | .1 | .2 | .3 | .4 | .5 |

Miles

| 0 | .1 | .2 | .3 | .4 | .5 |

Kilometers

NORTH

Red-winged Blackbird (female)
Photo by John Pennoyer

NEARBY PLACES TO VISIT

Moose Lake Chamber - Moose Lake, 800-635-3680, 218-485-4145
Willard Munger State Trail - Moose Lake, 612-296-6699, 800-263-0586

OUR NOTES

Date visited   What we liked

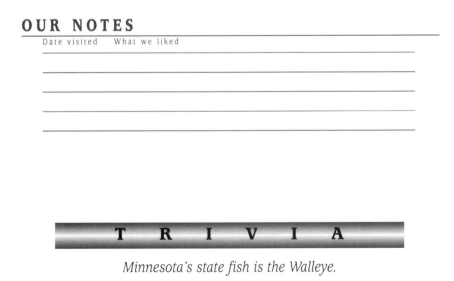

Minnesota's state fish is the Walleye.

Scenic State Park
HCR 2 Box 17
Bigfork, MN 56628
218-743-3362

DIRECTIONS

The park is located 7 miles east of Bigfork on County Road 7.

ABOUT THE PARK

Scenic State Park was created in 1921 and is comprised of 2,649 acres. This area is thought to have been used for seasonal hunting by the Ojibway, but it is doubtful that they had a permanent presence here. During the late 1800s this area was logged, and settlers moved in to attempt farming. In the early 1920s, area residents wanted the remaining birch and pines to be preserved, and requested state protection of the land. When the park was created it was very remote, and it received very little development until the Civilian Conservation Corps (CCC) came to the park during the depression to build buildings and help with other developments.

IF YOU GO . . .

Bring your hiking shoes! For a peaceful afternoon hike, head southeast from the Chase Point Campground until you pick up the self-guided interpretive trail that heads out onto Chase Point. The trail is quite scenic, offering views of Sandwick Lake and Coon Lake.

SCENIC STATE PARK

FACILITIES

Visitor Center:	seasonal Visitor Center on Coon Lake
Picnic Area:	picnic area on Coon Lake

RECREATION

Children's play area:	no
Volleyball courts:	no
Horseshoe pits:	no
Swimming:	swimming beach on Coon Lake
Fishing:	lake fishing
	fishing pier on Coon Lake
Boating:	2 drive-in boat access points to Coon Lake
	boat and canoe rental

CAMPGROUND

Campsites:	120 drive-in campsites
Electric:	17 electric campsites
Hike or carry-in:	6 backpack campsites
Canoe campsites:	1 canoe campsite
Dump station:	yes
Toilets:	flush toilets
Showers:	yes
Group Campground:	primitive group campsite
Guest House:	lake shore house on Sandwick Lake
	4 bedrooms sleeping 10 people
	there is also 1 3/4 bathrooms and a kitchen

TRAILS

Hiking Trails:	14 miles
Hiking Club Trail:	2.9 miles, starting near the park office
Biking Trails:	2 paved miles
Cross-country Ski:	10 miles
Warming house:	yes
Snowshoe rental:	yes
Snowmobile Trails:	12 miles
Horse Trails:	no
Horse Campsites:	no

INTERPRETIVE PROGRAMS

A park naturalist provides interpretive programs during the summer months.
Visitors should check the bulletin boards for schedules.

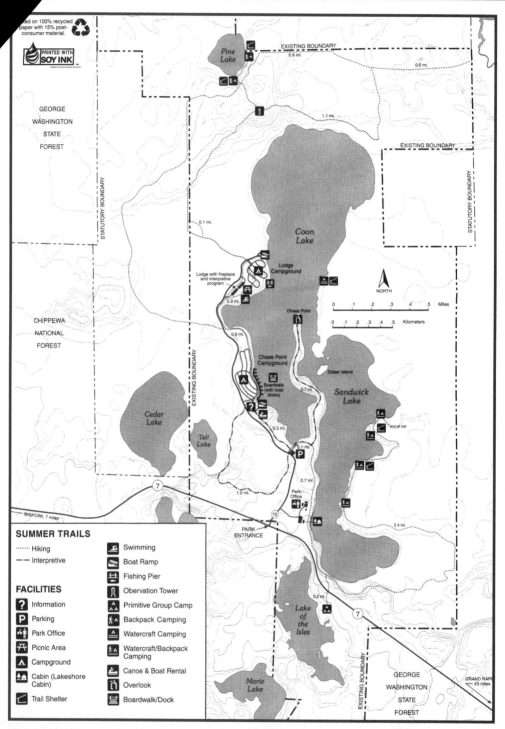

SUMMER TRAILS

- .... Hiking
- —·—· Interpretive

FACILITIES

- ? Information
- P Parking
- Park Office
- Picnic Area
- Campground
- Cabin (Lakeshore Cabin)
- Trail Shelter

- Swimming
- Boat Ramp
- Fishing Pier
- Obervation Tower
- Primitive Group Camp
- Backpack Camping
- Watercraft Camping
- Watercraft/Backpack Camping
- Canoe & Boat Rental
- Overlook
- Boardwalk/Dock

SCENIC STATE PARK

Photo by Dudley Edmondson

NEARBY PLACES TO VISIT

Edge of the Wilderness Scenic Byway - Grand Rapids, 218-326-9607
Forest History Center - Grand Rapids, 218-327-4482
Grand Rapids Visitor & Convention Bureau
    Grand Rapids, 800-472-6366, 218-326-9607
Judy Garland Birthplace Museum - Grand Rapids, 800-664-5839, 218-327-9276
Taconite State Trail - Grand Rapids, 612-296-6699, 218-327-4408

OUR NOTES

Date visited   What we liked

TRIVIA

The Common Loon is Minnesota's state bird.

Schoolcraft State Park
HCR 4 Box 181
Deer River, MN 56636
218-566-2383

DIRECTIONS

From Grand Rapids, go west on Highway 2 to County Road 6, then south to County Road 65. Next, go west to County Road 74, and north to the park entrance.

ABOUT THE PARK

Schoolcraft State Park, 295 acres, was established in 1959. The park is small, and situated in a nicely wooded area along the Mississippi River.

The park was named for Henry Rowe Schoolcraft, who, in 1832, became the first European to see the headwaters of the Mississippi River. Schoolcraft is believed to have camped in the park area on his trip up the river. He was also an Indian agent to the Ojibway, and put together many writings about the customs, history, and legends of the Indians.

There are signs that prehistoric people once lived in the park. Later, in the days of river travel, the southern edge of the park was a rest stop for those journeying on the Mississippi River. This part of the park was also a logging camp while the area was being logged, and is the site of a homestead dated back to 1898.

IF YOU GO . . .

Bring your boat! Schoolcraft State Park is located along the Mississippi and Vermillion Rivers. There is a boat launch on the Mississippi, and the fishing is excellent in either river.

SCHOOLCRAFT STATE PARK

FACILITIES

Visitor Center: no
Picnic Area: picnic area along the Mississippi River

RECREATION

Children's play area: no
Volleyball courts: no
Horseshoe pits: no
Swimming: no
Fishing: fishing on the Mississippi and Vermillion Rivers
Boating: drive-in boat access to the Mississippi River

CAMPGROUND

Campsites: 37 drive-in campsites
Electric: no
Hike or carry-in: no
Canoe campsites: 12 campsites along the Mississippi River
Dump station: no
Toilets: pit toilets
Showers: no
Group Campground: 1 primitive group campground

TRAILS

Hiking Trails: 2 miles
Hiking Club Trail: 1.8 miles, starting at the picnic area parking lot
Biking Trails: no
Cross-country Ski: no
Snowmobile Trails: no
Horse Trails: no
Horse Campsites: no

INTERPRETIVE PROGRAMS

There is no park naturalist at Schoolcraft State Park, but there is a short self-guided interpretive trail.

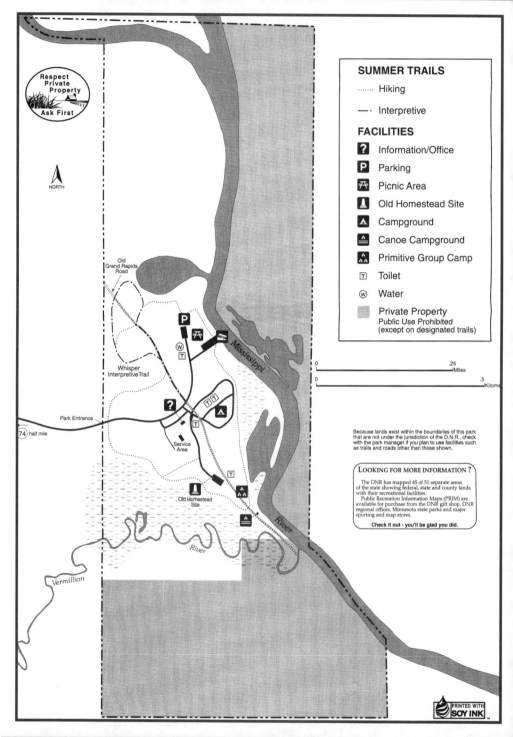

Respect Private Property Ask First

NORTH

SUMMER TRAILS

...... Hiking

—-· Interpretive

FACILITIES

? Information/Office

P Parking

⛽ Picnic Area

Old Homestead Site

▲ Campground

Canoe Campground

Primitive Group Camp

T Toilet

W Water

Private Property
Public Use Prohibited
(except on designated trails)

0 .25 Miles

0 .5 Kilome

Old Grand Rapids Road

Whisper Interpretive Trail

Park Entrance

(74) half mile

Service Area

Old Homestead Site

Mississippi

River

River

Vermillion

Because lands exist within the boundaries of this park that are not under the jurisdiction of the D.N.R., check with the park manager if you plan to use facilities such as trails and roads other than those shown.

LOOKING FOR MORE INFORMATION ?

The DNR has mapped 45 of 51 separate areas of the state showing federal, state and county lands with their recreational facilities.
Public Recreation Information Maps (PRIM) are available for purchase from the DNR gift shop, DNR regional offices, Minnesota state parks and major sporting and map stores.

Check it out - you'll be glad you did.

PRINTED WITH SOY INK

White-tailed Deer   Photo by Dudley Edmondson

NEARBY PLACES TO VISIT

Cass County & Walker Museum Historical Society's - Walker, 218-547-7251
Forest History Center - Grand Rapids, 218-327-4482
Grand Rapids Visitor & Convention Bureau
   Grand Rapids, 800-472-6366, 218-326-9607
Judy Garland Birthplace Museum - Grand Rapids, 800-664-5839, 218-327-9276
Leech Lake Area Tourism Bureau - Walker, 218-654-3150
Leech Lake Area Chamber - Walker, 800-833-1118, 218-547-1313
Leech Lake Hunting Area - Federal Dam, 218-654-3998
Taconite State Trail - Grand Rapids, 612-296-6699, 218-327-4408

OUR NOTES

Date visited   What we liked

TRIVIA

It has been said the Longfellow used Henry Schoolcraft's research in the writing of The Legend of Hiawatha.

Soudan Underground Mine State Park
Box 335
Soudan, MN 55782
218-753-2245

DIRECTIONS

The park is located just off Highway 169 in Soudan.

ABOUT THE PARK

Soudan Underground Mine State Park was created in 1963, and covers 1,300 acres.

Iron Ore was discovered in Soudan in the 1880s. The Soudan Mine began operation in 1884, and by the 1890s had progressed from an open mine to an underground mine. The mine closed in 1963 when taconite and shipping made the mine unprofitable. The United State Steel Corporation then donated the mine, and additional acreage, to the park system. Since only 10% of the mine can be seen from the surface, it is sometimes called the "state park down under."

IF YOU GO . . .

Tour! The highlight of the park is the tour of the underground mine, available from Memorial Day to Labor Day. There is a fee for a 1.5 hour tour.

SOUDAN UNDERGROUND MINE STATE PARK

FACILITIES

Visitor Center: seasonal Visitor Center
Picnic Area: yes

RECREATION

Children's play area: no
Volleyball courts: no
Horseshoe pits: no
Swimming: no
Fishing: no
Boating: no

CAMPGROUND

Campsites: no
Electric: no
hike or carry: no
Canoe campsites: no
Dump station: no
Toilets: flush toilets
Showers: no
Group Campground: no

TRAILS

Hiking Trails: 5 miles
Hiking Club Trail: 2.5 miles, starting at the Visitor Center
Biking Trails: no
Cross-country Ski: no
Snowmobile Trails: no
Horse Trails: no
Horse Campsites: no

INTERPRETIVE PROGRAMS

There is a Visitor Center which offers a movie telling about the history and use of the mine. There is also a nature trail that winds through the pit mines.

SOUDAN UNDERGROUND MINE STATE PARK

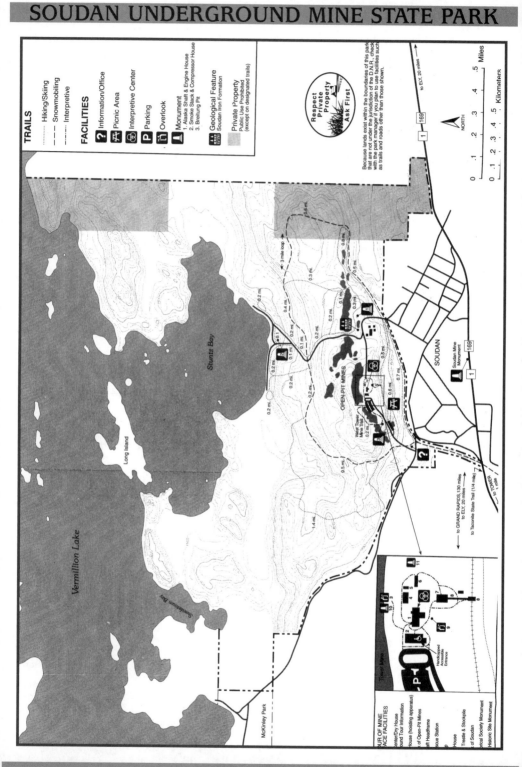

Photo by Dudley Edmondson

NEARBY PLACES TO VISIT

Tower-Soudan Historical Society - Tower, 218-753-3041

OUR NOTES

Date visited   What we liked

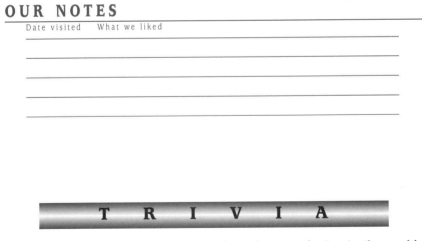

*Soudan Underground Mine is the only underground mine in the world
that can be toured. It is also the deepest and oldest iron ore mine.*

Split Rock Lighthouse State Park
2010A Highway 61 E
Two Harbors, MN 55616
218-226-3065

DIRECTIONS

The park is located 20 miles north of Two Harbors on Highway 61.

ABOUT THE PARK

Six ships were wrecked near Split Rock River during a storm on Lake Superior in 1905. As a result, in 1910, the federal government commissioned to have a lighthouse constructed there. The lighthouse remained in operation until 1969, when more advanced technology made it obsolete. The lighthouse was deemed surplus federal property in 1971, and was given to the state. The Minnesota Historical Society took over operation of the site In 1976, and opened a history center ten years later. The state also maintains the approximately 1,900 acres adjacent to the lighthouse.

IF YOU GO . . .

Bring your camera! From the picnic area, head northeast along Lake Superior toward the lighthouse. A visit to the park would not be complete without seeing the lighthouse and the lighthouse keeper's home, which offers lots of picturesque views of both the lighthouse and the lake. Head back to the picnic area and, if time allows, take a hike along the Day Hill Trail. Check out the scenic overlooks, and try to find out who built the stone fireplace.

SPLIT ROCK LIGHTHOUSE STATE PARK

FACILITIES

Visitor Center: Visitor Center run by the Minnesota Historical Society

Picnic Area: picnic area with an enclosed shelter

RECREATION

Children's play area: no
Volleyball courts: no
Horseshoe pits: no
Swimming: no
Fishing: fishing on Lake Superior or Split Rock Creek
Boating: carry-in boat access to Lake Superior

CAMPGROUND

Campsites: drive campsites are not available
Electric: no
Hike or carry-in: 20 cart-in campsites
4 backpack campsites
Canoe campsites: no
Dump station: no
Toilets: flush toilets
Showers: yes
Group Campground: no

TRAILS

Hiking Trails: 12 miles
Hiking Club Trail: 6.2 miles, starting at the Trail Center.
Biking Trails: 6 miles
Cross-country Ski: 8 miles
Warming house: yes
Snowmobile Trails: no
Horse Trails: no
Horse Campsites: no

INTERPRETIVE PROGRAMS

There is a History Center next to the site with information and a video about the lighthouse. The historical society has refurbished the lighthouse and the keeper's house to its 1920s appearance. There is a 6 mile self-guided interpretive trail.

SPLIT ROCK LIGHTHOUSE STATE PARK

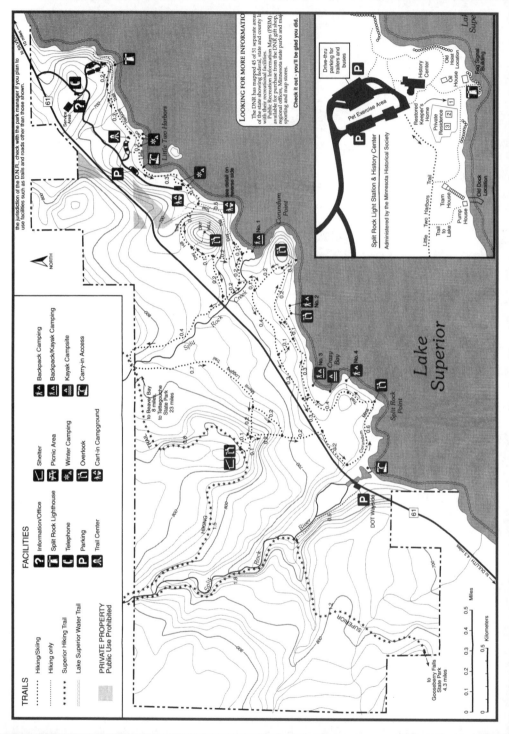

Split Rock Lighthouse
Photo by Dudley Edmondson

NEARBY PLACES TO VISIT

3M/Dwan Museum - Two Harbors, 218-834-4898
Canal Park Marine Museum - Duluth, 218-727-2497, 218-720-5271
Duluth Children's Museum - Duluth, 218-733-7543, 218-733-7548
Glensheen Mansion - Duluth, 218-724-8864, 888-454-4536
Gooseberry Falls - Two Harbors, 218-834-3855, 218-834-3787
Great Lakes Fur Trade Museum & Shop - Two Harbors, 218-834-3323
Karpeles Manuscript Library Museum - Duluth, 218-728-0630
Lake County Historical Museum - Two Harbors, 218-834-4898
Lake Superior Museum of Transportation - Duluth, 218-733-7590
Lighthouse Point & Harbor Museum - Two Harbors, 218-834-4898
Split Rock Lighthouse Historic Site - Two Harbors, 218-226-6372
St Louis County Historical Society - Duluth, 218-733-7580
St Louis County Heritage & Arts Center - Duluth, 218-727-8025
Superior Hiking Trail - Two Harbors, 218-834-4436, 218-834-2700
William A. Irvin Ore Boat Tour - Duluth, 218-722-7876, 800-628-8385

OUR NOTES

Date visited   What we liked

T R I V I A

The devastating Lake Superior storm in November of 1905
damaged 29 vessels and instigated the building of the lighthouse
at Split Rock which was in use from 1910 to 1969.

Temperance River State Park
Box 33
Schroeder, MN 55612
218-663-7476

DIRECTIONS

The park is located 1 mile north of Schroeder on Highway 61.

ABOUT THE PARK

Temperance River State Park contains only 534 acres, making it one of the smaller parks in the system. The park was created by the highway department in 1934, after the completion of Highway 61, and became property of the park system in 1957. It is adjacent to 2,500 acres of the Cross River Wayside, and there is a trail system throughout the entire area.

The river was originally known as "kawimbash," or Deep Hollow River, but was renamed Temperance, since there is no sandbar at its mouth (a humorous reference to the double meaning of the word "bar"). This area was originally visited by Europeans during the 17th century, and by the 1800s, many fur trading posts had been established along Lake Superior.

IF YOU GO . . .

Plan on some hiking! The trail system is extensive, so make sure you get a map before heading out. Head up the river from the parking area along Highway 61, and follow the trail to Hidden Falls, or follow along the south side of the river to another waterfall. The Superior Hiking trail crosses through the area, and connects with the other trails in the park. If time allows, head over to the Cross River, where the trail continues.

FACILITIES

Visitor Center:	no
Picnic Area:	picnic area on Lake Superior

RECREATION

Children's play area:	yes
Volleyball courts:	no
Horseshoe pits:	no
Swimming:	no
Fishing:	fishing on the Temperance River and Lake Superior
Boating:	carry-in boat access to Lake Superior

CAMPGROUND

Campsites:	50 drive campsites
Electric:	no
Bike or carry-in:	3 carry-in campsites
Canoe campsites:	no
Dump station:	no
Toilets:	flush toilets
Showers:	yes
Group Campground:	no

TRAILS

Hiking Trails:	8 miles access to the Superior Hiking Trail
Biking Club Trail:	1.8 miles, following along the Temperance River
Biking Trails:	no
Cross-country Ski:	12 miles
Snowmobile Trails:	5 miles
Horse Trails:	no
Horse Campsites:	no

INTERPRETIVE PROGRAMS

There are no interpretive programs in the park.

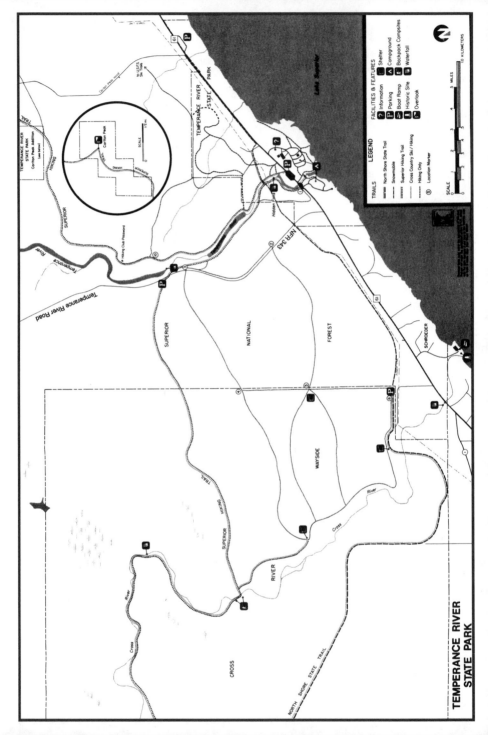

TEMPERANCE RIVER
STATE PARK

Temperance River
Photo by Dudley Edmondson

NEARBY PLACES TO VISIT

North Shore Commercial Fishing Museum - Tofte, 218-663-7804
Lutsen-Tofte Tourism Assoc - Tofte, 218-663-7804, 888-616-6784

OUR NOTES

Date visited   What we liked

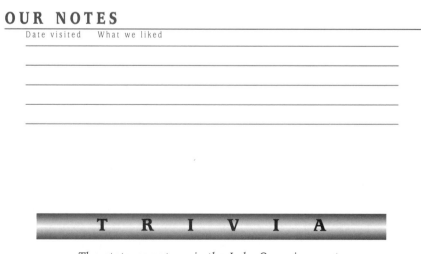

T R I V I A

The state gemstone is the Lake Superior agate.

Tettegouche State Park
474 Highway 61 E
Silver Bay, MN 55614
218-226-3539

DIRECTIONS

The park is located 4.5 miles northeast of Silver Bay on Highway 61.

ABOUT THE PARK

Tettegouche State Park was established in 1979, and is comprised of 8,468 acres. The area was logged from the turn of the century until 1910, when it was sold to a group of Duluth businessmen called the "Tettegouche Club." The land was eventually sold to one of the group's members, who preserved it until 1971, when it was sold to another family. The Nature Conservancy helped in negotiations to make the land a state park in 1979.

Visitors should explore not only Lake Superior, but also the inland lakes and Baptism River, both of which are accessible by trail. The Baptism River has three waterfalls, including the highest one located entirely in Minnesota. The park also features many scenic overlooks and destinations, including Mount Baldy, Raven Rock, and Mosquito Creek. Visitors can also hike back to Mic Mac Lake and see the Tettegouche camp, a series of log buildings which date back to the loggers who came to the area.

There is a free rest area along Highway 61 in the park. The park headquarters is also located here, providing information not only for Tettegouche, but also for the north shore.

IF YOU GO . . .

Plan to spend a few days on Mic Mac Lake! Tettegouche State Park has some log cabins available for rent. These are hike-in only cabins but will provide a wonderful base from which to explore the park.

For those people with limited time, plan on a hike up to High Falls. From the rest area, head southwest along Lake Superior to the mouth of the Baptism River, then follow the trail away from the lake until Two Steps Falls, and up to High Falls. Cross the river, and head back to Two Steps Falls. Cross the river again, and backtrack to the rest area.

TETTEGOUCHE STATE PARK

FACILITIES

Visitor Center:	Visitor Center and rest area on Highway 61
Picnic Area:	picnic area overlooking Lake Superior
	picnic area at Nipisquit Lake

RECREATION

Children's play area:	no
Volleyball courts:	no
Horseshoe pits:	no
Swimming:	no
Fishing:	6 lakes, Baptism River, and numerous streams
Boating:	drive-in boat access to Lax Lake

CAMPGROUND

Campsites:	29 drive-in campsites
Electric:	no
Hike or carry-in:	5 walk-in campsites
Canoe campsites:	no
Dump station:	no
Toilets:	flush toilets
Showers:	yes
Group Campground:	no
Tettegouche State Park	accessible only by hiking or skiing
Historic Cabins:	rented individually or as a group
	have electricity, a kitchenette and a woodstove
	water must be pumped at a well in the area
	central building with flush toilets and showers
	cabin A: sleeps 6 people in 2 rooms
	cabin B&C: sleeps 6 people in 3 rooms
	cabin D: sleeps 2 people in 1 room

TRAILS

Hiking Trails:	17 miles
	self guided hiking trail
Hiking Club Trail:	2 miles, starting at the self-guided interpretive
	trail near the rest area parking lot
Biking Trails:	1.5 miles
Cross-country Ski:	12 miles
	4 skate/ski miles
Warming house:	yes
Snowmobile Trails:	7 miles
Horse Trails:	no
Horse Campsites:	no

INTERPRETIVE PROGRAMS

There are no interpretive programs available in the park, but the Visitor Center does offer some exhibits, in addition to a self-guided nature trail.

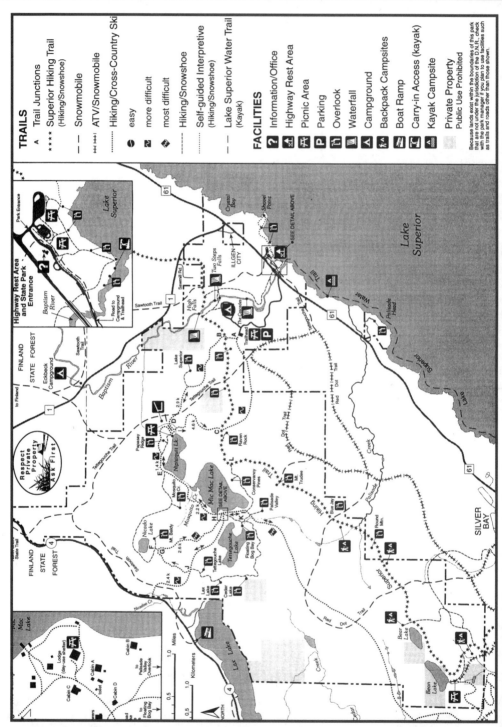

Tettegouche State Park   Photo by Dudley Edmondson

NEARBY PLACES TO VISIT

3M/Dwan Museum - Two Harbors, 218-834-4898
Baptism River High Falls - Silver Bay, 218-226-3539
Beaver Bay Tourism Info Center - Beaver Bay, 218-226-3317
Gooseberry Falls - Two Harbors, 218-834-3855, 218-834-3787
Great Lakes Fur Trade Museum & Shop - Two Harbors, 218-834-3323
Lake County Historical Museum - Two Harbors, 218-834-4898
Lighthouse Point & Harbor Museum - Two Harbors, 218-834-4898
Silver Bay Chamber - Silver Bay, 218-226-4870
Split Rock Lighthouse Historic Site - Two Harbors, 218-226-6372
Superior Hiking Trail - Two Harbors, 218-834-4436, 218-834-2700

OUR NOTES

Date visited   What we liked

TRIVIA

Illgen City at the intersection of Highway 61 & Highway 1 is the birthplace of 3M. Tettegouche is the location of the highest waterfall located entirely in the state (not on the Canadian border) at 80 feet.

PARK	ACREAGE
Banning State Park	6,237 acres
Charles A. Lindberg State Park	330 acres
Crow Wing State Park	2,042 acres
Father Hennepin State Park	318 acres
Interstate State Park	293 acres
Lake Maria State Park	1,590 acres
Mille Lacs Kathio State Park	10,585 acres
St. Croix State Park	34,037 acres
Savanna Portage State Park	15,818 acres
Wild River State Park	6,803 acres

CENTRAL REGION

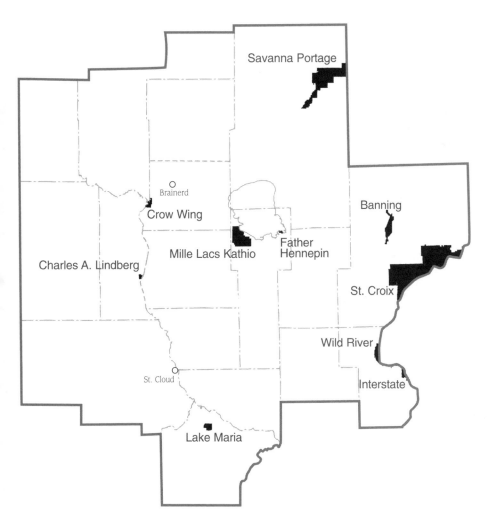

Savanna Portage

Brainerd

Crow Wing

Banning

Charles A. Lindberg

Mille Lacs Kathio

Father Hennepin

St. Croix

Wild River

St. Cloud

Interstate

Lake Maria

BANNING STATE PARK

Banning State Park
Box 643
Sandstone, MN 55072
320-245-2668

DIRECTIONS

From Minneapolis/St. Paul, take Interstate 35 north to exit 195, then go east on Highway 23 to the park entrance.

ABOUT THE PARK

Banning State Park was established in 1963 and currently contains 6,237 acres. Ten miles of the Kettle River, designated a "wild and scenic river," are adjacent to the park. This portion of the river is highly scenic, and is comprised of five spectacular segments: Blueberry Slide, Mother's Delight, Dragon's Tooth, Little Banning, and Hell's Gate.

The village of Banning was established in the early 1890s, when sandstone was quarried at Hell's Gate. The quarry was rebuilt after the Hinckley fire of 1894, and by 1896 the village of Banning had grown considerably. The demand for sandstone dwindled after the turn of the century, and the quarry was forced to cease operations. By 1918 the village of Banning had ceased to exist. Today, all that remains of the village are some foundations near the river bank and a few ruins at the quarry.

IF YOU GO . . .

Bring your hiking boots! For a good hike, park at the picnic area/boat landing, from which you can see the Blueberry Slide Rapids. From there, take the Quarry Loop trail along the Kettle River. This loop passes by the Mother's Delight rapids, Dragon's Tooth rapids, Little Banning rapids, and the ruins from the old quarry. Follow the short Hell's Gate Trail to see the Hell's Gate rapids. From there, backtrack to the High Bluff Trail, which leads, after merging with another trail, to the Wolf Creek Falls. Backtrack along the trail to the campground, and follow the Spur Trail back to the parking lot.

BANNING STATE PARK

FACILITIES

Visitor Center:	no
Picnic Area:	7 picnic areas

RECREATION

Children's play area:	small playground located in the campground
Volleyball courts:	no
Horseshoe pits:	no
Swimming:	no
Fishing:	river fishing on the Kettle River
Boating:	canoeing and kayaking on the Kettle River
	drive-in boat access to the Kettle River
	carry-in access on Highway 23

CAMPGROUND

Campsites:	34 drive-in campsites
Electric:	11 electric campsites
Hike or carry-in:	1 backpack campsite
Canoe campsites:	4 canoe campsites on the Kettle River
Dump station:	no
Toilets:	flush toilets
Showers:	yes
Group Campground:	no
Camper Cabin:	inquire at the park headquarters

TRAILS

Hiking Trails:	17 miles
Hiking Club Trail:	2.6 miles, starting at the picnic area
Biking Trails:	no
Cross-country Ski:	12 miles
Snowmobile Trails:	6 miles
Horse Trails:	no
Horse Campsites:	no

INTERPRETIVE PROGRAMS

There are no interpretive programs available in the park.

BANNING STATE PARK

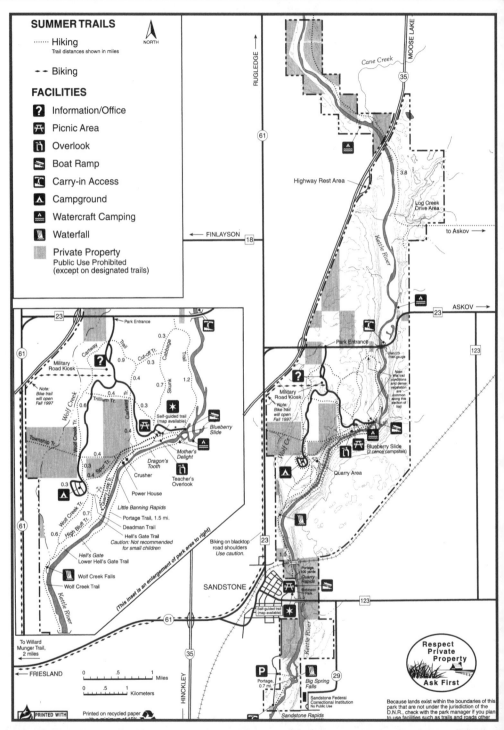

SUMMER TRAILS

↑ NORTH

········ Hiking
Trail distances shown in miles

– – Biking

FACILITIES

? Information/Office

⊞ Picnic Area

📷 Overlook

🛥 Boat Ramp

⛵ Carry-in Access

⛺ Campground

⛺ Watercraft Camping

💧 Waterfall

Private Property
Public Use Prohibited
(except on designated trails)

← FINLAYSON

RUGLEDGE

Cane Creek

MOOSE LAKE

35

3.8

Highway Rest Area

Log Creek
Drive Area

to Askov →

ASKOV →

61

18

123

Kettle River

Park Entrance

Military Road Kiosk
Note: Bike trail will open Fall 1997

? Military Road Kiosk
Note: Bike trail will open Fall 1997

Blueberry Slide
(2 canoe campsites)

Quarry Area

Park Entrance
Note: Wet trail conditions and dense vegetation are common along this section of trail

Hwy 23 river gauge

23

23

Cutoff Tr.
Cartway Trail
0.3
0.9
0.3
Cabbage Trail
0.4
0.7
Skunk Trail
1.2
0.4
Trillium Tr.
0.6
0.4
0.3
Self-guided trail (map available)
Blueberry Slide

Cartway Tr.

Mother's Delight

Dragon's Tooth
0.3
0.4
Crusher
Spur Tr.
Teacher's Overlook
Power House

Wolf Creek
Wolf Creek Tr.
Township Tr.
0.4
0.3
0.4

Quarry Loop Tr.

Little Banning Rapids
Portage Trail, 1.5 mi.
0.7
Deadman Trail
Hell's Gate Trail
Caution: Not recommended for small children

High Bluff Tr.
0.6

Hell's Gate
Lower Hell's Gate Trail

💧 Wolf Creek Falls
Wolf Creek Trail

Kettle River

(This inset is an enlargement of park area to right)

SANDSTONE

Biking on blacktop road shoulders
Use caution.

1.6

Portage, 100 yards
Quarry Rapids
Robinson Park

123

Self-guided trail (map available)

To Willard Munger Trail, 2 miles

← FRIESLAND

23
61

0   .5   1 Miles
0   .5   1 Kilometers

HINCKLEY
35

61

Portage, 0.7 mi.
P

Big Spring Falls
29

Sandstone Federal Correctional Institution
No Public Use

Kettle River

Sandstone Rapids

Respect Private Property
Ask First

Because lands exist within the boundaries of this park that are not under the jurisdiction of the D.N.R., check with the park manager if you plan to use facilities such as trails and roads other

♻ PRINTED WITH

Printed on recycled paper

Least Chipmunk   Photo by Dudley Edmondson

NEARBY PLACES TO VISIT

Hinckley Chamber of Commerce - Hinckley, 320-384-7837
Hinckley Convention & Visitor's Bureau - Hinckley, 800-996-4566, 320-384-0126
Hinckley Fire Museum - Hinckley, 320-384-7338
History and Art Center - Sandstone, 320-245-2271, 320-245-5241
North West Company Fur Post - Pine City, 320-629-6356, 612-296-5434
Pine County Historical Museum - Askov, 320-838-3792
Sandstone Chamber - Sandstone, 320-245-2271
St Croix State Park - Hinckley, 320-384-6591
Willard Munger State Trail - Moose Lake, 612-296-6699, 800-263-0586

OUR NOTES

Date visited   What we liked

_____

_____

_____

_____

_____

T R I V I A

Kettle River was Minnesota's first designated Scenic Wild River.

CHARLES A. LINDBERG STATE PARK

Charles A. Lindberg State Park
PO Box 364
Little Falls, MN 56345
320-632-9050

DIRECTIONS
The park is located on the south side of Little Falls, off Lindbergh Drive.

ABOUT THE PARK
Charles A. Lindbergh State Park was created in 1931 when the family of Charles A. Lindbergh Sr., father of the famous aviator Charles Lindbergh Jr., donated 110 acres of land for the creation of a park.

The park is rich in history. Besides the connections with the famous Lindberg family, there are prehistoric burial mounds and artifacts, which date back as far as 1,000 BC, that have been found here. During the first part of the 19th century the Red River Oxcart Trail, which moved goods from St. Paul to Pembina, ND, passed near this area. The Civilian Conservation Corps (CCC) came to the park during the depression.

Across the road from the main park is the house where Charles Jr. spent his summers. The house was built in 1906 and is now owned and maintained by the Minnesota Historical Society. Beside the house, which contains many original furnishings, the ice house and chauffeur's residence still remain. There is also the Lindberg History Center, open daily during the summer months, which depicts the careers and lives of the Lindbergh family.

Just southeast of the park is the Charles Weyerhaeuser Museum, which is maintained by the Morrison County Historical Society. The museum, which is free and open year round, portrays the area from prehistoric times through its development.

IF YOU GO . . .
Plan to tour! The Charles Lindbergh house, History Center, and the Weyerhaeuser Museum are all worth the time to explore. There are also some trails down to Pike Creek. From the picnic area, head across the bridge and go either north or south for some scenic overlooks. Both trails loop back around, but the trail to the north is longer and heads back to the campground.

CHARLES A. LINDBERG STATE PARK

FACILITIES

Visitor Center: no
Picnic Area: yes, with an enclosed shelter

RECREATION

Children's play area: at the picnic area
Horseshoe pits: yes
Volleyball courts: yes
Swimming: no
Fishing: river fishing on the Mississippi River
Boating: canoeing on Pike Creek
                         boating & boat access on the Mississippi River

CAMPGROUND

Campsites: 38 drive-in campsites
Electric: 15 electric campsites
Hike or carry-in: no
Canoe Campsites: 2 canoe campsites on the Pike Creek, just up
                         from the Mississippi River

Dump station: yes
Toilets: flush toilets
Showers: yes
Group Campground: group campsite

TRAILS

Hiking Trails: 6 miles
Hiking Club Trail: 2.5 miles, starting at the picnic area
Biking Trails: no
Cross-country Ski: 6 miles
Snowmobile Trails: no
Horse Trails: no
Horse Campsites: no

INTERPRETIVE PROGRAMS

There is no interpretive program available in the park.

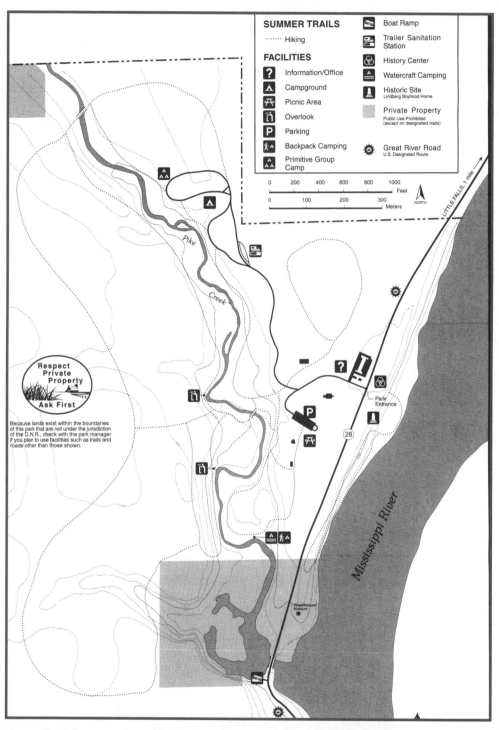

SUMMER TRAILS

...... Hiking

FACILITIES

? Information/Office

△ Campground

⊼ Picnic Area

ṅ Overlook

P Parking

⋏⋏ Backpack Camping

⋏⋏ Primitive Group Camp

Boat Ramp

Trailer Sanitation Station

History Center

Watercraft Camping

Historic Site
Lindberg Boyhood Home

Private Property
Public Use Prohibited
(except on designated trails)

Great River Road
U.S. Designated Route

| 0 | 200 | 400 | 600 | 800 | 1000 |
Feet

| 0 | 100 | 200 | 300 |
Meters

NORTH

LITTLE FALLS, 1 mile

Pike

Creek

Respect Private Property
Ask First

Because lands exist within the boundaries of this park that are not under the jurisdiction of the D.N.R., check with the park manager if you plan to use facilities such as trails and roads other than those shown.

Park Entrance

26

Mississippi River

Weyerhaeuser Museum

Photo by Dudley Edmondson

NEARBY PLACES TO VISIT

C.A. Weyerhaeuser Memorial Museum - Little Falls, 320-632-4007
Charles A. Lindbergh House & History Center - Little Falls, 320-632-3154
Christie Home Museum - Long Prairie, 320-732-2918
Dewey-Radke House - Little Falls, 320-632-2341, 320-632-8902
Great River Road - Little Falls Scenic Byway - Little Falls, 320-632-5155
Little Falls Tourism & Convention Bureau - Little Falls, 800-325-5916, 320-632-5642
Minnesota Military Museum - Little Falls, 320-632-7374
Todd County Historical Museum - Long Prairie, 320-732-4426

OUR NOTES

Date visited   What we liked

T R I V I A

In the Dakota language Minnesota means cloudy waters or sky-tinted waters.

CROW WING STATE PARK

Crow Wing State Park
7100 State Park Road SW
Brainerd, MN 56401
218-829-8022

DIRECTIONS

The park is located 9 miles south of Brainerd on Highway 371.

ABOUT THE PARK

Crow Wing State Park was established in 1959 and contains 2,042 acres of beautiful land. Visitors can explore this unique site which represents much of the history and growth of Minnesota Indians, fur trading, logging, and settlers. The park is now on the National Historic Places Register.

The park is located at the point that the Crow Wing and Mississippi Rivers join, a natural meeting place for river travelers. In 1768, there was an historic battle between the Dakota and Ojibway Indians here, the evidence of which can still be seen. The Northwest Company and the American Fur Company both had posts located here. During the 1840s, the settlement of Crow Wing, which grew up around the trading posts, could boast of three competing missions: one Catholic, one Episcopalian, and one Lutheran. Over the years, Crow Wing transformed its economy from fur trading to logging. The river gave the sawmills power, and transported the wood further down river. In the early 1870s the railroad river crossing was situated in the community of Brainerd, north of Crow Wing. It didn't take long for the population to desert Crow Wing and move to Brainerd.

The remains of Crow Wing's missions and cemeteries are still visible in the park, and visitors can hike along part of the Red River Ox Cart Trail, which brought goods and settlers to western Minnesota and North Dakota.

IF YOU GO . . .

Come for a hike! Park at the south picnic area, which is only a short distance from a worthwhile interpretive display. Follow the trail to the north, along the Mississippi River, to two historical sites. For a shorter route, cut across to the north picnic parking area, and follow the trail south back to the south picnic parking area. For a longer route, keep going east to the boat launch, then to the campground, and back around to the south picnic area.

CROW WING STATE PARK

FACILITIES

Visitor Center:	visitor orientation exhibit
Picnic Area:	2 picnic areas, 1 with a shelter

RECREATION

Children's play area:	yes
Horseshoe pit:	yes
Volleyball court:	yes
Swimming:	no
Fishing:	fishing on the Crow Wing & Mississippi Rivers
Boating:	boating and canoeing on both rivers
	boat launch
	canoe and boat rentals

CAMPGROUND

Campsites:	61 drive-in campsites
Electric:	12 electric campsites
Hike or carry-in:	no
Canoe campsites:	1 campsite on the Mississippi River
Dump station:	yes
Toilets:	flush toilets
Showers:	yes
Group Campground:	1 primitive group campsite
Camping cabins:	yes

TRAILS

Hiking Trails:	18 miles
Hiking Club Trail:	2.3 miles, starting at the interpretive display
Biking Trails:	no
Cross-country Ski:	6.4 miles
Snowmobile Trails:	6 miles
Horse Trails:	no
Horse Campsites:	no

INTERPRETIVE PROGRAMS

The park offers a visitor orientation exhibit that explains the history of the area, and some self-guiding interpretive trails.

CROW WING STATE PARK

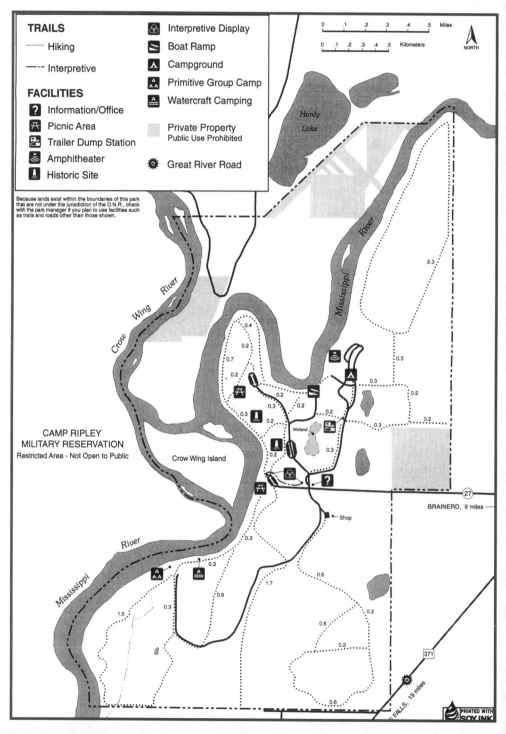

TRAILS

.... Hiking

—··— Interpretive

FACILITIES

? Information/Office

🎪 Picnic Area

Trailer Dump Station

Amphitheater

Historic Site

Interpretive Display

Boat Ramp

Campground

Primitive Group Camp

Watercraft Camping

Private Property
Public Use Prohibited

Great River Road

Because lands exist within the boundaries of this park that are not under the jurisdiction of the D.N.R., check with the park manager if you plan to use facilities such as trails and roads other than those shown.

Miles
0 .1 .2 .3 .4 .5

Kilometers
0 .1 .2 .3 .4 .5

NORTH

Hardy Lake

Mississippi River

Crow Wing River

CAMP RIPLEY
MILITARY RESERVATION
Restricted Area - Not Open to Public

Crow Wing Island

Wetland

Shop

BRAINERD, 9 miles

27

371

FALLS, 19 miles

Yellow-headed Blackbird (male)
Photo by Dudley Edmondson

NEARBY PLACES TO VISIT

Brainerd Lakes Area Convention and Visitor's Bureau
    Brainerd, 800-450-2838, 218-829-2838
Crow Wing County Historical Museum - Brainerd, 218-829-3268
Deep-Portage Conservation Reserve - Hackensack, 218-682-2325
Northland Arboretum - Brainerd, 218-963-4762
Paul Bunyan State Trail - Baxter, 218-828-2561

OUR NOTES

Date visited   What we liked

T R I V I A

Crow Wing is the geographic center of the state.

Father Hennepin State Park
Box 397
Isle, MN 56342
320-676-8763

DIRECTIONS

The park is located 1 mile west of Isle on Highway 27.

ABOUT THE PARK

The 318 acre Father Hennepin State Park was established in 1941 through tax forfeited lands. It is a small park, but its access to Mille Lacs Lake makes it quite popular.

Historically, Lake Mille Lacs has been home to prehistoric peoples, and many Native Americans. The park was named for Father Louis Hennepin, a Jesuit priest and the first European to visit the region. He was captured by Native Americans and brought to Lake Mille Lacs in 1679 and released in 1681.

IF YOU GO . . .

Come for a hike! The hiking club trail starts at the east picnic area, and follows the shore of Lake Mille Lacs. Along the way there are several great spots to enjoy the beauty of the lake. The trail goes to the west picnic area, where a quick swim on a hot day would be great. You can hike back along the lake or follow the trail out of the west parking lot through the woods.

FATHER HENNEPIN STATE PARK

FACILITIES

Visitor Center: no
Picnic Area: 2 picnic areas with shelters

RECREATION

Children's play area: yes
Horseshoe pit: no
Volleyball courts: yes
Swimming: swimming beach on Lake Mille Lacs
Fishing: fishing on Lake Mille Lacs
                                fishing pier on Lake Mille Lacs
Boating: boating on Lake Mille Lacs
                                2 boat ramps onto Lake Mille Lacs

CAMPGROUND

Campsites: 2 campgrounds
                                total of 103 drive-in campsites
Electric: 30 electric campsites
Hike or carry-in: no
Canoe campsites: no
Dump station: yes
Toilets: flush toilets
Showers: yes
Group Campground: group campground with 6 campsites

TRAILS

Hiking Trails: 4 miles
Hiking Club Trail: 2 miles, start at the east picnic area parking lot
Biking Trails: 12 miles of paved trails near the park
Cross-country Ski: 2.5 miles
Snowmobile Trails: 1.5 miles
Horse Trails: no
Horse Campsites: no

INTERPRETIVE PROGRAMS

There are no interpretive programs available at Father Hennepin State Park, but there are programs available at nearby Mille Lacs Kathio State Park.

FATHER HENNEPIN STATE PARK

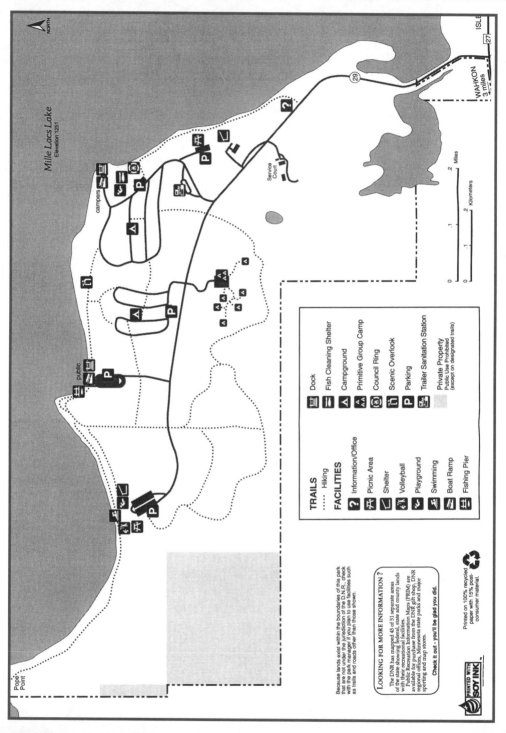

Mille Lacs Lake
Elevation 1251

Pope's Point

campers

public

Service Court

29

27

ISLE

WAHKON
3 miles

TRAILS
······ Hiking

FACILITIES

? Information/Office
⛑ Picnic Area
🏕 Shelter
🏐 Volleyball
🛝 Playground
🏊 Swimming
🚤 Boat Ramp
🎣 Fishing Pier

🛶 Dock
🚿 Fish Cleaning Shelter
⛺ Campground
▲▲ Primitive Group Camp
🔥 Council Ring
🔭 Scenic Overlook
P Parking
🚽 Trailer Sanitation Station

Private Property
Public Use Prohibited
(except on designated trails)

Miles
Kilometers
0   .1   .2

Because lands exist within the boundaries of this park that are not under the jurisdiction of the D.N.R., check with the park manager if you plan to use facilities such as trails and roads other than those shown.

LOOKING FOR MORE INFORMATION ?

The DNR has mapped 45 of 51 separate areas of the state showing federal, state and county lands with their recreational facilities.
Public Recreation Information Maps (PRIM) are available for purchase from the DNR gift shop, DNR regional offices, Minnesota state parks and major sporting and map stores.

Check it out - you'll be glad you did.

Printed on 100% recycled paper with 15% post-consumer material.

PRINTED WITH
SOY INK™

Pileated Woodpecker
Photo by Dudley Edmondson

NEARBY PLACES TO VISIT

Kathio State Park - 320-532-3523
Mille Lacs Indian Museum - Onamia, 320-532-3632
Soo Line Trail - Onamia

OUR NOTES

Date visited   What we liked

T R I V I A

Mille Lacs Lake has a shoreline of approximately 100 miles and 200 square miles of water surface. It is the second largest lake in the state.

Interstate State Park
Box 254
Taylors Falls, MN 55084
612-465-5711

DIRECTIONS

The park is located on Highway 8, 1 mile south of Taylors Falls.

ABOUT THE PARK

Interstate State Park consists of 293 well-used acres. It is situated along the St. Croix River, just south of Taylors Falls. This park was established in 1895, making it the second oldest park in the system. There is another state park right across the river, in Wisconsin, that was developed at the same time.

The area surrounding the park is full of history. Hiking through the northern end of the park will show numerous examples of the geological turmoil that has marked the area, including the fascinating "potholes." Prehistoric people are known to have inhabited the area as many as 6,000 years ago. More recently, the Dakota and Ojibway made use of the area. The first Europeans probably visited the area around 1680 while exploring the St. Croix River. The river became an important trade route not only for the fur traders, but for the logging of the white pine forests. In the late 1830s the first business was established in what would become Taylors Falls.

IF YOU GO . . .

Plan to tour! First, go to the Visitor Center on the edge of Taylors Falls. Starting from the parking lot, take the trail down to the "potholes." Wander through the pothole area, and imagine the forces that created them. Next, check out the two scenic overlooks along the St. Croix River. Follow the trail back to the parking lot along the service road. It is not unusual to find rock climbers scaling these cliffs — on a beautiful day the cliffs are alive with climbers — while down below the spectators gather to watch.

INTERSTATE STATE PARK

FACILITIES

Visitor Center:
Picnic Area:

seasonal
large picnic area with 1 open shelter and
1 enclosed shelter

RECREATION

Children's play area:
Horseshoe pit:
Volleyball courts:
Swimming:
Fishing:
Boating:

no
no
yes
no
fishing on the St. Croix River
drive-in boat access to the St. Croix River
canoe rental and shuttle service
excursion boats are available in Taylors Falls

CAMPGROUND

Campsites:
Electric:
Hike or carry-in:
Canoe campsites:
Dump station:
Toilets:
Showers:
Group Campground:

37 drive-in campsites
22 electric campsites
no
no
yes
flush toilets
yes
1 primitive group campsite

TRAILS

Hiking Trails:
Hiking Club Trail:

4 miles
1.5 miles, start at the north end of the park
near the glacial potholes

Biking Trails:
Cross-country Ski:
Snowmobile Trails:
Horse Trails:
Horse Campsites:

no
no
no
no
no

INTERPRETIVE PROGRAMS

In addition to exhibits, park naturalists offer interpretive programs on a seasonal basis. Visitors should check the bulletin boards around the park for daily schedules.

INTERSTATE STATE PARK

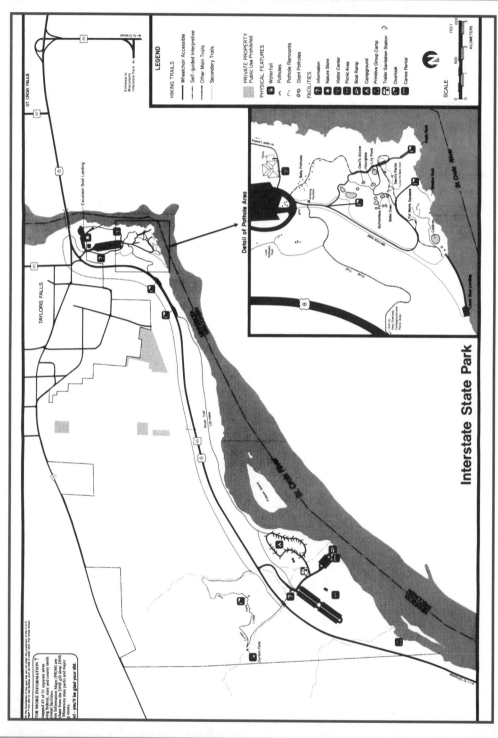

Osprey   Photo by Dudley Edmondson

NEARBY PLACES TO VISIT

W H C Folsom House - Taylors Falls, 612-465-3125
Wild River State Park - Center City, 612-583-2125
William O'Brien State Park - Marine on St. Croix, 612-433-0500

OUR NOTES

Date visited   What we liked

_____

_____

_____

_____

_____

T   R   I   V   I   A

The Minnesota state motto is L' Etoile du Nord, which translates to Star of the North.

Lake Maria State Park
RR 1 Box 128
Monticello, MN 55362
320-878-2325

DIRECTIONS

The park is located 8 miles from Interstate 94 on County Road 39.

ABOUT THE PARK

Lake Maria State Park was established in 1963 and encompasses 1,590 wooded acres. The park has been designed for hikers, backpackers, and horseback riders, in an effort to increase recreational use of park lands close to the Twin Cities. The park contains several lakes, and a hardwood forest with many old oaks.

IF YOU GO . . .

Bring your skis and a camera! The winter sports here are excellent, with 22 miles of ski trails winding through wonderful hardwood forests and along the many small lakes within the park. After your ski, warm up in the trail center and go for a skate on the rink.

LAKE MARIA STATE PARK

FACILITIES

Visitor Center: no
Picnic Area: yes

RECREATION

Children's play area: no
Horseshoe pit: no
Volleyball courts: yes
Swimming: no
Fishing: lake fishing
Boating: drive access to Maria Lake carry-in access to
                          Bjorkland Lake
                          boat rental

CAMPGROUND

Campsites: no
Electric: no
Bike or carry-in: 16 backpack campsites
Canoe campsites: no
Dump station: no
Toilets: pit toilets
Showers: no
Camper cabin: walk-in log camper cabin sleeps 6 people
                          no cooking facilities or electricity
Group Campground: 2 primitive group campsites

TRAILS

Hiking Trails: 14 miles
Hiking Club Trail: 2 miles, starting at the Trail Center
Biking Trails: no
Cross-country Ski: 22 miles
                          5 miles of skate/ski trails
Warming house: yes
Snowmobile Trails: no
Sliding hill: yes
Skating: yes
Horse Trails: 6 miles
Horse Campsites: no

INTERPRETIVE PROGRAMS

Lake Maria has a trail/Interpretive Center with interpretive displays, which can be used for group meetings. It has a woodstove for winter use.

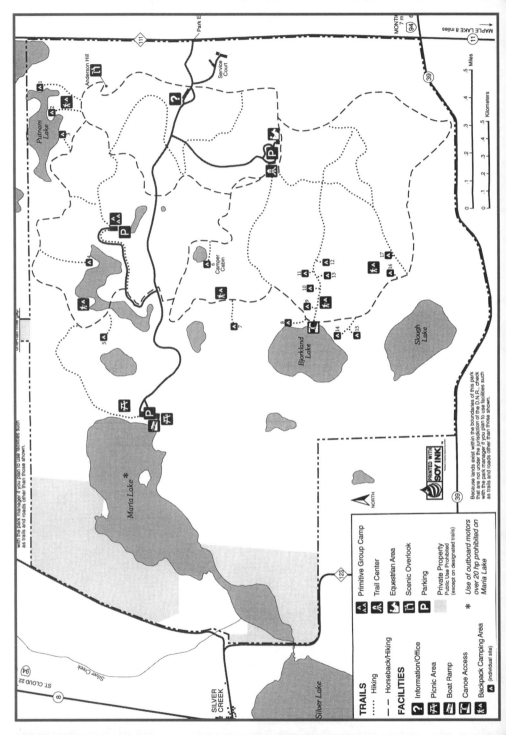

TRAILS

· · · · · Hiking

– – – Horseback/Hiking

FACILITIES

? Information/Office

🏕 Picnic Area

Boat Ramp

Canoe Access

🏕 Backpack Camping Area

▲ (individual site)

🏕 Primitive Group Camp

🏃 Trail Center

🐎 Equestrian Area

🏠 Scenic Overlook

P Parking

Private Property
Public Use Prohibited
(except on designated trails)

* Use of outboard motors
over 20 hp prohibited on
Maria Lake

Because lands exist within the boundaries of this park
that are not under the jurisdiction of the D.N.R., check
with the park manager if you plan to use facilities such
as trails and roads other than those shown.

with the park manager if you plan to use facilities such
as trails and roads other than those shown.

NORTH

Maria Lake *

Putnam Lake

Bjorkland Lake

Slough Lake

Silver Lake

Silver Creek

Anderson Hill

Service Court

Camper Cabin

MAPLE LAKE 8 miles

MONT... 7 m...

ST. CLOUD 22

SILVER CREEK

PRINTED WITH SOY INK

American Kestrel (male)
Photo by Dudley Edmondson

NEARBY PLACES TO VISIT

Elk River Area Chamber - Elk River, 612-441-3110
Little Mountain Settlement Museum - Monticello, 612-295-2950, 612-295-2950
Munsinger Gardens - St Cloud, 320-255-7238
Sherburne County Historical Society - Becker, 612-261-4433, 612-441-1880
Stearns County Heritage Center - St Cloud, 320-253-8424
Wright County Historical Society/Museum - Buffalo, 612-682-7323, 800-362-3667

OUR NOTES

Date visited   What we liked

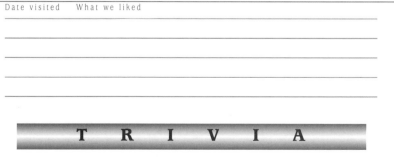

T R I V I A

In the Algonquin language Mississippi means great water.

Mille Lacs Kathio State Park
15066 Kathio State Park Road
Onamia, MN 56359
320-532-3523

DIRECTIONS

To find the park entrance, take Highway 169 to County Road 26.

ABOUT THE PARK

With 10,585 acres, Mille Lacs Kathio State Park is Minnesota's fourth largest park. The northern boundary of the park is Lake Mille Lacs, a very popular tourist area. The park, founded in 1957, also contains lakes Shakopee and Ogechie.

Nineteen archeological sites have been identified within the park, some dating back 4,000 years. There is evidence that there was once a permanent settlement on Ogechie Lake and the Rum River. The Dakota Indians are also known to have inhabited this area. Father Louis Hennepin, one of the early white explorers, was a captive of the Dakota in 1680, and lived with them near the Rum River for six months. By the early 1700s the Dakota were heading west while the Ojibway moved in from the east. There is a legend of a great battle between the Dakota and the Ojibway, but no evidence has been found to support the tale. The Ojibway still inhabit the region, and just north of the park, on Highway 169, the Mille Lacs Indian Museum provides Ojibway cultural information.

Loggers came into the area during the mid-1800s. The white and red pine were cut and floated to the sawmills on Lake Mille Lacs, or down the Rum River to the Mississippi River. The park is now forested with a second growth of trees, but a few stands of old growth still exist.

IF YOU GO . . .

For a different type of adventure, bring your canoe! The Rum River, which starts at Mille Lacs Lake, flows through the park, and continues down to the Mississippi River near Anoka. Launch your canoe in Mille Lacs Lake, and catch the Rum which feeds into Ogechie Lake, located in the heart of the State Park. Paddle on through the lake to the south, where the Rum empties out. A short paddle down the river will get you to a canoe campsite. The following day, an easy paddle will take you to Shakopee Lake. There is a boat landing on the southeast end of the lake.

MILLE LACS KATHIO STATE PARK

FACILITIES

Visitor Center:	year round Interpretive Center
Picnic Area:	picnic area on Ogechie Lake

RECREATION

Children's play area:	available in the campground
Volleyball courts:	no
Horseshoe pits:	no
Swimming:	swimming beach on Ogechie Lake
Fishing:	both lake and river fishing
	fish cleaning house in the campground
Boating:	drive-in boat access to both Shakopee Lake and the Rum River
	boat and canoe rental

CAMPGROUND

Campsites:	68 drive-in campsites
Electric:	no
Hike or carry-in:	no
Canoe campsites:	on the Rum River
Dump station:	yes
Toilets:	flush toilets
Showers:	yes
Group Campground:	primitive group campground

TRAILS

Hiking Trails:	35 miles
	2 miles of interpretive trails
Hiking Club Trail:	3.6 miles, starting at Kathio Visitor Center
Biking Trails:	no
Cross-country Ski:	18 miles
Heated trail center:	yes
Sliding hill:	yes
Snowmobile Trails:	19 miles
Horse Trails:	27 miles
Horse Campsites:	20 horse campsites

INTERPRETIVE PROGRAMS

The park's Visitor Center provides information on the cultural and natural history of the area, and naturalist led programs are available in the park. Check bulletin boards for schedules.

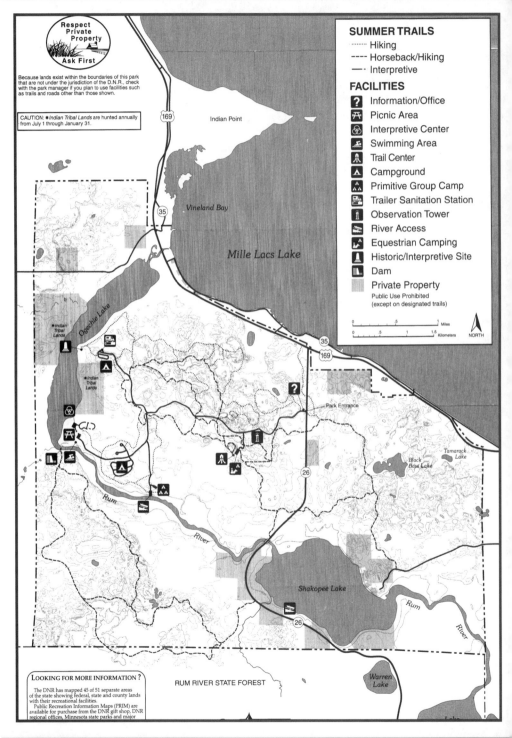

Respect Private Property Ask First

Because lands exist within the boundaries of this park that are not under the jurisdiction of the D.N.R., check with the park manager if you plan to use facilities such as trails and roads other than those shown.

CAUTION: ● *Indian Tribal Lands* are hunted annually from July 1 through January 31.

SUMMARY TRAILS

········· Hiking

------ Horseback/Hiking

—·— Interpretive

FACILITIES

?	Information/Office
🎪	Picnic Area
⊕	Interpretive Center
🏊	Swimming Area
🏕	Trail Center
⛺	Campground
⛺⛺	Primitive Group Camp
🚐	Trailer Sanitation Station
🗼	Observation Tower
🛶	River Access
🐴	Equestrian Camping
🏛	Historic/Interpretive Site
🏭	Dam
	Private Property

Public Use Prohibited (except on designated trails)

Indian Point

Vineland Bay

Mille Lacs Lake

Ogechie Lake

● *Indian Tribal Lands*

● *Indian Tribal Lands*

Park Entrance

Tamarack Lake

Black Bass Lake

Rum

River

Shakopee Lake

Rum

River

Warren Lake

LOOKING FOR MORE INFORMATION ?

The DNR has mapped 45 of 51 separate areas of the state showing federal, state and county lands with their recreational facilities.
Public Recreation Information Maps (PRIM) are available for purchase from the DNR gift shop, DNR regional offices, Minnesota state parks and major

RUM RIVER STATE FOREST

Trumpeter Swan   Photo by Dudley Edmondson

NEARBY PLACES TO VISIT

Father Hennepin State Park - Isle, 320-676-8763
Mille Lacs Indian Museum - Onamia, 320-532-3632
Soo Line Trail - Onamia

OUR NOTES

Date visited   What we liked

Archeologists have determined that copper tools were made by Native Americans in the area of Mille Lacs Kathio State Park.

St. Croix State Park
RR 3 Box 450
Hinckley, MN 55037
320-384-6591

DIRECTIONS

The park is located 16 miles east of Hinckley on Highway 48.

ABOUT THE PARK

St. Croix State Park was established in 1943, and, with 34,037 acres, is the largest State Park in Minnesota. The land was logged during the late 19th and early 20th centuries, during which time logging camps were located along the St. Croix River and at St. John's Landing. When the land had been logged, the farmers moved in to make use of the cleared land. The soil in the area, however, was poor, and farming was a struggle. During the depression the federal government purchased poor farm lands and turned them into recreational areas. The government purchased the land, and had the Civilian Conservation Corps (CCC) build roads, campgrounds, and buildings.

The St. Croix River was an important early trade route, with prehistoric peoples known to have been in the area at least 3,000 years ago. The Dakota Indians were inhabiting the area when the first traders arrived in the 17th century. The Ojibway Indians later took the area from the Dakota, and they continued to live in the area until the 1930s.

The park's eastern boundary is the St. Croix River, 21 miles of which is designated a "National Wild and Scenic River." The western boundary is made up by the Kettle River, which is also classified as "Wild and Scenic." There are at least 10 other streams that flow through the park.

IF YOU GO . . .

Bring everything! There is so much to do that you will have trouble deciding what to do first. Try a bike ride from the campground over to Lake Clayton for a swim, and on the way back check out the Yellowbanks Civilian Conservation Corps (CCC) camp. Launch a canoe in the Kettle River, and paddle down to the St. Croix River for a variety of campsites. Horses are welcome, with miles of trails heading out from the equestrian area. For a hike, try the Kettle Rapids Trail, starting at Big Eddy, and offering several good overlooks of the river. Circle back along the trail to the Chapel Grove and eventually back to Big Eddy.

ST. CROIX STATE PARK

FACILITIES

isitor Center:	seasonal Visitor Center
icnic Area:	picnic area with an enclosed shelter

RECREATION

hildren's play area:	available at the picnic area near Lake Clayton
orseshoe pits:	yes
olleyball courts:	yes
wimming:	swimming beach on Lake Clayton
ishing:	fishing on the St. Croix and Kettle Rivers and Hay and Crooked Creeks
oating:	6 canoe landings on St. Croix and Kettle Rivers canoe rental

CAMPGROUND

ampsites:	Riverview Campground, 55 drive-in sites Paint Rock Springs Campground, 66 drive-in sites Old Logging Trail Campground 50 drive-in sites
lectric:	Riverview Campground 42 electric sites
ike or carry-in:	4 walk-in campsites at Riverview Campground 2 backpack sites
anoe campsites:	12 primitive canoe sites, 4 sites on the Kettle River and 8 sites on the St.Croix River canoe rental and canoe shuttle
ump station:	yes
oilets:	flush toilets
howers:	yes
roup Campground:	8 primitive group campsites
lodern group center:	2 centers are available from Memorial Day to Labor Day; a third center, St. John's Landing, is not open to the public at this time
ead of the Rapids:	10 barracks that sleep up to 11 people staff quarters for 9 people 3 bathrooms, dinning hall and kitchen, craft building, athletic fields and private beach minimum of 50 people
orway Point:	comprised of 4 villages each with a lodge and bathrooms 6 cabins sleeping 8 and a counselors cabin sleeping 2 people there is 1 central sanitation building, kitchen and dining hall, craft building, athletic fields and private swimming beach minimum of 75 people

ST. CROIX STATE PARK

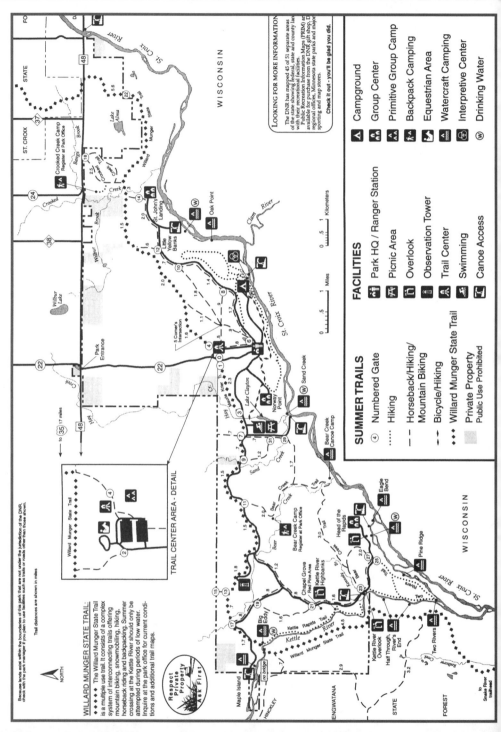

uest House:	guest house sleeps up to 15 people
	6 bedrooms, 2 bathrooms, dining roon
	kitchen

| abins: | 5 cabins sleep 2 adults each |
| | kitchen, half-bath, no linens |

TRAILS

iking Trails:	127 miles
iking Club Trail:	4 miles, starting at the St. Croix Lodge
king Trails:	6 paved miles
	24 miles of mountain bike trails
	bike rental
ross-country Ski:	21 miles
arming house:	yes
owmobile Trails:	80 miles
orse Trails:	75 miles
orse Campsites:	50 horse campsites

INTERPRETIVE PROGRAMS

he park offers a year round naturalist, an Interpretive Center with exhibits on e cultural and natural history of the park, and two self-guided interpretive trails. neck with the Interpretive Center for further information. Groups may arrange becial interpretive programs with the park staff in advance.

NEARBY PLACES TO VISIT

Banning State Park - Sandstone, 320-245-2668
North West Company Fur Post - Pine City, 320-629-6356, 612-296-5434
Hinckley Chamber of Commerce - Hinckley, 320 384-7837
Hinckley Convention/Visitor's Bureau - Hinckley, 800-996-4566, 320-384-0126
Hinckley Fire Museum - Hinckley, 320-384-7338
History and Art Center - Sandstone, 320-245-2271, 320-245-5241
Sandstone Chamber - Sandstone, 320-245-2271
Willard Munger State Trail - Moose Lake, 612-296-6699, 800-263-0586

OUR NOTES

Date visited   What we liked

Savanna Portage State Park
HCR 3, Box 591
McGregor, MN 55760
218-426-3271

DIRECTIONS

The park is located 7 miles northeast of McGregor on Highway 65. Take Highway 65 to County Road 14 and then take County Road 36 for 10 miles.

ABOUT THE PARK

Savanna Portage State Park, created in 1961, contains 15,818 acres of bogs, marshes, lakes, rivers, and rolling hills. The park also provides a wealth of recreational activities, including hiking, swimming, boating, fishing, snowmobiling, and skiing.

The Savanna Portage was developed centuries before the first traders came to the area, as a way to traverse between the Mississippi River and the St. Louis River watershed, and onto the Great Lakes. Traders would come up the East Savanna River by pushing themselves with poles for 12 miles. Next, the canoes were pushed through a quagmire to a pole "highway," where the canoes could be pushed through the tamarack swamp while the men carried the goods. Finally, the portage moved to higher ground, making the trek easier until they reached the West Savanna River, Big Sandy Lake, and Mississippi River. The portage took an average of five days to complete!

IF YOU GO . . .

Bring your snowmobile or skis! Savanna Portage State Park has 61 miles of snowmobile trails available, and 16 miles of hardwood forested ski trails to be explored.

SAVANNA PORTAGE STATE PARK

FACILITIES

Visitor Center: no
Picnic Area: picnic area on Loon Lake with a shelter

RECREATION

Children's play area: available in the campground and Loon Lake picnic area
Volleyball courts: yes
Horseshoe pits: yes
Swimming: swimming beach on Loon Lake
Fishing: lake fishing & fishing pier on Lake Shumway
Boating: drive-in boat access to Loon Lake and Lake Shumway
carry-in access to Remote Lake
boat and canoe rental

trout

CAMPGROUND

Campsites: 60 drive-in campsites
Electric: 18 electric campsites
Hike or carry-in: 6 backpacking campsites
1 walk-in campsite
Canoe campsites: no
Dump station: yes
Toilets: flush toilets
Showers: yes
Group Campground: 1 primitive group campsite on Savanna Lake
Camping cabins: inquire at park headquarters

TRAILS

Hiking Trails: 17 miles
Hiking Club Trail: 5.3 miles, starting at the Shumway Campground or the boat landing
Biking Trails: 10 miles for mountain bikes
Cross-country Ski: 17 miles
2 skate/ski miles
Warming house: yes
Snowmobile Trails: 60 miles
Horse Trails: no
Horse Campsites: no

INTERPRETIVE PROGRAMS

There are no interpretive programs available in the park.

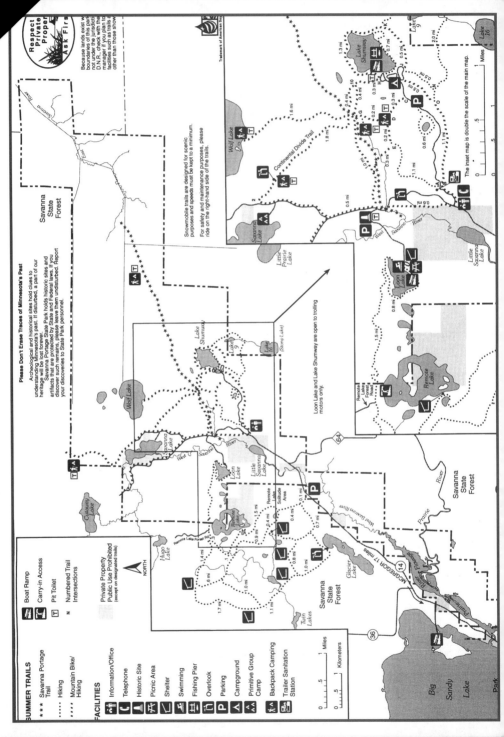

SUMMER TRAILS

* * * Savanna Portage Trail
· · · · · Hiking
· · · · · Mountain Bike/ Hiking
N Numbered Trail Intersections

FACILITIES

Information/Office
Telephone
Historic Site
Picnic Area
Shelter
Swimming
Fishing Pier
Overlook
Parking
Campground
Primitive Group Camp
Backpack Camping
Trailer Sanitation Station

Boat Ramp
Carry-in Access
Pit Toilet

Private Property Public Use Prohibited (except on designated trails)

NORTH

Please Don't Erase Traces of Minnesota's Past

Archeological and historical sites hold clues to understanding Minnesota's past. If disturbed, a part of our heritage will be lost forever.
Savanna Portage State Park holds historic sites and artifacts that are protected by State and Federal laws. If you discover such remains, please leave them undisturbed. Report your discoveries to State Park personnel.

Snowmobile trails are designed for scenic purposes and speeds must be kept to a minimum.
For safety and maintenance purposes, please ride on the right-hand side of the trails.

Loon Lake and Lake Shumway are open to trolling motors only.

The inset map is double the scale of the main map.

SAVANNA PORTAGE STATE PARK

Photo by Dudley Edmondson

NEARBY PLACES TO VISIT

Longlake Conservation Center Trail - Palisade, 218-927-7364
McGregor Chamber - McGregor, 218-768-3692
Remote Lake Solitude Area - McGregor, 218-426-3407

OUR NOTES

Date visited   What we liked

TRIVIA

Savanna Portage State Park has a "grand portage" of 6 miles. This was the final link to the upper Mississippi watershed connecting the East and West Savanna Rivers.

Wild River State Park
19755 Park Trail
Center City, MN 55012
612-583-2125

DIRECTIONS

The park is located 14 miles east of Interstate 35 on Highway 95.

ABOUT THE PARK

Wild River State Park was established in 1973 to protect the natural resources of the area. The park contains 6,803 acres, much of which was donated by Northern States Power. The park received its name from the St. Croix River, designated a "Wild and Scenic River" in 1968.

The area along the St. Croix River has long been inhabited by Native Americans. The river was part of the fur trading routes, and several posts were established along the river. Samuel's Fur Post and Connor's Goose Creek Post were active in the area until 1847. The land was logged at the end of the 19th century, and the remains of Never's Dam, which was used by loggers, can still be seen near the river.

IF YOU GO . . .

Come for a hike! Start out from the Visitor Center and follow the hiking club trail north along the St. Croix River. Plan to spend some time at the Old Never's Dam site on the river, and then follow the trail up to the picnic area. From there, follow the Old Logging Trail back to the Visitor Center.

WILD RIVER STATE PARK

FACILITIES

Visitor Center:	year round Visitor Center
Picnic Area:	picnic area with an enclosed shelter

RECREATION

Children's play area:	no
Volleyball courts:	no
Horseshoe pits:	no
Swimming:	no
Fishing:	fishing on the St. Croix River
Boating:	2 drive-in boat accesses to the St. Croix River
	canoe rental
	canoe shuttles

CAMPGROUND

Campsites:	96 drive-in campsites
Electric:	17 electric campsites
Hike or carry-in:	8 backpack campsites
Canoe campsites:	8 canoe campsites
Dump station:	yes
Toilets:	flush toilets
Showers:	yes
Group Campground:	primitive group campsite
Guest house:	house available for 8 people
	2 bedrooms, bathroom, and kitchen
Camping cabins:	2, each with a capacity for 6 people

TRAILS

Hiking Trails:	35 miles
Hiking Club Trail:	3.3 miles, starting at the Visitor Center
Biking Trails:	no
Cross-country Ski:	35 miles
	ski rental
Warming house:	yes
Snowmobile Trails:	no
Snowshoe rental:	yes
Horse Trails:	20 miles
Horse Campsites:	20 horse campsites

INTERPRETIVE PROGRAMS

There is a year round interpretive program at Wild River State Park. Visitors should check the bulletin boards for schedules. The Visitor Center overlooking the St. Croix River valley offers a weather station, displays, exhibits, and slide shows.

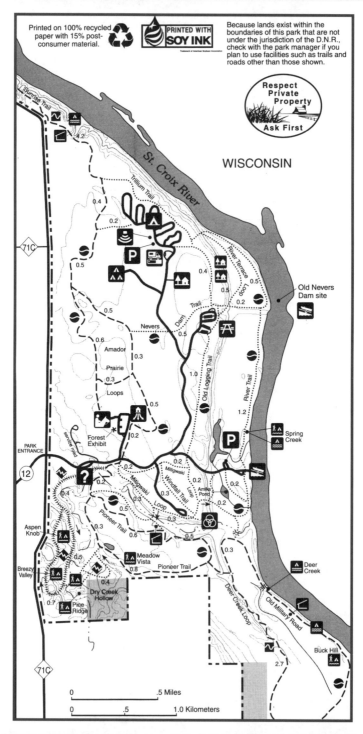

Printed on 100% recycled paper with 15% post-consumer material.

PRINTED WITH SOY INK

Because lands exist within the boundaries of this park that are not under the jurisdiction of the D.N.R., check with the park manager if you plan to use facilities such as trails and roads other than those shown.

Respect Private Property Ask First

WISCONSIN

St. Croix River

Sunrise Trail

Trillium Trail

0.4

0.2

71C

0.5

River Terrace Loop

Old Nevers Dam site

0.4

0.5

0.5

0.5

0.2

Dam Trail

Nevers

0.5

0.5

0.6

Amador

Prairie

0.3

Loops

0.3

Old Logging Trail

River Trail

0.5

1.0

1.2

Spring Creek

Forest Exhibit

0.2

0.5

PARK ENTRANCE

12

?

0.2

0.2

0.2

0.2

Milligwaki

Windfall Loop

Amik Pond

0.2

0.2

0.4

Milgwaki Trail

0.3

0.3

Loop

0.5

Pioneer Trail

0.3

0.6

0.5

0.3

Aspen Knob

Meadow Vista

Pioneer Trail

Deer Creek

0.5

0.8

Breezy Valley

0.4

Dry Creek Hollow

0.7

Pine Ridge

Deer Creek Loop

Old Military Road

Buck Hill

2.7

71C

0   .5 Miles

0   .5   1.0 Kilometers

Wild River State Park
Photo by author

NEARBY PLACES TO VISIT

Interstate State Park - Taylors Falls, 612-465-5711
W H C Folsom House - Taylors Falls, 612-465-3125

OUR NOTES

Date visited   What we liked

T R I V I A

Minnesota State Parks have 450 registered landmarks.

PARK	ACREAGE
Big Stone Lake State Park	1,118 acres
Blue Mounds State Park	2,028 acres
Camden State Park	1,745 acres
Flandreau State Park	805 acres
Fort Ridgely State Park	584 acres
Kilen Woods State Park	228 acres
Lac Qui Parle State Park	530 acres
Lake Shetek State Park	1,109 acres
Minneopa State Park	1,145 acres
Monson Lake State Park	187 acres
Sibley State Park	2,926 acres
Split Rock Creek State Park	400 acres
Upper Sioux Agency State Park	1,280 acres

SOUTHWESTERN REGION

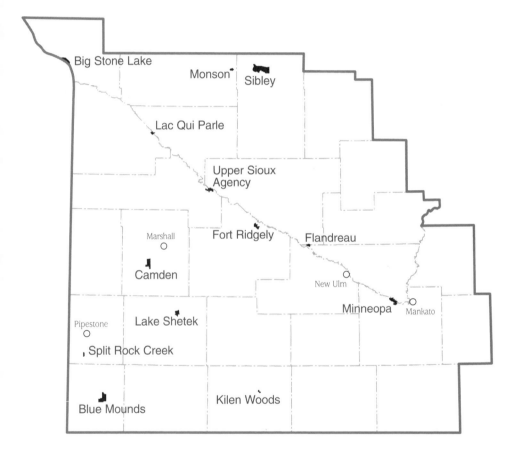

Big Stone Lake

Monson

Sibley

Lac Qui Parle

Upper Sioux
Agency

Marshall

Fort Ridgely

Flandreau

Camden

New Ulm

Pipestone

Lake Shetek

Minneopa

Mankato

Split Rock Creek

Blue Mounds

Kilen Woods

Big Stone Lake State Park
RR 1 Box 153
Ortonville, MN 56278
320-839-3663

DIRECTIONS

The park entrance is located about 6 miles northwest of Ortonville, on Highway 7.

ABOUT THE PARK

Big Stone Lake State Park's 1,118 acres are located along Big Stone Lake, the source of the Minnesota River. The park has two parts: the Meadowbrook area, which offers a campground picnic area, and boat launch, and the Bonanza area, with an Interpretive Center, swimming area, picnic grounds, and boat launching site. The park has the distinction of being the most westerly in Minnesota — looking across the lake, visitors can see South Dakota!

Fossils and remains of aquatic life have been found in the area surrounding Big Stone Lake, so it is thought that the area was once submerged. Prehistoric peoples are known to have inhabited the area, and many artifacts have been found near the park. Traces of ancient tools with Viking inscriptions were discovered, and there are stories of large stones with Runic writings. If these stones can be found, it could provide proof of ancient Viking explorations.

IF YOU GO . . .

Bring your fishing pole! Fishing and boating are quite popular in the park, with boat launches in both areas. When you arrive in the park, check out the Interpretive Center — it is well worth visiting.

BIG STONE LAKE STATE PARK

FACILITIES

Visitor Center:	yes
Picnic Area:	2 picnic areas

RECREATION

Children's play area:	yes
Volleyball courts:	no
Horseshoe pits:	yes
Swimming:	swimming beach on Big Stone Lake
Fishing:	lake fishing in Big Stone Lake
Boating:	boating on Big Stone Lake
	2 boat launching areas

CAMPGROUND

Campsites:	42 drive-in campsites
Electric:	10 electric campsites
Hike or carry-in:	no
Canoe campsites:	no
Dump station:	yes
Toilets:	flush toilets
Showers:	yes
Group Campground:	1 campsite

TRAILS

Hiking Trails:	1.5 miles
Hiking Club Trail:	1.5 miles, starting at the picnic area parking lot
Biking Trails:	no
Cross-country Ski:	no
Snowmobile Trails:	3.5 miles
Horse Trails:	no
Horse Campsites:	no

INTERPRETIVE PROGRAMS

There are no interpretive programs available in the park.

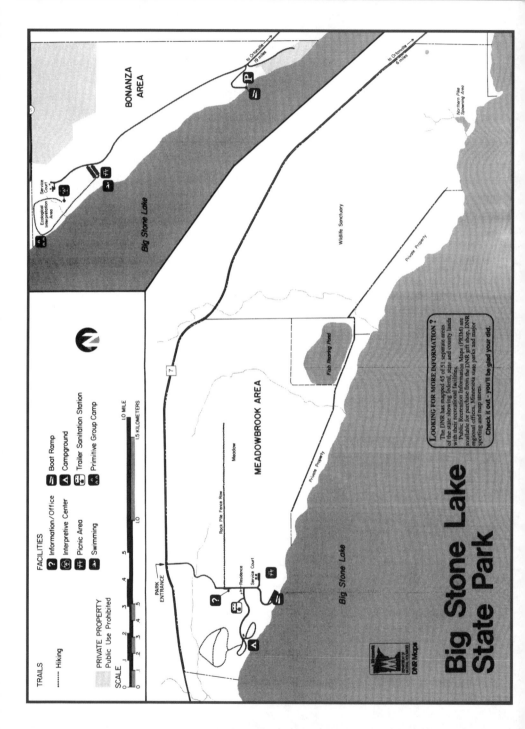

Big Stone Lake State Park

TRAILS

······ Hiking

PRIVATE PROPERTY
Public Use Prohibited

SCALE

FACILITIES

2 Information/Office
(i) Interpretive Center
π Picnic Area
🏊 Swimming

🚤 Boat Ramp
▲ Campground
🚻 Trailer Sanitation Station
🏕 Primitive Group Camp

BONANZA AREA

Big Stone Lake

Service Court
Ecological Interpretation Area

to Ortonville 9 miles

P

to Ortonville 6 miles

Northern Pike Spawning Area

Wildlife Sanctuary

Private Property

MEADOWBROOK AREA

Fish Rearing Pond

Meadow

Rock Pile Fence Row

Private Property

PARK ENTRANCE

Residence
Service Court

2

Big Stone Lake

DNR Maps

LOOKING FOR MORE INFORMATION ?

The DNR has mapped 45 of 51 separate areas of the state showing federal, state and county lands with their recreational facilities.
Public Recreation Information Maps (PRIM) are available for purchase from the DNR gift shop, DNR regional offices, Minnesota state parks and major sporting and map stores.
Check it out - you'll be glad your did.

Yellow Warbler (male)   Photo by Dudley Edmondson

NEARBY PLACES TO VISIT

Big Stone County Historical Museum - Ortonville, 320-839-3359, 320-839-3206
Big Stone Lake Area Chamber - Ortonville, 800-568-5722

OUR NOTES

Date visited   What we liked

T R I V I A

Fossilized sharks' teeth have been found in the area surrounding Big Stone Lake.

BLUE MOUNDS STATE PARK

Blue Mounds State Park
RR 1 Box 52
Luverne, MN 56156
507-283-4892

DIRECTIONS

The park is located 6 miles north of Interstate 90 on Highway 75, or 16 miles south of Pipestone on Highway 75.

ABOUT THE PARK

The 2,028 acre Blue Mounds State Park got its name from the large Sioux quartzite cliff that rises up from the prairie. The mound looked blue to the settlers that passed by, so they named it "Blue Mound." This area was never plowed, due to the rock outcroppings, but there was some animal grazing and the introduction of foreign weeds. There is currently a program in place to bring the prairie back to its original state so that visitors can experience the tall prairie grasses and wildflowers of a native prairie.

Buffalo are an important part of the history of the prairie, and it is known that the Plains Indians went out onto the prairie to hunt the buffalo. There is a legend that the Indians would drive buffalo over the cliff at Blue Mounds, but there has never been any evidence to support the claim. The park is still home to a herd of buffalo, which visitors can view from a stand near the buffalo pen.

An interesting park mystery is the line of 1,250 feet of rocks located in the southern end of the park. Who put them there (and why) has never been answered, but the stones are said to line up with the sun during the spring and fall equinoxes.

The two lakes in the park were formed by two dams on the Mound Creek, which were built by the Works Progress Administration (WPA). Thousands of trees were planted around the lakes and campground during the 1950s.

IF YOU GO . . .

Check out the buffalo! Park at the swimming beach and hike to the viewing stand at the buffalo range. From there, follow the Mound trail through the prairie grasses along the eastern edge of the buffalo range. Take the Upper Mound trail to the Interpretive Center, which is open May through September. After leaving the center, follow the Upper Cliffline trail back to the swimming beach and jump in the lake to cool off after the hike.

BLUE MOUNDS STATE PARK

FACILITIES

Visitor Center: Interpretive Center
Picnic Area: open area for picnicking

RECREATION

Children's play area: yes
Horseshoe pit: yes
Volleyball courts: yes
Swimming: swimming beach on Lower Mound Lake
Fishing: lake fishing
Boating: boating, but there is no drive-in access
                        canoe rentals

CAMPGROUND

Campsites: 73 drive-in campsites
Electric: 40 electric campsites
Hike or carry-in: 14 cart-in campsites
Canoe campsites: no
Dump station: yes
Toilets: flush toilets
Showers: yes
Group Campground: primitive group campsite

TRAILS

Hiking Trails: 13 miles
Hiking Club Trail: 6.2 miles, starting at the picnic area shelter
Biking Trails: no
Cross-country Ski: no
Snowmobile Trails: 7 miles
Horse Trails: no
Horse Campsites: no

INTERPRETIVE PROGRAMS

There is an Interpretive Center within the park which was built in 1976. There is also an amphitheater near the campground.

BLUE MOUNDS STATE PARK

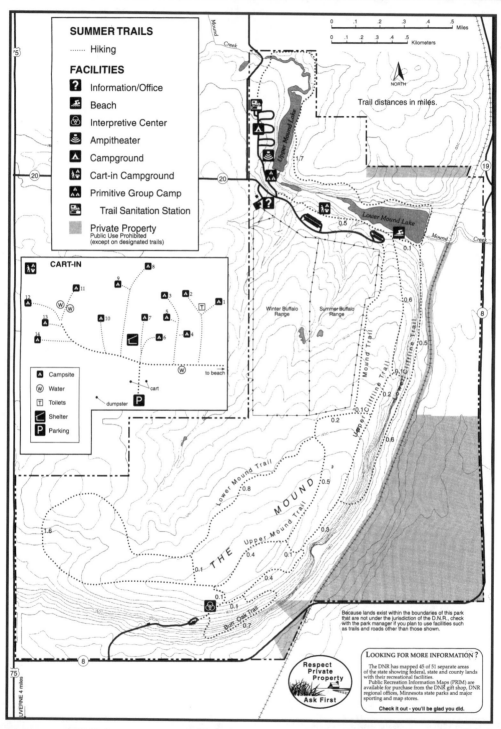

SUMMER TRAILS

..... Hiking

FACILITIES

? Information/Office
🏊 Beach
Interpretive Center
Ampitheater
▲ Campground
Cart-in Campground
Primitive Group Camp
Trail Sanitation Station

Private Property
Public Use Prohibited
(except on designated trails)

Trail distances in miles.

NORTH

CART-IN

▲ Campsite
W Water
T Toilets
Shelter
P Parking

to beach

cart

dumpster

Winter Buffalo Range
Summer Buffalo Range

Upper Mound Lake

Lower Mound Lake

Mound Creek

Mound Creek

Lower Mound Trail

Upper Mound Trail

Upper Cliffline Trail

Lower Cliffline Trail

Mound Trail

THE MOUND

Buff Oak Trail

1.7

0.5

0.1

0.6

0.5

0.1

0.6

0.2

0.8

0.5

0.3

0.4

0.1

0.4

0.1

0.1

0.7

1.6

Because lands exist within the boundaries of this park that are not under the jurisdiction of the D.N.R., check with the park manager if you plan to use facilities such as trails and roads other than those shown.

Respect Private Property
Ask First

LOOKING FOR MORE INFORMATION ?

The DNR has mapped 45 of 51 separate areas of the state showing federal, state and county lands with their recreational facilities.
Public Recreation Information Maps (PRIM) are available for purchase from the DNR gift shop, DNR regional offices, Minnesota state parks and major sporting and map stores.

Check it out - you'll be glad you did.

Blue Mounds State Park   Photo by author

NEARBY PLACES TO VISIT

Fort Pipestone - Pipestone, 507-825-4474
Hinkly House Museum - Luverne, 507-283-8294, 507-283-4061
Luverne Convention/Visitor's Bureau - Luverne, 507-283-4061, 888-283-4061
Pipestone Chamber - Pipestone, 507-825-3316, 800-336-6125
Pipestone County Historical Museum - Pipestone, 507-825-2563
Pipestone Falls - Pipestone, 507-825-5463
Pipestone National Monument - Pipestone, 507-825-5464
Rock County History Museum at Masonic Temple Site
    Luverne, 507-283-8294, 507-283-4061
Split Rock Creek State Park - Jasper, 507-348-7908

OUR NOTES

Date visited   What we liked

_____

_____

_____

_____

_____

Although no known burial mounds exist within Blue Mounds State Park,
more than 10,000 Indian burial mounds were once located in the state.
Many of these mounds have been destroyed.

Camden State Park
RR 1 Box 49
Lynd, MN 56152
507-865-4530

DIRECTIONS

To get to the park entrance, take Highway 23 southwest of Marshall for 10 miles, then go 10 miles north on US Highway 14.

ABOUT THE PARK

Camden State Park was established in 1935 and has 1,745 acres. The park, located in a beautiful wooded valley created by the Redwood River, has long been an oasis for travelers crossing the prairies.

Prehistoric peoples are believed to have built semi-permanent villages in this area as far back as 8,000 years ago. The American Fur Company established a post here during the 1830s. Settlers began coming into the valley during the late 1840s, and they named the valley Camden after their previous home of Camden, New Jersey. After the Dakota Uprising of 1862 the town thrived, until the railroad bypassed Camden, causing the town to decline. By the 1930s the village was history.

Favorite park activities include hiking, fishing, and swimming. During the depression the park benefited from the skills of the Civilian Conservation Corps (CCC). This area is a wonderful change from the prairie.

IF YOU GO . . .

Bring your walking shoes or horse! There is an abundance of trails along the river valley that provide scenic trips for both the rider and the hiker. Try exploring Camden State Park in the spring, when there is an abundance of wildflowers in both the woodlands and the prairie areas of the park. The Valley comes alive in the fall, when the color from the maples, basswoods, and cottonwoods make for great viewing.

CAMDEN STATE PARK

FACILITIES

Visitor Center:	no
Picnic Area:	3 picnic areas 2 with shelters

RECREATION

Children's play area:	no
Horseshoe pit:	yes
Volleyball court:	yes
Swimming:	spring-fed swimming pond
Fishing:	trout fishing and fishing pier on Brawner Lake
Boating:	boat ramp on Brawner Lake

CAMPGROUND

Campsites:	80 drive-in campsites
Electric:	29 electric campsites
Hike or carry-in:	no
Canoe campsites:	no
Dump station:	yes
Toilets:	flush toilets
Showers:	yes
Group Campground:	primitive group campground

TRAILS

Hiking Trails:	14.8 miles
Hiking Club Trail:	2.4 miles, starting at the Visitor Center
Biking Trails:	4.2 miles
Cross-country Ski:	8 kilometers and 2.2 kilometers of skate/ski
Warming shelter:	yes
Snowmobile Trails:	7.6 miles
Horse Trails:	10.2 miles
Horse Campsites:	12 campsites accommodating up to 50 people

INTERPRETIVE PROGRAMS

Interpretive programs are available during the summer.

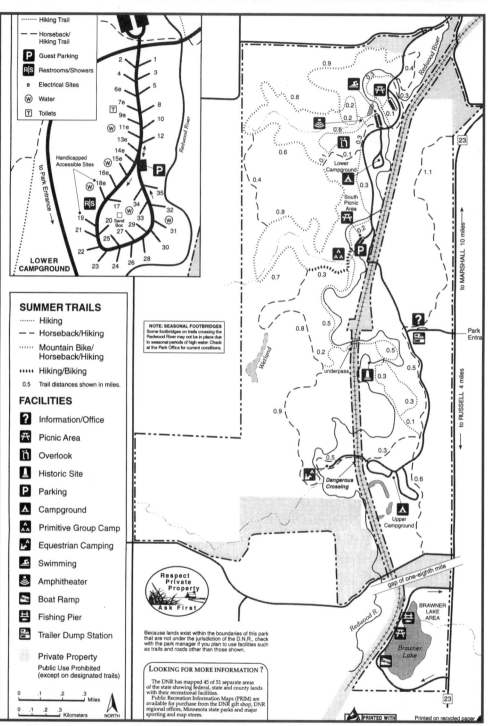

Legend (upper left):
- ⋯⋯ Hiking Trail
- — — Horseback/Hiking Trail
- P Guest Parking
- R|S Restrooms/Showers
- e Electrical Sites
- W Water
- T Toilets

Handicapped Accessible Sites

LOWER CAMPGROUND

Sand Box

Redwood River

to Park Entrance

SUMMER TRAILS
- ⋯⋯ Hiking
- — — Horseback/Hiking
- ⋯⋯ Mountain Bike/ Horseback/Hiking
- ⋄⋄⋄⋄ Hiking/Biking
- 0.5 Trail distances shown in miles.

FACILITIES
- ? Information/Office
- 🍴 Picnic Area
- 🔭 Overlook
- ▮ Historic Site
- P Parking
- ▲ Campground
- ▲▲ Primitive Group Camp
- 🏕 Equestrian Camping
- 🏊 Swimming
- 🎵 Amphitheater
- ⛵ Boat Ramp
- ☰ Fishing Pier
- 🚐 Trailer Dump Station
- ░░ Private Property
  Public Use Prohibited (except on designated trails)

NOTE: SEASONAL FOOTBRIDGES
Some footbridges on trails crossing the Redwood River may not be in place due to seasonal periods of high water. Check at the Park Office for current conditions.

Respect Private Property Ask First

Lower Campground

South Picnic Area

Wetland

underpass

Dangerous Crossing

Upper Campground

gap of one-eighth mile

BRAWNER LAKE AREA

Brawner Lake

Redwood R.

Redwood River

Park Entrance

to MARSHALL 10 miles →

to RUSSELL 4 miles →

23

Because lands exist within the boundaries of this park that are not under the jurisdiction of the D.N.R., check with the park manager if you plan to use facilities such as trails and roads other than those shown.

LOOKING FOR MORE INFORMATION ?
The DNR has mapped 45 of 51 separate areas of the state showing federal, state and county lands with their recreational facilities.
Public Recreation Information Maps (PRIM) are available for purchase from the DNR gift shop, DNR regional offices, Minnesota state parks and major sporting and map stores.

0 .1 .2 .3 Miles
0 .1 .2 .3 Kilometers
NORTH

PRINTED WITH — Printed on recycled paper

CAMDEN STATE PARK

Camden State Park   Photo by author

NEARBY PLACES TO VISIT

Historic Osbeck House - Lake Benton, 507-368-9343
Laura Ingalls Wilder Museum - Walnut Grove, 507-859-2358
Lyon County Museum - Marshall, 507-537-6580
Marshall Convention and Visitor's Bureau - Marshall, 507-537-1865

OUR NOTES

Date visited   What we liked

TRIVIA

Minnesota encompasses 84,068 square miles of which 4,059 square miles are water. Minnesota has the most square miles of water of any state.

Flandreau State Park
1300 Summit Ave.
New Ulm, MN 56073
507-354-3519

DIRECTIONS

The park is adjacent to (and partially within) the city of New Ulm, located several blocks southwest of Highway 15.

ABOUT THE PARK

The 805 acre Flandreau State Park was named to honor Charles Flandreau, a Minnesota lawyer and Indian agent during the 1860s.

Artifacts, campsites, buffalo bones, and petroglyphs have been found in the area surrounding the Cottonwood River, proving that Native Americans once lived there. Buffalo bones are still being found in fresh gravel washouts. Explorers and fur traders used the area until the 1830s, when the first settlers starting arriving.

During the 1930s, shortly after the park was established, the Civilian Conservation Corps (CCC) planted trees throughout the park. They also built three dams (later destroyed by flooding), a beach house, and trails. During World War II the park was the site of a prisoner of war camp.

IF YOU GO . . .

Bring your hiking shoes! Head down to the parking area at the sand-bottomed swimming pool, and follow the trail heading to the west, which meets up with the Cottonwood trail. This is a self-guided interpretive trail that follows the Cottonwood River and then circles back to the swimming area.

FLANDREAU STATE PARK

FACILITIES

Visitor Center:	no
Picnic Area:	large picnic area with enclosed shelter

RECREATION

Children's play area:	yes
Horseshoe pit:	yes
Volleyball court:	yes
Swimming:	swimming pool with sand bottom
Fishing:	river fishing on the Cottonwood River
Boating:	carry-in boat access to the Cottonwood River

CAMPGROUND

Campsites:	57 drive-in campsites
Electric:	35 electric campsites
Bike or carry-in:	no
Canoe campsites:	no
Dump station:	yes
Toilets:	flush toilets
Showers:	yes
Group Campground:	1 primitive group campground
Modern Group Center:	accommodates up to 105 people in 7 barracks
	staff quarters sleep 6
	fully equipped dining room and kitchen
	available from Memorial Day to Labor Day
	50 person minimum

TRAILS

Hiking Trails:	8.5 miles
Hiking Club Trail:	2.8 miles, start at beach house
Biking Trails:	no
Cross-country Ski:	7.5 miles
Warming house:	yes
Snowmobile Trails:	1.3 miles
Horse Trails:	no
Horse Campsites:	no

INTERPRETIVE PROGRAMS

There is no interpretive program available in the park.

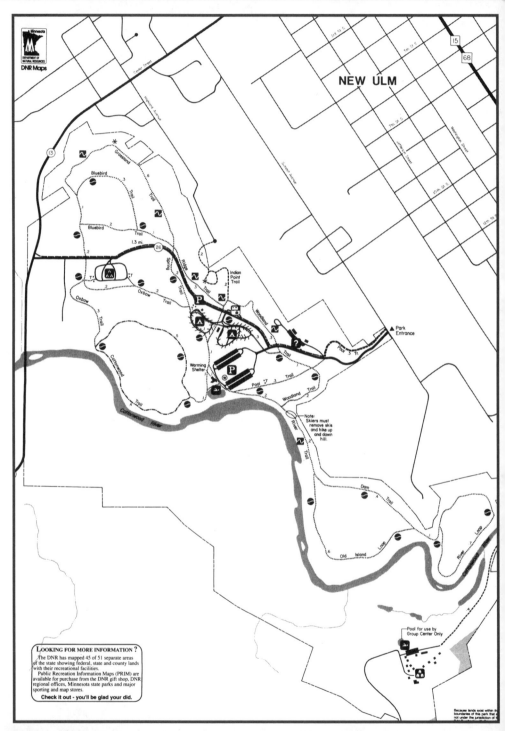

NEW ULM

Park Entrance

Note: Skiers must remove skis and hike up and down hill.

Pool for use by Group Center Only

LOOKING FOR MORE INFORMATION ?

The DNR has mapped 45 of 51 separate areas of the state showing federal, state and county lands with their recreational facilities.

Public Recreation Information Maps (PRIM) are available for purchase from the DNR gift shop, DNR regional offices, Minnesota state parks and major sporting and map stores.

Check it out - you'll be glad your did.

Flandreau State Park

Photo by author

NEARBY PLACES TO VISIT

A. Schell Museum of Brewing - New Ulm, 507-354-5528
Brown County Historical Museum - New Ulm, 507-354-2016
Glockenspiel - New Ulm, 507-354-4217, 888-463-9856
Harkin Store - New Ulm, 507-354-8666, 507-354-2016
Hermann Monument - New Ulm, 507-359-8344
Lind House - New Ulm, 507-354-4949, 507-359-1807
Minnesota Music Hall of Fame - New Ulm, 507-354-7305
New Prague Chamber - New Prague, 612-758-4360
New Ulm Convention and Visitor's Bureau - New Ulm, 507-354-4217, 888-463-9856
Nicollet County Historical Museum/Treaty Site History Center - St Peter, 507-931-2160
Sleepy Eye Depot Museum - Sleepy Eye, 507-794-5053
Turner Hall - New Ulm, 507-354-4916
Wanda Gag House - New Ulm, 507-359-2632

OUR NOTES

Date visited   What we liked

T R I V I A

Minnesota was the second state to establish a state park system.

Fort Ridgely State Park
RR 1 Box 65
Fairfax, MN 55332
507-426-7840

DIRECTIONS

The park is located 6 miles south of Fairfax on Highway 4.

ABOUT THE PARK

Fort Ridgely State Park commemorates the US military garrison of the same name, which was built in 1853. The fort was situated along the bluffs of the Minnesota River, and provided protection for the settlers in the area. It played a major role in the Dakota Uprising of 1862, when it was attacked by over 400 Dakota Indians. The old fort site was bought by the state in 1896 to memorialize the conflict, and a monument was erected. Additional acreage was purchased in 1911, and the site was turned into a state park. The park received development help from the Civilian Conservation Corps (CCC), who located their camp near the rustic campsite area.

Since 1975, the Minnesota Historic Society has maintained an Interpretive Center in the park, which features exhibits and information about life at the Fort. During the summer the park hosts the Fort Ridgely Historic Festival, which offers a re-creation of a military rendezvous and encampment, music, food and other entertainment.

IF YOU GO . . .

Plan to tour! Park at the old fort site and check out the Interpretive Center and excavated ruins. There are miles of trails across the street for both the hiker and horseback rider. Try the River Bluff trail in either direction for some scenic overlooks of the Minnesota River Valley.

FORT RIDGELY STATE PARK

FACILITIES

Visitor Center:	no
Picnic Area:	3 picnic areas: 1 with an open shelter 1 with an enclosed shelter
Warming Shelter:	enclosed picnic shelter serves as a warming shelter in winter

RECREATION

Children's play area:	at the upper picnic area
Horseshoe pits:	yes
Volleyball courts:	yes
Golf Course:	9 hole course in park golf club rentals
Swimming:	no
Fishing:	stream fishing
Boating:	no

CAMPGROUND

Campsites:	33 drive-in campsites
Electric:	8 electric campsites
Hike or carry-in:	4 walk-in campsites
Canoe campsites:	no
Dump station:	no
Toilets:	flush toilets
Showers:	yes
Group Campground:	ground campsite

TRAILS

Hiking Trails:	11 miles
Hiking Club Trail:	2.6 miles, starting at the upper picnic shelter
Biking Trails:	no
Cross-country Ski:	4 miles
Snowmobile Trails:	7 miles
Horse Trails:	7 miles
Horse Campsites:	20 campsites

INTERPRETIVE PROGRAMS

The park's Interpretive Center is maintained through the Minnesota Historic Society.

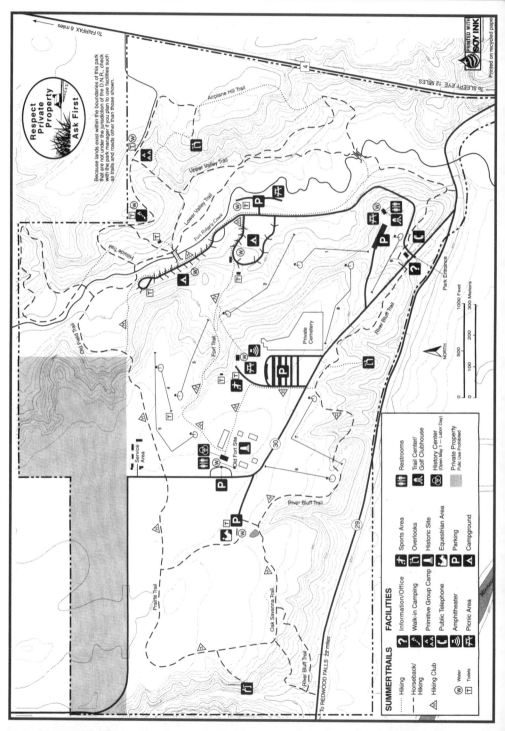

Fort Ridgely State Park   Photo by author

NEARBY PLACES TO VISIT

A. Schell Museum of Brewing - New Ulm, 507-354-5528
Brown County Historical Museum - New Ulm, 507-354-2016
Gifillan Estate - Morgan, 507-644-2490, 507-249-3451
Glockenspiel - New Ulm, 507-354-4217, 888-463-9856
Harkin Store - New Ulm, 507-354-8666, 507-354-2016
Hermann Monument - New Ulm, 507-359-8344
Lind House - New Ulm, 507-354-4949, 507-359-1807
Lower Sioux Agency Historic Site - Morton, 507-697-6321
Minnesota Music Hall of Fame - New Ulm, 507-354-7305
New Ulm Convention/Visitor's Bureau
     New Ulm, 507-354-4217, 888-463-9856
Redwood County Museum - Redwood Falls, 507-637-3329
Redwood Regional TCB - Redwood Falls, 800-657-7070, 507-637-2828
Renville County Historical Museum - Morton, 507-697-6147
Sleepy Eye Depot Museum - Sleepy Eye, 507-794-5053
Turner Hall - New Ulm, 507-354-4916
Wanda Gag House - New Ulm, 507-359-2632

OUR NOTES

Date visited   What we liked

TRIVIA

Fort Ridgely State Park is the only park to operate its own golfcourse.

Kilen Woods State Park
RR 1 Box 122
Lakefield, MN 56150
507-662-6258

DIRECTIONS

The park is located 9 miles northeast of Lakefield on County Road Highway 24.

ABOUT THE PARK

Kilen Woods State park consists of about 200 acres of wooded hillsides and valley, located along the Des Moines River. The land was purchased from Agil Kilen, for whom the park was named, in 1945.

This area was inhabited by prehistoric people approximately 6,000 years ago, although little is known about them. The Dakota eventually moved into the area, and were living here when the first explorers came to the area in the mid 1700s. Joseph Nicollet explored the Des Moines River during the 1830s, and settlers moved into the area after the treaty of Traverse de Sioux in 1851. During the Dakota Uprising of 1862 twenty settlers were killed and the fearful settlers abandoned the area.

IF YOU GO . . .

Come for a hike! Start your hike at the picnic area along the Sioux Trail, which wanders through the prairie grasses. Next, catch the Connector trail, which joins the Rock Creek Trail, and head towards the Des Moines River. Be sure to check out the Dinosaur Ridge Overlook, and then head back towards the picnic area.

KILEN WOODS STATE PARK

FACILITIES

sitor Center:	multi-purpose year round shelter with facilities
cnic Area:	2 picnic areas

RECREATION

iildren's play area:	no
orseshoe pits:	yes
olleyball courts:	yes
vimming:	no
shing:	river fishing
oating:	boat access to the Des Moines River

CAMPGROUND

ampsites:	33 drive-in campsites
ectric:	11 electric campsites
ke or carry-in:	4 walk-in campsites
anoe campsites:	3 canoe campsites
ump station:	yes
oilets:	flush toilets
nowers:	yes
roup Campground:	1 group campsite

TRAILS

king Trails:	5 miles
king Club Trail:	2 miles, start at the east end of the picnic area parking lot
king Trails:	no
ross-country Ski:	1.5 miles
iding Hill:	yes
arming house:	yes
nowmobile Trails:	3.5 miles
orse Trails:	no
orse Campsites:	no

INTERPRETIVE PROGRAMS

nere is no interpretive program available in park.

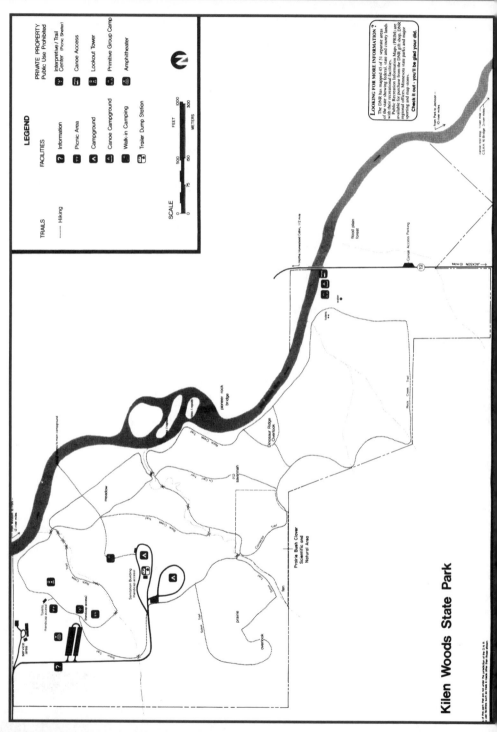

LEGEND

TRAILS

------- Hiking

FACILITIES

? Information

Picnic Area

Campground

Canoe Campground

Walk-in Camping

Trailer Dump Station

PRIVATE PROPERTY
Public Use Prohibited

Interpretive / Trail Center (Picnic Shelter)

Canoe Access

Lookout Tower

Primitive Group Camp

Amphitheater

SCALE

FEET
METERS

LOOKING FOR MORE INFORMATION ?
The DNR has mapped 45 of 51 separate areas of the state showing federal, state and county lands with their recreational facilities.
Public Recreation Information Maps (PRIM) are available for purchase from the DNR gift shop, DNR regional offices, Minnesota state parks and major sporting and map stores.
Check it out - you'll be glad your did.

Kilen Woods State Park

Red-tailed Hawk
Photo by Dudley Edmondson

NEARBY PLACES TO VISIT

Cottonwood County Historical Museum - Windom, 507-831-1134
Jackson County Historical Museum - Lakefield, 507-662-5505
Jeffers Petroglyphs - Bingham Lake, 507-678-2311
Mountain Lake Heritage House, Inc. - Mountain Lake, 507-427-2023, 507-427-3368
Windom Area Chamber - Windom, 507-831-2752, 800-794-6366

OUR NOTES

Date visited   What we liked

T R I V I A

The state muffin is blueberry. The state mushroom is the morel.

LAC QUI PARLE STATE PARK

Lac Qui Parle State Park
RR 5 Box 74A
Montevideo, MN 56265
320-752-4736

DIRECTIONS
The park is located 5 miles northwest of Watsonvia, on Highway 59 & County Road 13.

ABOUT THE PARK
Lac Qui Parle State Park was established in 1939 and covers 530 acres. The park is located at the point that the Lac Qui Parle River joins with the Minnesota River and was created when the flood control project of 1936 was enacted. The Works Progress Administration (WPA) created a picnic shelter, toilets and roads in the park. The park is situated next to the 27,000 acre Lac Qui Parle Wildlife Management area.

Lac Qui Parle translates to "lake which speaks," and the lake is the dominant feature of the park. Thousands of geese and other waterfowl descend upon the park in the fall, making for great birdwatching.

IF YOU GO . . .
Come prepared for fishing. Since the park is located at the junction of two major waterways, there are many choice spots to try your luck with a fishing pole.

LAC QUI PARLE STATE PARK

FACILITIES

Visitor Center: no
Picnic Area: picnic area with open shelter

RECREATION

Children's play area: no
Volleyball courts: no
Horseshoe pits: no
Swimming: yes
Fishing: lake and river fishing
Boating: drive-in boat access

CAMPGROUND

Campsites: 42 drive-in campsites
Electric: 22 electric campsites
Hike or carry-in: 11 walk-in campsites
                       3 back pack campsites
Canoe campsites: no
Dump station: yes
Toilets: flush toilets
Showers: yes
Group Campground: yes

TRAILS

Hiking Trails: 6 miles
Hiking Club Trail: 2 miles, starting at the canoe landing
Biking Trails: no
Cross-country Ski: 5 miles
Warming house: yes
Snowmobile Trails: no
Horse Trails: 6 miles
Horse Campsites: 5 campsites

INTERPRETIVE PROGRAMS

There are no interpretive programs available in the park.

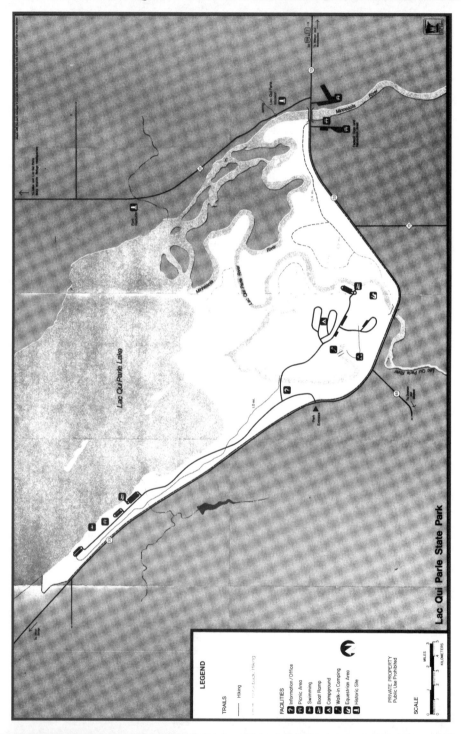

Lac Qui Parle State Park

LEGEND

TRAILS

········· Hiking

FACILITIES

🛈 Information / Office
⛱ Picnic Area
🏊 Swimming
🚤 Boat Ramp
△ Campground
🚶 Walk-in Camping
🐎 Equestrian Area
🏛 Historic Site

PRIVATE PROPERTY
Public Use Prohibited

SCALE

LAC QUI PARLE STATE PARK

Franklin's Gull   Photo by Dudley Edmondson

NEARBY PLACES TO VISIT

Granite Falls Area Chamber - Granite Falls, 320-564-4039
Historic Chippewa City - Montevideo, 320-269-7636
Lac Qui Parle Mission/Fort Renville - Montevideo, 320-269-7636
Lac Qui Parle County Historic Center - Madison, 320-598-7678
Milan Arv Hus Museum - Milan, 320-734-4868, 320-734-4829
Montevideo Area Chamber - Montevideo, 800-269-5527, 320-269-5527
Olof Swensson Farm - Montevideo, 320-269-7636

OUR NOTES

Date visited   What we liked

Lac Qui Parle Sioux Mission was established in 1835. This is about the time the first dictionary of the Sioux language was completed and that cloth was first made.

Lake Shetek State Park
RR 1 Box 164
Currie, MN 56123
507-763-3256

DIRECTIONS

The park is located 14 miles northeast of Slayton or 13 miles south of Tracy on County Road 38.

ABOUT THE PARK

Lake Shetek State Park was established in 1929 and covers 1,109 acres.

Lake Shetek, the headwaters of the Des Moines River, is the largest lake in the southwestern part of Minnesota. The area's first settlement occurred in the 1850s, but never grew very large. During the Dakota Uprising of 1862, 15 local settlers were killed and the rest abandoned their homes. Since farming the prairie was difficult and unsuccessful, settlers did not permanently return to the area until the early 1900s. The state park was created as a memorial to the people who were killed in the uprising, and to serve as an important recreational service to the community. The Civilian Conservation Corps (CCC) worked on many park projects during the depression, including the bath house, beach, and causeway to Loon Island.

In the park, visitors can view the relocated "Koch" cabin, home of the Koch family during the Dakota Uprising. There are also four pioneer cabin sites along the interpretive trail. The Shetek monument is made from granite and marks the burial site of the settlers killed during the uprising.

IF YOU GO . . .

Come for a hike! After a picnic overlooking Lake Shetek, take the trail heading north to the boat ramp. From there, a self-guided interpretive trail heads out and circles Loon Island. There is another trail from the boat landing back to the picnic area and the swimming beach, which has a changing house for those wishing to cool off.

LAKE SHETEK STATE PARK

FACILITIES

Visitor Center:	seasonal
Picnic Area:	picnic area with 2 shelters

RECREATION

Children's play area:	yes
Volleyball courts:	yes
Horseshoe pits:	yes
Swimming:	swimming beach on Lake Shetek
Fishing:	fishing in Lake Shetek
Boating:	drive-in boat access to Lake Shetek
	boat rental

CAMPGROUND

Campsites:	2 campgrounds:
	Wolf Point has 78 drive-in campsites
	Prairie Campground has 20 primitive campsites
Electric:	67 electric campsites in Wolf Point
Hike or carry-in:	10 primitive hike-in campsites
Canoe campsites:	no
Dump station:	yes
Toilets:	flush toilets
Showers:	yes
Group Campground:	2 primitive campgrounds
Modern Group Center:	Zuya Group Center
	3 barracks that sleep 22 people each
	recreation hall sleeps 14
	also a dining hall, kitchen, and bathrooms
	minimum of 50 people
	available from Memorial Day to Labor Day
Camper Cabin:	accommodates 6 people, with electricity

TRAILS

Hiking Trails:	8 miles
Hiking Club Trail:	1 mile, starting at the boat ramp parking area
Biking Trails:	3 miles
Cross-country Ski:	3 miles
Warming house:	yes
Snowmobile Trails:	5 miles
Horse Trails:	no
Horse Campsites:	no

INTERPRETIVE PROGRAMS

The park offers a self-guided interpretive trail around Loon Lake in addition to programs during the summer months. The Interpretive Center is open throughout the summer with displays, maps, and artifacts. Check bulletin boards for schedules.

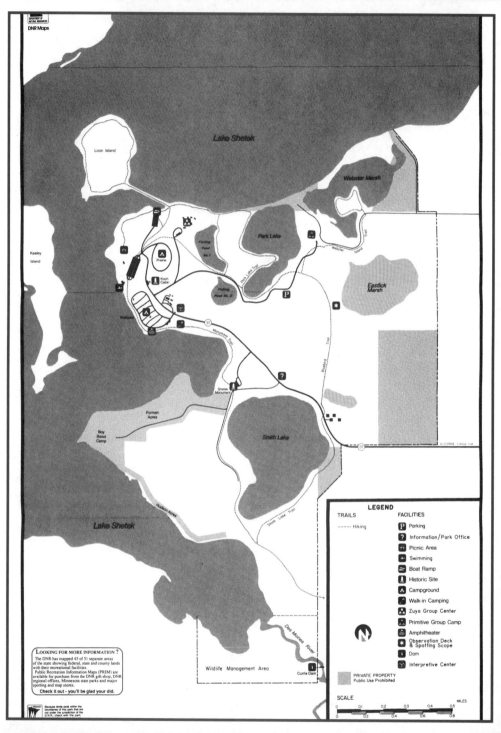

DNR Maps

Lake Shetek

Loon Island

Webster Marsh

Park Lake

Keeley Island

Fishing Pond No. 1

Prairie

Koch Cabin

Fishing Pond No. 2

Eastlick Marsh

Park Lake Trail

Webster Woods Trail

Wolford

37

Monument Trail

Bluebird Trail

Shetek Monument

Forman Acres

Boy Scout Camp

Smith Lake

To CURRIE 2 miles →

37

Halvorl Acres

Lake Shetek

Smith Lake Trail

Des Moines River

LEGEND

TRAILS

.... Hiking

FACILITIES

- 🅿 Parking
- ? Information / Park Office
- 🏕 Picnic Area
- 🏊 Swimming
- ⛵ Boat Ramp
- 🏛 Historic Site
- △ Campground
- 🚶 Walk-in Camping
- Zuya Group Center
- Primitive Group Camp
- Amphitheater
- ★ Observation Deck & Spotting Scope
- Dam
- Interpretive Center

PRIVATE PROPERTY
Public Use Prohibited

Wildlife Management Area

Currie Dam

LOOKING FOR MORE INFORMATION ?
The DNR has mapped 45 of 51 separate areas of the state showing federal, state and county lands with their recreational facilities.
Public Recreation Information Maps (PRIM) are available for purchase from the DNR gift shop, DNR regional offices, Minnesota state parks and major sporting and map stores.

Check it out - you'll be glad your did.

Because lands exist within the boundaries of this park that are not under the jurisdiction of the D.N.R. check with the park

SCALE

0   0.1   0.2   0.3   0.4   MILES
0   0.2   0.4   0.6   0.8

Lake Shetek State Park   Photo by author

NEARBY PLACES TO VISIT

End-O-Line Railroad Park and Museum - Currie, 507-763-3708
Lake Shetek State Park - Currie, 507-763-3256
Marshall Convention and Visitor's Bureau - Marshall, 507-537-1865
McCone 1880 Sod House Exhibit/Sod House on the Prairie - Sanborn, 507-723-5138
Murray County Historical Museum - Slayton, 507-836-6533
Westbrook Heritage House Museum - Westbrook, 507-274-5222

OUR NOTES

Date visited   What we liked

T R I V I A

Minnesota has....
2010 species of shrubs, trees and plants,
403 species of breeding and migratory birds,
144 species of fish,
81 species of mammals, and
29 species of reptiles.

Minneopa State Park
RR 9 Box 143
Mankato, MN 56001
507-625-4388

DIRECTIONS

The park is located 5 miles west of Mankato on either Highway 169 or Highway 68.

ABOUT THE PARK

Minneopa State Park, established in 1905, contains 1,145 acres of land along the south side of the Minnesota River and the Minneopa Creek gorge. The largest waterfall in southern Minnesota is located in the park, just a short hike from the parking area.

Prior to the 1850s, when the first white settlers came, this area was home to a semi permanent Dakota settlement. Miner Porter built a summer resort near the falls in 1858, but the Civil War and the Dakota Uprising of 1862 interfered with the business, and it was later abandoned. Park visitors can still see the remains of the Seppmann windmill, which was built in 1864 and operated as a grist mill until it was struck by lightning. During the 1870s a small village was established near the Minneopa Creek, but natural disasters plagued the village and it soon disappeared. Visitors can also see examples of Works Progress Administration (WPA) labor near the picnic area. A campground along the Minnesota River was developed in 1960.

IF YOU GO . . .

Check out the falls! The falls along Minneopa Creek are a must — be sure to bring your picnic basket and camera. The picnic area is surrounded by hardwood trees, just a short distance from the double waterfalls. The park also offers a short trail system that wanders around the creek and the falls.

MINNEOPA STATE PARK

FACILITIES

Visitor Center: seasonal
Picnic Area: 3 picnic areas

RECREATION

Children's play area: no
Horseshoe pits: yes
Volleyball courts: yes
Swimming: no
Fishing: fishing in both the Minneopa Creek and the
                           Minnesota River
Boating: carry-in boat access to the Minnesota River

CAMPGROUND

Campsites: 62 drive-in campsites
Electric: 6 electric campsites
Hike or carry-in: no
Canoe campsites: no
Dump station: no
Toilets: flush toilets
Showers: yes
Group Campground: primitive group campground

TRAILS

Hiking Trails: 4.5 miles
Hiking Club Trail: 3.5 miles, starting at the trail head parking lot
                           near the campground
Biking Trails: no
Cross-country Ski: 4 miles
Snowmobile Trails: no
Horse Trails: no
Horse Campsites: no

INTERPRETIVE PROGRAMS

There are no interpretive programs available in the park.

MINNEOPA STATE PARK

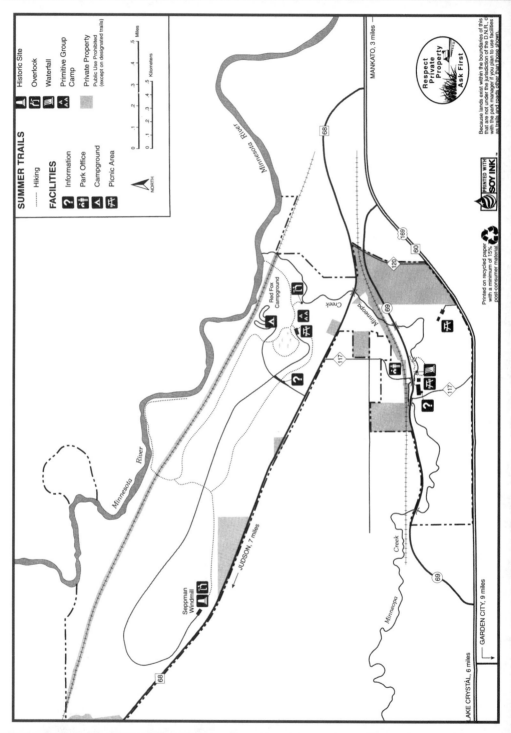

SUMMER TRAILS

...... Hiking

FACILITIES

? Information

Park Office

Campground

Picnic Area

Historic Site

Overlook

Waterfall

Primitive Group Camp

Private Property
Public Use Prohibited
(except on designated trails)

NORTH

Miles

Kilometers

Minnesota River

Minneopa Creek

Red Fox Campground

Seppman Windmill

MANKATO, 3 miles

169

60

120

69

68

117

117

69

JUDSON, 7 miles

LAKE CRYSTAL, 6 miles

GARDEN CITY, 9 miles

Minneopa Creek

Because lands exist within the boundaries of this that are not under the jurisdiction of the D.N.R., check with the park manager if you plan to use facilities as trails and roads other than those shown.

Respect Private Property
Ask First

Printed on recycled paper with a minimum of 15% post-consumer material.

PRINTED WITH SOY INK

Minneopa State Park
Photo by author

NEARBY PLACES TO VISIT

African Sports and Museum - Mankato, 507-386-1548
Alexander Faribault House - Faribault, 507-334-7913, 507-332-2121
Blue Earth County Historical Society - Mankato, 507-345-5566
Mankato Area Convention and Visitor's Bureau - Mankato, 800-657-4733, 507-345-4519
MN Valley Regional Library-Maud Hart Lovelace Collection - Mankato, 507-387-1856
R. D. Hubbard House - Mankato, 507-345-5566
Red Jacket Trail - Mankato, 507-387-8627
Rice County Historical Society Museum - Faribault, 507-332-2121
Sakatah Singing Hills State Trail - Mankato, 612-296-6699
Watonwan County Historical Museum - Madelia, 507-642-3247

OUR NOTES

Date visited   What we liked

T R I V I A

The Seppmann windmill could grind up to 150 bushels of wheat in a day.

MONSON LAKE STATE PARK

Monson Lake State Park
RR 1 Box 53
Sunberg, MN 56289
320-366-3797

DIRECTIONS

The park is located 20 miles northwest of Willmar on Highway 104.

ABOUT THE PARK

Monson Lake State Park was created in 1923 as a memorial to a local pioneer family, the Brobergs, that were killed in the Dakota Uprising of 1862. All members of the family were killed, except for a 16 year old daughter. Visitors can read her eye-witness account and see the sites of the pioneer cabins in the park.

The park is very small, containing only 187 acres. The hikes are short, but the park offers visitors solitude, bird watching, camping, and fishing.

IF YOU GO . . .

Bring a boat, fishing pole, and a good book! This park is small, but Monson Lake offers excellent fishing for walleye, northern pike, and bass. Keep your eyes peeled for pelicans, herons, shorebirds, and waterfowl.

MONSON LAKE STATE PARK

FACILITIES

Visitor Center: no
Picnic Area: yes

RECREATION

Children's play area: no
Volleyball courts: no
Horseshoe pits: no
Swimming: no
Fishing: fishing on Monson Lake
Boating: drive-in boat access to Monson Lake

CAMPGROUND

Campsites: 20 drive-in campsites
Electric: no
Hike or carry-in: no
Canoe campsites: no
Dump station: no
Toilets: pit toilets
Showers: no
Group Campground: no

TRAILS

Hiking Trails: 1 mile
Hiking Club Trail: 1 mile, starting at the picnic area
Biking Trails: no
Cross-country Ski: no
Snowmobile Trails: no
Horse Trails: no
Horse Campsites: no

INTERPRETIVE PROGRAMS

There are no interpretive programs available in the park.

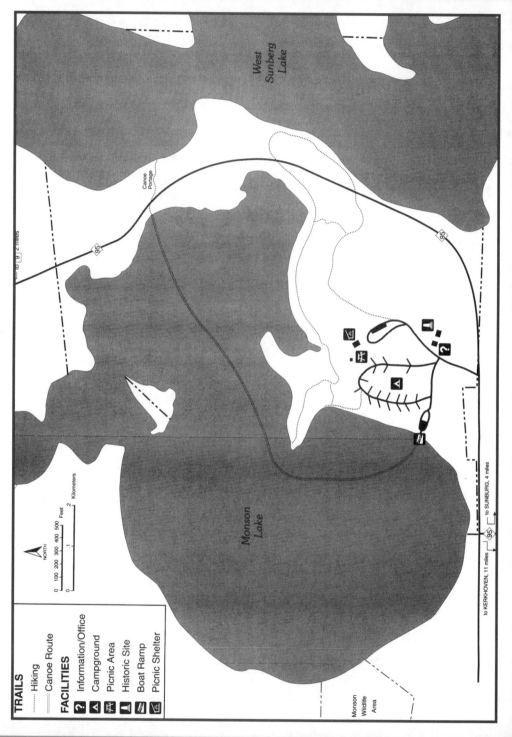

TRAILS
- ------- Hiking
- ≈≈≈ Canoe Route

FACILITIES
- **?** Information/Office
- **▲** Campground
- **⛱** Picnic Area
- **▮** Historic Site
- **//** Boat Ramp
- **⛺** Picnic Shelter

West Sunberg Lake

Canoe Portage

95

95

Monson Lake

Monson Wildlife Area

to KERKHOVEN, 11 miles

to SUNBURG, 4 miles

95

to Hwy 9, 2 miles

NORTH

0 100 200 300 400 500 Feet

0 .1 .2 Kilometers

Common Loon   Photo by Dudley Edmondson

NEARBY PLACES TO VISIT

Glacial Lakes State Trail - Willmar, 612-296-6157
Glacial Ridge Trail Association - Glenwood, 800-782-9937
Kandiyohi County Historical Museum - Willmar, 320-235-1881
Memorial Room in City Auditorium - Willmar, 320-235-1854
Mikkelson Collection, Inc. - Willmar, 320-231-0384
Monongalia Historical Society & Museum - New London, 320-354-2990
Pope County Historical Museum - Glenwood, 320-634-3293
Sibley State Park - New London, 320-354-2055
Sperry House - Willmar, 320-235-1881
Swift County Historical Museum - Benson, 320-843-4467
Willmar Chamber - Willmar, 320-235-0300

OUR NOTES

Date visited   What we liked

Minnesota has the largest number of Loons in the lower 48 states.

SIBLEY STATE PARK

Sibley State Park
800 Sibley State Park Road NE
New London, MN 56273
320-354-2055

DIRECTIONS
The park is located 15 miles north of Willmar on Highway 71.

ABOUT THE PARK
Sibley State Park was established in 1919 through the efforts of Peter Broberg, the only member of his family to survive the Dakota Uprising of 1862. The 2,926 acres that comprise the park are named for the first governor of Minnesota, Henry Hastings Sibley.

Mount Tom, elevation of 1375 feet, is located within the park. Fragments of pipes have been found there, causing speculation that it had some spiritual significance to the Dakota Indians.

Before the Depression, lack of funds caused the park to fall into disrepair. In 1935 the Veterans Conservation Corps came to the park and made numerous repairs, leaving behind a wonderful legacy of buildings and park developments.

IF YOU GO . . .
Bring your hiking shoes! Take the trail north out of the campground, and stop at Little Mount Tom for a scenic view before heading north. The trail will head to the east for another scenic view before heading towards Mount Tom, the highest spot for miles. The view from Mount Tom is of the surrounding prairie and farm lands. The trail heads north before curving south and back to Lake Andrew. After the hike, a swim in Lake Andrew might be in order.

SIBLEY STATE PARK

FACILITIES

Visitor Center: Interpretive/Visitor center
Picnic Area: picnic area with an open shelter

RECREATION

Children's play area: yes
Volleyball court: yes
Horseshoe pits: yes
Swimming: swimming beach on Lake Andrew
Fishing: lake fishing, fishing pier on Lake Andrew
Boating: drive-in boat access to Lake Andrew
                       boat and canoe rental

CAMPGROUND

Campsites: 138 drive-in campsites
Electric: 52 electric campsites
Hike or carry-in: no
Canoe campsites: no
Dump station: yes
Toilets: flush toilets
Showers: yes
Group Campground: primitive group campsite
Modern Group Center: 6 barracks that sleep 18 people each
                       staff quarters for 12
                       modern sanitation building, kitchen and dining
                       hall, crafts building, and athletic field
                       available from Memorial Day to Labor Day
                       minimum of 50 people

TRAILS

Hiking Trails: 18 miles
Hiking Club Trail: 3.3 miles, starting at the Interpretive Center
Biking Trails: 5 paved miles
                       bike rentals
Cross-country Ski: 10 miles
                       2 miles of skate ski
Warming house: yes
Sliding hill: yes
Snowmobile Trails: 6 miles
Horse Trails: 9 miles
Horse Campsites: horse riders group camp

INTERPRETIVE PROGRAMS

Sibley State Park supports a year round interpretive program and Interpretive
Center. Check the bulletin boards for schedules.

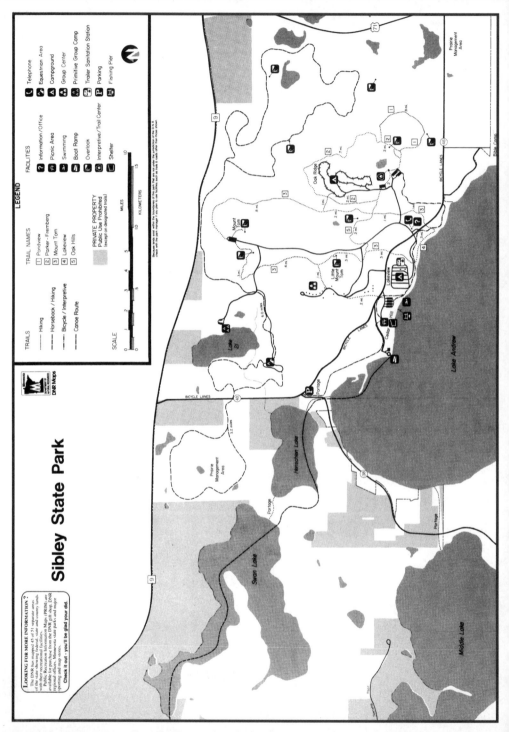

Sibley State Park

LOOKING FOR MORE INFORMATION ?

The DNR has mapped 45 of 51 separate areas of the state, showing federal, state and county lands with their recreational facilities.

Public Recreation Information Maps (PRIM) are available for purchase from the DNR gift shop, DNR regional offices, Minnesota state parks and major sporting and map stores.

Check it out - you'll be glad your did.

LEGEND

TRAILS

········· Hiking

- - - Horseback / Hiking

—·—·— Bicycle / Interpretive

——— Canoe Route

TRAIL NAMES

1 Parkview
2 Parker - Fremberg
3 Mount Tom
4 Lakeview
5 Oak Hills

PRIVATE PROPERTY
Public Use Prohibited
(except on designated trails)

FACILITIES

? Information/Office
🛈 Picnic Area
🏊 Swimming
🚤 Boat Ramp
🔭 Overlook
ⓘ Interpretive/Trail Center
🏠 Shelter

📞 Telephone
🐎 Equestrian Area
🏕 Campground
🏢 Group Center
🏕 Primitive Group Camp
🚽 Trailer Sanitation Station
🅿 Parking
🎣 Fishing Pier

SCALE

MILES
0 1 2 3 4 5

KILOMETERS
0 .5 1.0 1.5

Gray Squirrel   Photo by Dudley Edmondson

NEARBY PLACES TO VISIT

Blue Mound State Park - Luverne, 507-283-4892
Fort Pipestone - Pipestone, 507-825-4474
Hinkly House Museum - Luverne, 507-283-8294, 507-283-4061
Luverne Convention/Visitor's Bureau - Luverne, 507-283-4061
Pipestone Chamber - Pipestone, 507-825-3316, 800-336-6125
Pipestone County Historical Museum - Pipestone, 507-825-2563
Pipestone Falls - Pipestone, 507-825-5463
Pipestone National Monument - Pipestone, 507-825-5464
Rock County History Museum at Masonic Temple Site
        Luverne, 507-283-8294, 507-283-4061

OUR NOTES

Date visited   What we liked

_____

_____

_____

_____

T R I V I A

Before statehood Minnesota flew 12 different flags:
France, England, Spain, Colony of Virginia, Northwest Territories, and the Territories of
Louisiana, Indiana, Illinois, Michigan, Missouri, Iowa, and Wisconsin.

Split Rock Creek State Park
RR 2 Box 102
Jasper, MN 56144
507-348-7908

DIRECTIONS

The park is located 6 miles south of Pipestone on Highway 23.

ABOUT THE PARK

Split Rock Creek was dammed in 1938, creating Split Rock Lake and the park. This 400 acre park provides numerous recreational activities for the residents of southwestern Minnesota.

The park is located just south of the Pipestone National Monument. Indians would come through this area on their way to gather pipestone, which was used in ceremonial pipes.

IF YOU GO . . .

Bring your binoculars! Split Rock Lake is the only sizable lake in the area, so it attracts many waterfowl and birds. There is a hiking trail along the lake with several spots for bird-watching. Check out Prairie Hill for an excellent view.

SPLIT ROCK CREEK STATE PARK

FACILITIES

Visitor Center: seasonal Interpretive Center
Picnic Area: picnic area on Split Rock Lake

RECREATION

Children's play area: available in the picnic area
Horseshoe pit: no
Volleyball court: yes
Swimming: swimming beach on Split Rock Lake
Fishing: fishing on Split Rock Lake
                           fishing pier on Split Rock Lake
Boating: drive-in boat access to Split Rock Lake

CAMPGROUND

Campsites: 26 drive-in campsites
Electric: 14 electric campsites
Hike or carry-in: 6 hike-in campsites
Canoe campsites: no
Dump station: yes
Toilets: flush toilets
Showers: yes
Group Campground: primitive group campground

TRAILS

Hiking Trails: 2 miles
Hiking Club Trail: 3.2 miles, starting at the picnic area
Biking Trails: no
Cross-country Ski: 2 miles
Snowmobile Trails: no
Horse Trails: no
Horse Campsites: no

INTERPRETIVE PROGRAMS

There is an interpretive program throughout the summer months. Visitors should check bulletin boards for schedules.

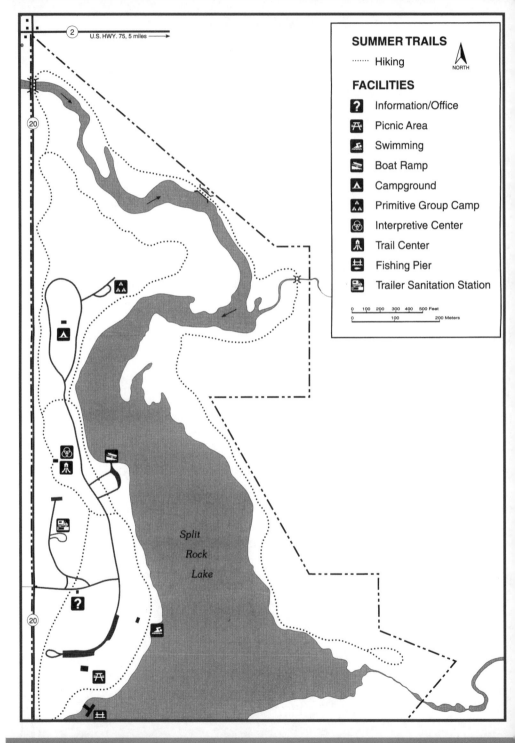

SUMMER TRAILS

...... Hiking

FACILITIES

? Information/Office

🛱 Picnic Area

🏊 Swimming

🛥 Boat Ramp

▲ Campground

⟑⟑ Primitive Group Camp

⊛ Interpretive Center

👤 Trail Center

🎏 Fishing Pier

▦ Trailer Sanitation Station

U.S. HWY. 75, 5 miles →

Split
Rock
Lake

American Goldfinch (male)   Photo by Dudley Edmondson

NEARBY PLACES TO VISIT

Blue Mound State Park - Luverne, 507-283-4892
Fort Pipestone - Pipestone, 507-825-4474
Hinkly House Museum - Luverne, 507-283-8294, 507-283-4061
Luverne Convention/Visitor's Bureau - Luverne, 507-283-4061
Pipestone Chamber - Pipestone, 507-825-3316, 800-336-6125
Pipestone County Historical Museum - Pipestone, 507-825-2563
Pipestone Falls - Pipestone, 507-825-5463
Pipestone National Monument - Pipestone, 507-825-5464
Rock County History Museum at Masonic Temple Site
    Luverne, 507-283-8294, 507-283-4061

OUR NOTES

Date visited   What we liked

Minnesota's state animal is the white-tailed deer.

Upper Sioux Agency State Park
RR 2 Box 92
Granite Falls, MN 56241
320-564-4777

DIRECTIONS

The park is located southeast of Granite Falls on Highway 67.

ABOUT THE PARK

Upper Sioux Agency State Park was established in 1963, and comprises 1,280 acres. The park commemorates the Upper Sioux, or Yellow Medicine Agency, which, along with the Lower Sioux, oversaw the Indian affairs when the Dakota were moved to their reservation after the 1851 treaty of Traverse Des Sioux. The Upper Sioux Agency was more successful and humane in their dealings with the Dakota. Because of this, many of the Upper Agency Dakota did not participate in the Dakota Uprising of 1862, but rather helped people to escape. The agency was burned during the Uprising.

As a part of the agency, many buildings were constructed in the area. After the agency disbanded following the uprising, settlers in the area dismantled many of the buildings for materials. When the park was created, there was only a partial employee residence and stables still standing. The Minnesota Historical Society gained control of the area in 1969, restored the residence, and exposed the foundations of several other buildings.

Visitors can hike trails along the Minnesota and the Yellow Medicine Rivers. There is an old steamboat landing along the Minnesota River, and the wooded hillsides along the rivers and the prairie on the bluffs provide a home for much wildlife.

IF YOU GO . . .

Plan to spend some time learning about the Dakota Uprising of 1862! Visit the site of the Upper Sioux Agency and the Interpretive Center. If time allows, hike the trail along the Minnesota River to the picnic area at the mouth of the Yellow Medicine River. There is also some good fishing here.

UPPER SIOUX AGENCY STATE PARK

FACILITIES

Visitor Center: Interpretive Center
Picnic Area: 2 picnic areas, 1 with a shelter

RECREATION

Children's play area: yes
Horseshoe pits: yes
Volleyball courts: yes
Swimming: no
Fishing: fishing in the Minnesota River and Yellow Medicine River
Boating: drive-in boat access to the Minnesota River

CAMPGROUND

Campsites: 45 drive-in campsites
Electric: no
Hike or carry-in: no
Canoe campsites: 1 canoe campsite
Dump station: no
Toilets: pit toilets
Showers: no
Group Campground: primitive group campsite

TRAILS

Hiking Trails: 19 miles
Hiking Club Trail: 4.5 miles, starting at the picnic area
Biking Trails: no
Cross-country Ski: no
Sliding Hill : yes
Warming house: yes
Snowmobile Trails: 16 miles
Horse Trails: 16 miles
Horse Campsites: group campsite

INTERPRETIVE PROGRAMS

There are no interpretive programs.

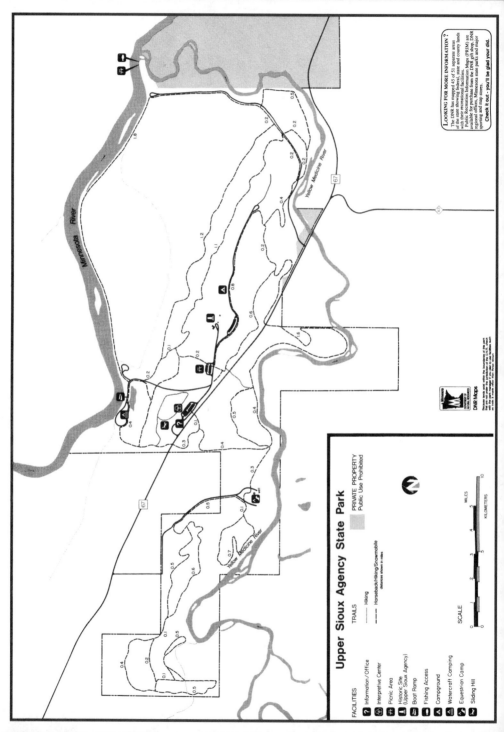

Upper Sioux Agency State Park

FACILITIES

🅘 Information / Office
🄸 Interpretive Center
🄳 Picnic Area
🄷 Historic Site (Upper Sioux Agency)
🄱 Boat Ramp
🄵 Fishing Access
🄲 Campground
🄰 Watercraft Camping
🄴 Equestrian Camp
🄹 Sliding Hill

TRAILS

········· Hiking
———— Horseback/Hiking/Snowmobile
distances shown in miles

PRIVATE PROPERTY
Public Use Prohibited

SCALE

MILES
0   1   2   3   4   5

KILOMETERS
0   5   10

DNR Maps

LOOKING FOR MORE INFORMATION?
The DNR has mapped 45 of 51 separate areas of the state showing federal, state and county lands with their recreational facilities.
Public Recreation Information Maps (PRIM) are available for purchase from the DNR gift shop, DNR regional offices, Minnesota state parks and major sporting and map stores.
Check it out - you'll be glad you did.

Upper Sioux Agency State Park   Photo by author

NEARBY PLACES TO VISIT

Granite Falls Area Chamber - Granite Falls, 320-564-4039
Historic Chippewa City - Montevideo, 320-269-7636
Lac Qui Parle Mission/Fort Renville - Montevideo, 320-269-7636
Minnesota's Machinery Museum - Hanley Falls, 507-768-3522, 507-768-3580
Montevideo Area Chamber - Montevideo, 800-269-5527, 320-269-5527
Olof Swensson Farm - Montevideo, 320-269-7636
Renville Museum - Renville, 320-329-3545, 320-329-3297
Yellow Medicine Cty Historical Museum - Granite Falls, 320-564-4479

OUR NOTES

Date visited   What we liked

_____

_____

_____

_____

_____

TRIVIA

There are at least 1,600 buildings in Minnesota's state parks, of which 564 are on the National Register of Historic Places.

PARK	ACREAGE
Beaver Creek Valley State Park	1,214 acres
Carley State Park	204 acres
Forestville/Mystery Cave State Park	2,691 acres
Frontenac State Park	2,186 acres
Great River Bluffs State Park	2,835 acres
John A. Latsch State Park	1,534 acres
Lake Louise State Park	781 acres
Myre-Big Island State Park	1,648 acres
Nerstrand Big Woods State Park	1,131 acres
Rice Lake State Park	1,056 acres
Sakatah Lake State Park	842 acres
Whitewater State Park	1,656 acres

SOUTHEASTERN REGION

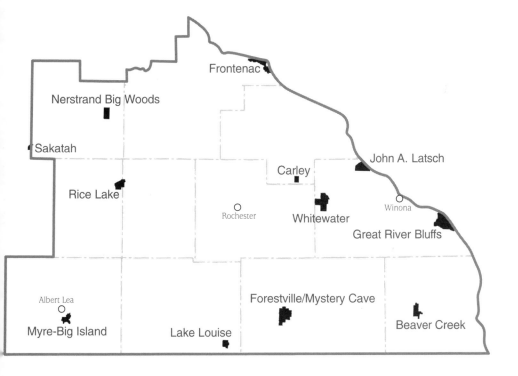

Frontenac

Nerstrand Big Woods

Sakatah

John A. Latsch

Carley

Rice Lake

○ Rochester

Winona ○

Whitewater

Great River Bluffs

Albert Lea ○

Forestville/Mystery Cave

Myre-Big Island

Lake Louise

Beaver Creek

Beaver Creek Valley State Park
RR 2 Box 57
Caledonia, MN 55921
507-724-2107

DIRECTIONS

The park is located 5 miles west of Caledonia on County Highway 76.

ABOUT THE PARK

Beaver Creek Valley State Park is located in the extreme southeastern section of the state. The park was established in 1937 and contains 1,214 acres. Beaver Creek flows through the park, with the valley walls rising above the stream up to 250 feet. From these porous valley walls run numerous fresh water springs.

Stone tools and a village site have been found in the park, so it is speculated that this area was once home to Native Americans. Homesteaders also settled in this area, and the remains of an old home site can still be seen. Schech's Mill, which was built in 1876, is the northern portion of the park's main attraction, aside from its abundant wildflowers.

Visitors should be warned that timber rattlesnakes inhabit the park. Though these snakes are seldom seen, if you do see one you should not attempt to capture or kill it. Move slowly away and inform the park staff of the sighting.

IF YOU GO . . .

Plan to tour! A worthwhile adventure is a tour of Schech's Mill. Learn about the different types of milling, and what is unique about this particular mill. After the tour, cast a fishing line into Beaver Creek for a brown trout.

BEAVER CREEK VALLEY STATE PARK

FACILITIES

isitor Center:	no
icnic Area:	50 tables in the picnic area with an enclosed shelter

RECREATION

hildren's play area:	yes
olleyball courts:	no
orseshoe pits:	no
wimming:	children's wading pool
ishing:	stream fishing
oating:	no

CAMPGROUND

ampsites:	42 drive-in campsites
lectric:	16 electric campsites
ike or carry-in:	6 walk-in campsites
anoe campsites:	no
ump station:	yes
oilets:	yes
howers:	yes
roup Campground:	primitive group campsite

TRAILS

iking Trails:	7.5 miles
iking Club Trail:	6.2 miles, starting at the park office
iking Trails:	no
ross-country Ski:	4 miles
nowmobile Trails:	no
orse Trails:	no
orse Campsites:	no

INTERPRETIVE PROGRAMS

here are no interpretive programs available in the park.

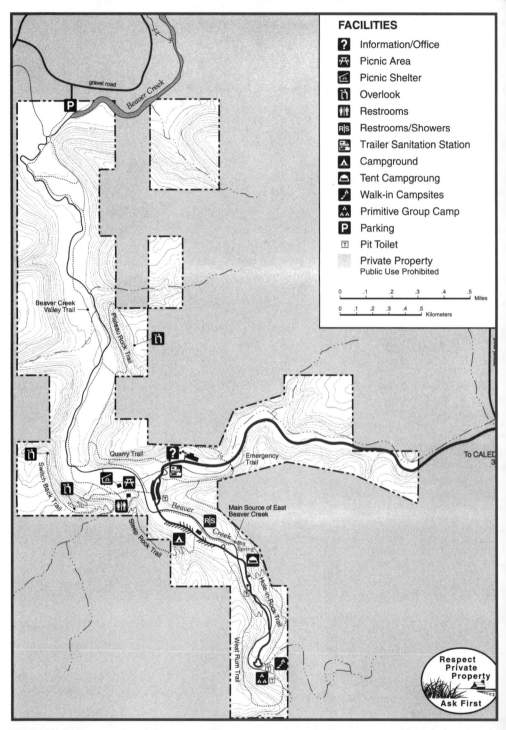

FACILITIES

?	Information/Office
	Picnic Area
	Picnic Shelter
	Overlook
	Restrooms
R|S	Restrooms/Showers
	Trailer Sanitation Station
A	Campground
	Tent Campground
	Walk-in Campsites
	Primitive Group Camp
P	Parking
	Pit Toilet
	Private Property Public Use Prohibited

Beaver Creek

gravel road

P

Beaver Creek
Valley Trail

Plateau Rock Trail

Quarry Trail

Switch Back Trail

Steep Rock Trail

Beaver

Creek

Big Spring

Emergency Trail

Main Source of East
Beaver Creek

To CALED
3

Hole-In-Rock Trail

West Rum Trail

Respect
Private
Property
Ask First

Northern Harrier   Photo by Dudley Edmondson

NEARBY PLACES TO VISIT

1877 Peterson Station Museum - Peterson, 507-895-2551
Bluff Country Drive Scenic Byway - Harmony, 800-428-2030, 507-886-2030
Caledonia Area Chamber of Commerce - Caledonia, 507-724-5477
Harmony Toy Museum - Harmony, 507-867-3380
Niagara Cave - Harmony, 507-886-6606, 800-837-6606
Root River State Trail - Lanesboro, 507-467-2552
Steam Engine Museum - Mabel, 507-493-5768, 319-735-5892

OUR NOTES

Date visited   What we liked

T R I V I A

*The 'driftless area' was a large area unaffected by
the glaciers that covered much of Minnesota.*

Carley State Park
RR 1 Box 256
Altura, MN 55910
507-537-3400

DIRECTIONS

The park is located 4 miles south of Plainview on County Road 4, and 10 miles northwest of Whitewater State Park.

ABOUT THE PARK

Carley State Park was established in 1949, and covers only 204 acres. It was named for State Senator James A. Carley, who donated the land in hopes of preserving a large stand of native white pine along the Whitewater River. Many of these trees were damaged during a severe hailstorm, and have been replaced by new plantings of white pine. These trees can be seen from the picnic area.

This area was once home to an agricultural band of Dakota Indians, who gave up their land in the Traverse de Sioux treaty of 1851. Following the signing of this treaty, white settlers came to the area.

IF YOU GO . . .

Bring your identification books. Hike along the trail following the Whitewater River. Watch for the wildflowers and listen for the bird songs. The remaining white pines can be seen from the observation platform.

CARLEY STATE PARK

FACILITIES

Visitor Center: no
Picnic Area: yes

RECREATION

Children's play area: in the picnic area
Volleyball courts: no
Horseshoe pits: no
Swimming: no
Fishing: stream fishing on the north branch of the Whitewater River
Boating: no

CAMPGROUND

Campsites: 20 drive-in campsites
Electric: no
Hike or carry-in: no
Canoe campsites: no
Dump station: no
Toilets: pit toilets
Showers: no
Group Campground: 3 primitive group camp campsites

TRAILS

Hiking Trails: 5 miles
Hiking Club Trail: 1.8 miles, starting the picnic area parking lot
Biking Trails: no
Cross-country Ski: 6 miles
Sliding hill: yes
Snowmobile Trails: no
Horse Trails: no
Horse Campsites: no

INTERPRETIVE PROGRAMS

There are no interpretive programs available at the park.

CARLEY STATE PARK

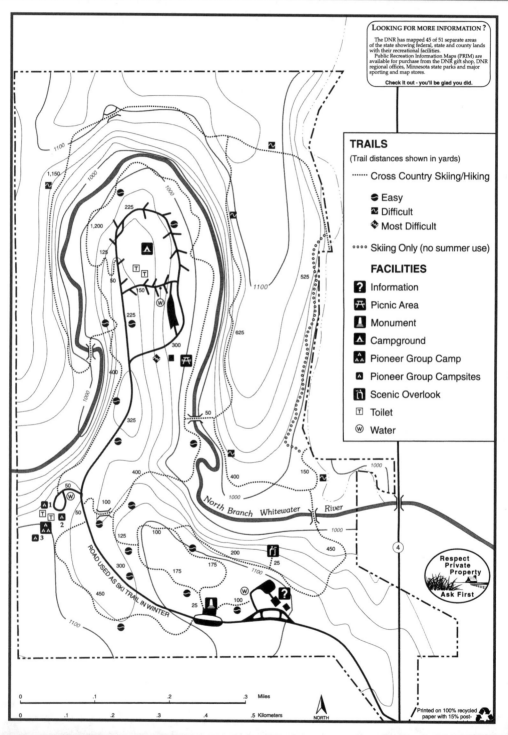

LOOKING FOR MORE INFORMATION ?

The DNR has mapped 45 of 51 separate areas of the state showing federal, state and county lands with their recreational facilities.

Public Recreation Information Maps (PRIM) are available for purchase from the DNR gift shop, DNR regional offices, Minnesota state parks and major sporting and map stores.

Check it out - you'll be glad you did.

TRAILS

(Trail distances shown in yards)

······ Cross Country Skiing/Hiking

● Easy

🔁 Difficult

◆ Most Difficult

°°°° Skiing Only (no summer use)

FACILITIES

? Information

🔀 Picnic Area

⬛ Monument

🔺 Campground

🔼🔼 Pioneer Group Camp

◼ Pioneer Group Campsites

🧍 Scenic Overlook

T Toilet

W Water

North Branch Whitewater River

ROAD USED AS SKI TRAIL IN WINTER

Respect Private Property Ask First

| 0 | .1 | .2 | .3 | Miles |

| 0 | .1 | .2 | .3 | .4 | .5 Kilometers |

NORTH

Printed on 100% recycled paper with 15% post-

CARLEY STATE PARK

Carley State Park — Photo by author

NEARBY PLACES TO VISIT

Douglas State Trail - Rochester, 507-285-7176
Heritage House of Rochester - Rochester, 507-286-9208, 507-282-2682
Olmsted County History Center - Rochester, 507-282-9447
Rochester Art Center - Rochester, 507-282-8629
Rochester Civic Music - Rochester, 507-285-8076, 507-281-6005
Rochester Civic Theatre - Rochester, 507-282-8481, 507-282-7633
Rochester Convention/Visitor's Bureau
    Rochester, 800-634-8277, 507-288-4331
Rochester Repertory Theatre - Rochester, 507-289-1737, 507-289-7800
Whitewater State Park - Altura, 507-932-3007

OUR NOTES

Date visited   What we liked

TRIVIA

Minnesota state parks cover almost 200,000 acres.

Forestville/Mystery Cave State Park
RR 2, Box 128
Preston, MN 55965
507-352-5111

DIRECTIONS

To find the park entrance, go 4 miles south of Highway 16 on County Road 16, and then 2 miles east on County Road 12.

ABOUT THE PARK

Forestville State Park was established in 1963 and encompasses 2,691 acres, including Mystery Cave.

The park was named for the town of Forestville, which had a population of 100 (and 20 buildings!) at its peak during the 1850s and 1860s. The town began to decline when the railroad bypassed it. The town store was the last business open, until one night it was locked intact and never reopened.

Since 1977 the Minnesota Historic Society has been restoring the town to its 1890s appearance, and offers costumed interpreters during the summer months. Besides the "old town," visitors can explore other historic sites, including the cemetery, school house, and grist mill.

Mystery Cave was purchased by the State of Minnesota in 1988, and added to Forestville State Park. In addition to being the longest cave in the state, it is the largest known limestone cave in existence, with over 12 miles of natural passageway. The entrance to the cave, which is open for tours in the summer, is located 6 miles from the park entrance.

IF YOU GO . . .

Plan to tour! In addition to touring Mystery Cave and exploring Forestville, the horseback riding is wonderful here. Ride up to Big Spring, the source of Canfield Creek, or over to the brickyard, which offers hitching posts.

FORESTVILLE/MYSTERY CAVE STATE PARK

FACILITIES

Visitor Center: no
Picnic Area: picnic area with enclosed shelter at Forestville
picnic area at Mystery Cave

RECREATION

Children's play area: no
Volleyball courts: no
Horseshoe pits: no
Swimming: no
Fishing: trout fishing in Canfield Creek, Forestville Creek, or the south branch of the Root River
Boating: no

CAMPGROUND

Campsites: 73 drive-in campsites
Electric: 23 electric campsites
Hike or carry-in: no
Canoe campsites: no
Dump station: yes
Toilets: flush toilets
Showers: yes
Group Campground: primitive group campsite

TRAILS

Hiking Trails: 16 miles
Hiking Club Trail: 3.4 miles, starting at the picnic shelter
Biking Trails: no
Cross-country Ski: 10 miles
winter warming shelter
Snowmobile Trails: 5.5 miles
Horse Trails: 16 miles
Horse Campsites: 80 unit campsite

INTERPRETIVE PROGRAMS

The park offers a summer Interpretive Center and council ring. Check with the park staff for a listing of activities.

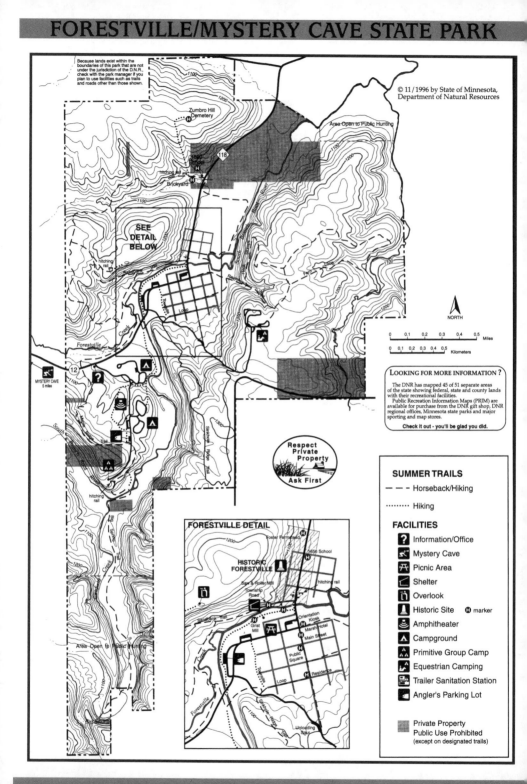

Because lands exist within the boundaries of this park that are not under the jurisdiction of the D.N.R., check with the park manager if you plan to use facilities such as trails and roads other than those shown.

© 11/1996 by State of Minnesota, Department of Natural Resources

Zumbro Hill Cemetery

Area Open to Public Hunting

118

hitching rail

Brickyard

SEE DETAIL BELOW

hitching rail

Forestville

MYSTERY CAVE 5 miles

12

NORTH

| 0 | 0.1 | 0.2 | 0.3 | 0.4 | 0.5 |
Miles

| 0 | 0.1 | 0.2 | 0.3 | 0.4 | 0.5 |
Kilometers

LOOKING FOR MORE INFORMATION?

The DNR has mapped 45 of 51 separate areas of the state showing federal, state and county lands with their recreational facilities.
Public Recreation Information Maps (PRIM) are available for purchase from the DNR gift shop, DNR regional offices, Minnesota state parks and major sporting and map stores.

Check it out - you'll be glad you did.

hitching rail

Respect Private Property
Ask First

SUMMER TRAILS

— — — Horseback/Hiking

·········· Hiking

FACILITIES

Information/Office

Mystery Cave

Picnic Area

Shelter

Overlook

Historic Site   Ⓗ marker

Amphitheater

Campground

Primitive Group Camp

Equestrian Camping

Trailer Sanitation Station

Angler's Parking Lot

Private Property
Public Use Prohibited
(except on designated trails)

FORESTVILLE DETAIL

Foster Farmstead

HISTORIC FORESTVILLE

1856 School

Saw & Roller Mill

hitching rail

Township Road

Orientation Kiosk

Grist Mill

Marsh Hotel

Main Street

Public Square

Residence

Loop

Area Open to Public Hunting

Unloading Spur

Eastern Kingbird
Photo by Dudley Edmondson

NEARBY PLACES TO VISIT

1877 Peterson Station Museum - Peterson, 507-895-2551
Historic Forestville - Preston, 507-765-2785
Lanesboro Historical Museum - Lanesboro, 507-467-2177, 507-467-2177
Lanesboro Office of Tourism - Lanesboro, 507-467-2696, 800-944-2670
Preston Area Tourism - Preston, 507-765-2100
Root River State Trail - Lanesboro, 507-467-2552
Spring Valley Methodist Church Museum
    Spring Valley, 507-346-7476, 507-346-7659
Washburn-Zittleman House Museum
    Spring Valley, 507-346-7659, 507-346-2763

OUR NOTES

Date visited   What we liked

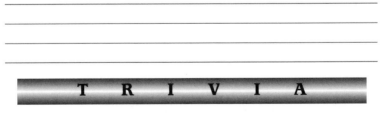

T R I V I A

Mystery Cave is the 36th largest cave in the country and the largest known limestone cave in the country. Mystery Cave is home to approximately 2,000 bats.

Frontenac State Park
RR 2 Box 134
Lake City, MN 55041
320-345-3401

DIRECTIONS

The park is located on Highway 61, 10 miles southeast of Red Wing.

ABOUT THE PARK

Frontenac State Park, located on Lake Pepin, consists of 2,186 acres situated along the river bluffs. The Mississippi River, which flows through the lake, is part of the migratory flyways, so the bird watching is excellent.

Archaeological excavations have discovered the habitations and burial sites of prehistoric people in the area, dating back to approximately 400 BC. Native Americans are known to have hunted and fished this area, parts of which were considered sacred. Father Louis Hennepin visited this area in 1680, and the French built a stockade known as Beaucharnois here in 1727. Two Jesuit missionaries established a fort there, which is thought to have been the first church in Minnesota. The fort was abandoned in 1736, when the British took control over all the French lands in North America. Despite continued efforts, the Minnesota Historical Society has not been able to find traces of either the fort or the mission.

During the late 1850s the town of Frontenac was founded. After the Civil War, as Mississippi River traffic increased, Frontenac blossomed into a fashionable summer resort town, with the three story Lake Side Hotel being especially popular among tourists. As railroad traffic increased, however, the river traffic decreased, leaving Frontenac to become a reminder of times past.

IF YOU GO . . .

Come for a hike! Head over to the picnic area located on shores of Lake Pepin. From there, follow the trails to the northwest, where there are several scenic overlooks. Since the Mississippi River is a flyway, you might be able to see some Bald Eagles.

FRONTENAC STATE PARK

FACILITIES

Visitor Center:	no
Picnic Area:	overlooking Lake Pepin with enclosed shelter

RECREATION

Children's play area:	no
Volleyball courts:	no
Horseshoe pits:	no
Swimming:	no
Fishing:	on Lake Pepin
Boating:	boating on Lake Pepin
	no boat access

CAMPGROUND

Campsites:	58 drive-in campsites
Electric:	19 electric campsites
Hike or carry-in:	6 campsites
Canoe campsites:	no
Dump station:	yes
Toilets:	flush toilets
Showers:	yes
Group Campground:	primitive campsite

TRAILS

Hiking Trails:	15 miles
Hiking Club Trail:	2.6 miles, starting at the picnic area kiosk
Biking Trails:	no
Cross-country Ski:	6 miles
Winter trail center:	yes
Snowmobile Trails:	8.4 miles
Horse Trails:	no
Horse Campsites:	no

INTERPRETIVE PROGRAMS

The park offers seasonal interpretive programs and exhibits. Check with the park staff for schedules.

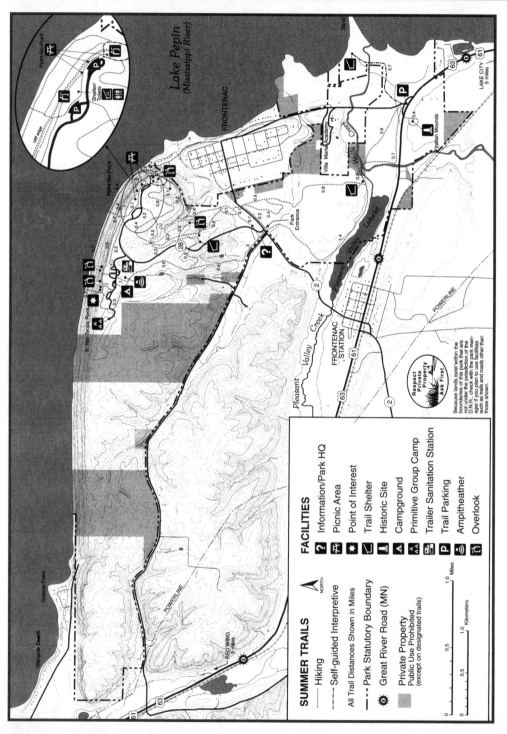

SUMMER TRAILS

⋯⋯ Hiking

--- Self-guided Interpretive

All Trail Distances Shown in Miles

--- Park Statutory Boundary

--- Great River Road (MN)

Private Property
Public Use Prohibited
(except on designated trails)

FACILITIES

- 🅿 Information/Park HQ
- 🌲 Picnic Area
- ✦ Point of Interest
- 📖 Trail Shelter
- 🏛 Historic Site
- 🔺 Campground
- 🔺🔺 Primitive Group Camp
- 🚽 Trailer Sanitation Station
- 🅿 Trail Parking
- 🔊 Ampitheather
- 🏠 Overlook

NORTH

Miles

Kilometers

Respect Private Property
Ask First

Because lands exist within the boundaries of this park that are not under the jurisdiction of the D.N.R., check with the park manager if you plan to use facilities such as trails and roads other than those shown.

Frontenac State Park   Photo by author

NEARBY PLACES TO VISIT

Arrowhead Bluffs Exhibits - Wabasha, 612-565-3829
Goodhue County Historical Society - Red Wing, 612-388-6024
Lake City Area Chamber - Lake City, 800-369-4123, 612-345-4128
Red Wing Visitor/Convention Bureau
    Red Wing, 612-385-5934, 800-498-3444
Wabasha County Museum - Lake City, 612-345-3987

OUR NOTES

Date visited   What we liked

TRIVIA

Minnesota is home to:
90,000 miles of shoreline, 25,000 miles of streams
15,391 lakes 10 acres or larger, 62 lakes greater than 5,000 acres

Great River Bluffs State Park
RR 4
Winona, MN 55987
507-643-6849

DIRECTIONS

The park is located 20 miles southeast of Winona. From Interstate 90, exit at County Road 12 and follow the signs.

ABOUT THE PARK

Great River Bluffs State Park was established in 1976 to protect the bluffland along the Mississippi River. The 2,835 acre park was originally named O.L. Kipp for Orrin Lansing Kipp, the highway commissioner that helped to establish Minnesota's trunk highway system. The park name was recently changed to Great River Bluffs.

This part of the state is known as the "driftless area" because no glaciers covered the land. There is evidence to suggest that prehistoric peoples inhabited the area for thousands of years. There are mounds along the bluffland, some of which were for burial, but the reasons for others has yet to be determined. Father Hennepin visited this area during his travels along the Mississippi River in 1680.

IF YOU GO . . .

Plan on hiking! The trails follow the ridges to many scenic overlooks of the Mississippi River and valleys. There is a 1 mile self-guided interpretive trail called the "King's Bluff Nature Trail," which ends at a scenic overlook. The fall colors are spectacular.

GREAT RIVER BLUFFS STATE PARK

FACILITIES

Visitor Center: no
Picnic Area: yes

RECREATION

Children's play area: available in the campground
Volleyball courts: no
Horseshoe pits: no
Swimming: no
Fishing: no
Boating: no

CAMPGROUND

Campsites: 38 drive-in campsites
Electric: no
Hike or carry-in: no
Canoe campsites: no
Dump station: no
Toilets: flush toilets
Showers: yes
Group Campground: primitive group campground

TRAILS

Hiking Trails: 7 miles
Hiking Club Trail: 2.5 miles, starting at small parking lot near the park entrance

Biking Trails: no
Cross-country Ski: 7 miles
Sliding hill: yes
Snowmobile Trails: no
Horse Trails: no
Horse Campsites: no

INTERPRETIVE PROGRAMS

There are no interpretive programs available in the park.

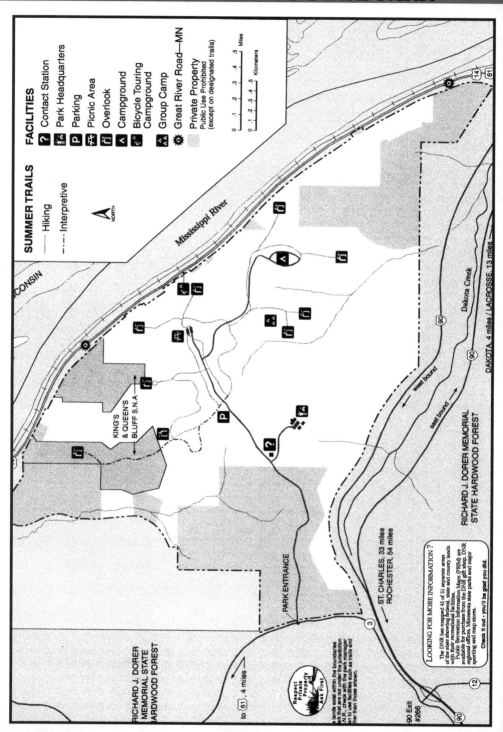

Great River Bluff State Park

Photo by author

NEARBY PLACES TO VISIT

Bluffside Park - Winona, 507-452-8550
Bunnell House Museum - Winona, 507-454-2723, 507-454-2723
Polish Cultural Institute - Winona, 507-454-3431
Winona Convention and Visitor's Bureau - Winona, 800-657-4972, 507-452-2272
Winona County Historical Museum - Winona, 507-454-2723

OUR NOTES

Date visited   What we liked

Great River Bluffs State Park has goat prairie which is where native prairie plants grow on steep slopes and survive extreme temperature changes.

John A. Latsch State Park
Highway 61
Winona, MN 55987
507-932-3007

DIRECTIONS

The park is located on Highway 61, approximately 12 miles northwest of Winona.

ABOUT THE PARK

John A. Latsch State Park consists of 1,534 acres along the bluffs of the Mississippi. There are three rocky bluffs at this point that shoot up 500 feet above the river. They came to be known as Mount Faith, Mount Hope, and Mount Charity. During the 1850s a steamboat landing and a small logging town were located in the area, but lock and dam #5 have erased all evidence of their existence. John A. Latsch, a prominent businessman, loved to fish beneath the "mountains." He purchased some of the land, and persuaded others to donate the rest to the state for the development of a state park.

IF YOU GO . . .

Bring your hiking shoes! Park at the picnic area and hike up the half mile trail along the ravine to the peaks of Faith, Hope, and Charity. The views are spectacular, and you can see for miles up and down the Mississippi River.

JOHN A. LATSCH STATE PARK

FACILITIES

Visitor Center: no
Picnic Area: picnic area

RECREATION

Children's play area: no
Volleyball courts: no
Horseshoe pits: no
Swimming: no
Fishing: no
Boating: no

CAMPGROUND

Campsites: there are no drive-in campsites available
Electric: no
Hike or carry-in: 10 walk-in campsites
Canoe campsites: no
Dump station: no
Toilets: pit toilets
Showers: no
Group Campground: no

TRAILS

Hiking Trails: 0.5 miles
Hiking Club Trail: no
Biking Trails: no
Cross-country Ski: no
Snowmobile Trails: no
Horse Trails: no
Horse Campsites: no

INTERPRETIVE PROGRAMS

There are no interpretive programs available in the park.

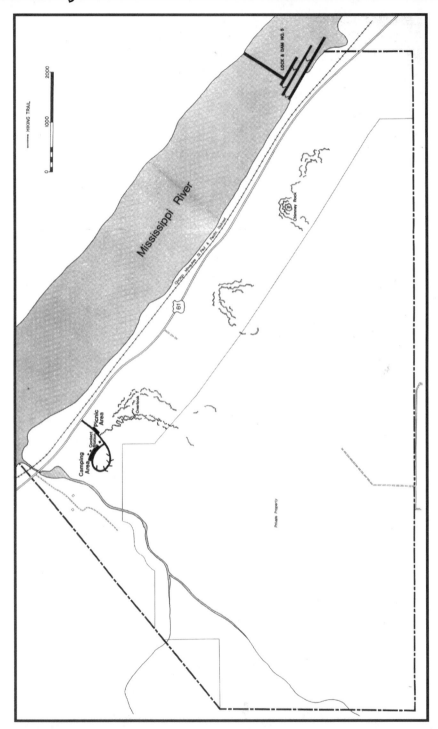

Rock Dove
Photo by Dudley Edmondson

NEARBY PLACES TO VISIT

Bluffside Park - Winona, 507-452-8550
Bunnell House Museum - Winona, 507-454-2723, 507-454-2723
Great River Bluffs State Park - Winona, 507-643-6849
Polish Cultural Institute - Winona, 507-454-3431
Whitewater State Park - Altura, 507-932-3007
Winona Convention and Visitor's Bureau - Winona, 800-657-4972, 507-452-2272
Winona County Historical Museum - Winona, 507-454-2723

OUR NOTES

Date visited   What we liked

_____
_____
_____
_____
_____

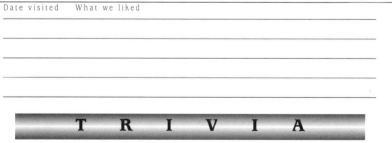

Our country's largest population of Blanding's Turtles is located near Wabasha.

Lake Louise State Park
RR 1, Box 184
Leroy, MN 55951
507-324-5249

DIRECTIONS
The park is located 1.5 miles north of LeRoy on County Road 14.

ABOUT THE PARK
Lake Louise State Park was created in 1963 and covers 781 acres. The park is located near the town of LeRoy, situated amid the rich farmland of southern Minnesota. It was founded in the 1850s near two spring fed streams, the Little Iowa and the Upper Iowa, which form the Upper Iowa River. In the 1850s the river was dammed at the confluence to provide power for a grist mill. A small village developed at the site, which grew into the town of LeRoy. After the town was moved a short distance to be located on the railroad, the grist mill closed, and the family that owned the mill and the mill pond donated the land to become a park. In 1962 the town of LeRoy donated the town park to the state, forming the nucleus of the state park, which has a long history of providing recreational opportunities to the local residents.

IF YOU GO . . .
Bring your horse or your hiking boots! There are miles of trails going through hardwood forests and old farm fields along both the Little Iowa River and the Upper Iowa River. After a day of exploring, the swimming beach on Lake Louise is a pleasant way to end the day.

LAKE LOUISE STATE PARK

FACILITIES

Visitor Center: no
Picnic Area: picnic area with a shelter

RECREATION

Children's play area: available in the campground
Volleyball courts: no
Horseshoe pits: no
Swimming: swimming beach on Lake Louise
Fishing: fishing on Lake Louise and on the Upper
                           Iowa River
Boating: carry-in boat access to Lake Louise

CAMPGROUND

Campsites: 22 drive-in campsites
Electric: 11 electric campsites
Hike or carry-in: no
Canoe campsites: no
Dump station: yes
Toilets: flush toilets
Showers: yes
Group Campground: primitive group campsite

TRAILS

Hiking Trails: 11 miles
                           1 mile self-guided interpretive trail
Hiking Club Trail: 3.5 miles, starting at the picnic area
Biking Trails: no
Cross-country Ski: 2 miles
Snowmobile Trails: 9 miles
Horse Trails: 10 miles
Horse Campsites: 6 horse campsites

INTERPRETIVE PROGRAMS

There are no programs available in the park.

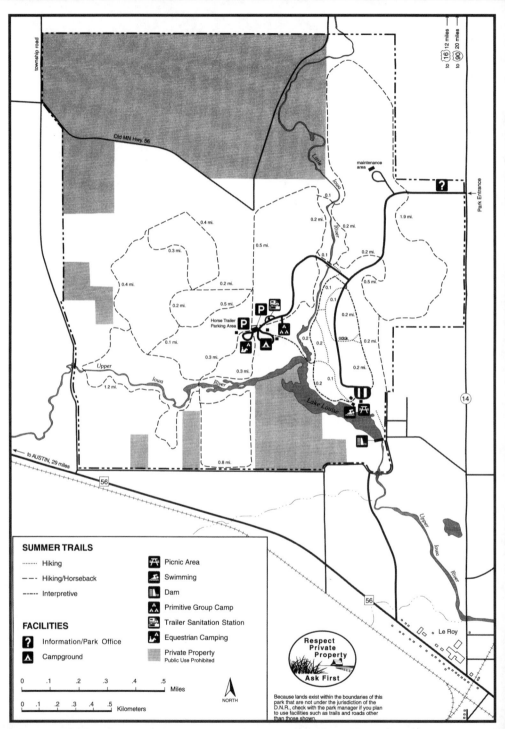

SUMMER TRAILS

.... Hiking

– – – Hiking/Horseback

–·–·– Interpretive

FACILITIES

? Information/Park Office

▲ Campground

🔺 Picnic Area

🏊 Swimming

🏭 Dam

⛺ Primitive Group Camp

🚐 Trailer Sanitation Station

🏇 Equestrian Camping

Private Property
Public Use Prohibited

0 .1 .2 .3 .4 .5
Miles

0 .1 .2 .3 .4 .5
Kilometers

NORTH

Respect
Private
Property
Ask First

Because lands exist within the boundaries of this
park that are not under the jurisdiction of the
D.N.R., check with the park manager if you plan
to use facilities such as trails and roads other
than those shown.

Sharp-shinned Hawk   Photo by Dudley Edmondson

NEARBY PLACES TO VISIT

Bluff Country Drive Scenic Byway - Harmony, 800-428-2030, 507-886-2030
Forestville/Mystery Cave State Park - Preston, 507-352-5111
Harmony Toy Museum - Harmony, 507-867-3380
Historic Forestville - Preston, 507-765-2785
Lanesboro Historical Museum - Lanesboro, 507-467-2177, 507-467-2177
Lanesboro Office of Tourism - Lanesboro, 507-467-2696, 800-944-2670
Niagara Cave - Harmony, 507-886-6606, 800-837-6606
Preston Area Tourism - Preston, 507-765-2100
Root River State Trail - Lanesboro, 507-467-2552
Shooting Star Scenic Byway - Adams
Spring Valley Methodist Church Museum - Spring Valley, 507-346-7476, 507-346-7659
Steam Engine Museum - Mabel, 507-493-5768, 319-735-5892
Washburn-Zittleman House Museum - Spring Valley, 507-346-7659, 507-346-2763

OUR NOTES

Date visited   What we liked

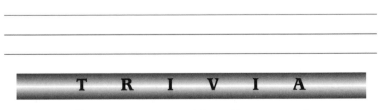

TRIVIA

Albert Lea was named for a lieutenant who published maps of southeastern Minnesota in 1835.

Myre-Big Island State Park
RR 3 Box 33
Albert Lea, MN 56007
320-373-5084

DIRECTIONS

The park is located 3 miles southeast of Albert Lea on County Road 38.

ABOUT THE PARK

Myre-Big Island State Park was established in 1947 through the efforts of a local resident named Owen Johnson. The park originally consisted of 116 acres and was primarily used for hiking and picnicking by local residents. After the development of interstates 90 and 35, the park gained visibility, and usage increased. Since then the park has grown to contain 1,648 acres and include a campground. The park was named for Helmer Myrethe, the state senator at the time of the park's creation.

Archeologists have found examples of human occupation in this area dating back as far as 9,000 years. The Interpretive Center houses one of the largest prehistoric artifact collections in the state.

Albert Lea Lake attracts many migrating waterfowl. Come in the fall to see the White Pelicans.

IF YOU GO . . .

Plan on spending some time exploring Big Island! From either the Big Island Campground or the picnic area, the Big Island trail circles the island. A short detour will take the hiker to the Owen Johnson Interpretive Center. The island is forested with hardwoods, making it quite beautiful in the fall.

MYRE-BIG ISLAND STATE PARK

FACILITIES

Visitor Center:	Owen Johnson Interpretive Center
Picnic Area:	picnic area on Big Island

RECREATION

Children's play area:	no
Volleyball courts:	no
Horseshoe pits:	no
Swimming:	no
Fishing:	on Albert Lea Lake
Boating:	boat access to Albert Lea Lake
	canoe rentals

CAMPGROUND

Campsites:	2 campgrounds
	total of 100 drive-in campsites
Electric:	32 campsites
Bike or carry-in:	4 backpack campsites
Canoe campsites:	no
Dump station:	yes
Toilets:	flush toilets
Showers:	yes
Group Campground:	Little Island Pioneer Group camp is a primitive campground
Semi-Modern Group Center:	New York Point Group Camp has a dining hall with facilities, a woodstove, craft building, and tent campsites
	maximum capacity is 100 people
	minimum of 20 is required
	available from the third weekend in May through the third weekend in September

TRAILS

Hiking Trails:	16 miles
Hiking Club Trail:	6.2 miles, starting at the picnic area
Biking Trails:	7 miles
Cross-country Ski:	8 miles
Warming house:	yes
Snowmobile Trails:	7 miles
Horse Trails:	no
Horse Campsites:	no

INTERPRETIVE PROGRAMS

On Big Island there is the Owen Johnson Interpretive Center, which maintains exhibits on natural history and the history of the area. Naturalists offer various seasonal programs, so visitors should check the bulletin boards for schedules.

Myre Big Island State Park

LEGEND

TRAILS

···········   Hiking
—·—·—   Interpretive

FACILITIES

? Information/Office
P Parking
Picnic Area
Interpretive Center (Owen Johnson)
Trailer Sanitation Station
Group Center (New York Point)
Primitive Group Camp (Little Island)
Campground
Backpack Campsite

SCALE

Albert Lea Lake

Great Marsh

PARK ENTRANCE

Myre-Big Island State Park   Photo by author

NEARBY PLACES TO VISIT

Albert Lea Community Theater - Albert Lea, 507-373-8593
Albert Lea Convention and Visitor's Bureau - Albert Lea, 800-345-8414, 507-373-3938
Albert Lea Story Lady Doll & Toy Museum - Albert Lea, 612-377-1820
Albert Lea Travel Information Center - Glenville, 507-448-3311
Freeborn County Historical Museum & Pioneer Village - Albert Lea, 507-373-8003
George A. Hormel Home - Austin, 507-433-4243
Hormel First Century & Spam Museum - Austin, 800-444-5713, 507-437-4563
Jay C. Hormel Nature Center - Austin, 507-437-7519
Lake Louise State Park - Le Roy, 507-324-5249
Le Sueur Cty History Society Museum - Elysian, 507-267-4620, 507-362-8350
Mower County Historical Center - Austin, 507-437-6082, 507-433-8150
W. W. Mayo House - Le Sueur, 507-665-3250

OUR NOTES

Date visited   What we liked
_____
_____
_____
_____
_____

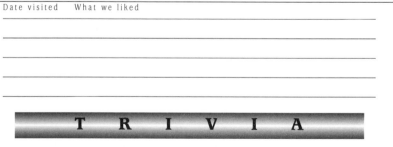

T R I V I A

Blue Earth is home to the statue of the Jolly Green Giant.
It stands 55.5 feet, weighs in at 8,000 pounds and has a shoe size of 78.

Nerstrand Big Woods
9700 170th St E
Nerstrand, MN 55052
507-334-8848

DIRECTIONS

The park is located 11 miles southeast of Northfield on Highway 246.

ABOUT THE PARK

Nerstrand Big Woods was established in 1945 and contains 1,131 acres. The park contains a remnant of the hardwood forests that once covered about 5,000 acres of the area. The first settlers created wood lots in five to ten acre parcels to protect their wood supply. During the 1930s, many of these wood lots were cut down. In the early 1940s, local residents wanted to protect the remaining woods and worked to create a state park.

Prairie Creek flows through the park, so visitors can hike to Hidden Falls and see picturesque waterfalls and examples of the limestone bedrock. Part of the park is used as a hardwood experimental station for the University of Minnesota.

IF YOU GO . . .

Come for a hike! The woods are spectacular any time of year, but plan on a hike either in the spring or the fall. From the picnic area, a short hike leads to Hidden Falls, from which miles of hiking are possible. The wildflowers and Prairie Creek's falls are a spring highlight and the fall colors of these hardwood trees makes a second trip necessary.

NERSTRAND BIG WOODS STATE PARK

FACILITIES

Visitor Center: seasonal Visitor Center
Picnic Area: yes

RECREATION

Children's play area: playground in the picnic area
Volleyball court: yes
Horseshoe pits: yes
Swimming: no
Fishing: no
Boating: no

CAMPGROUND

Campsites: 52 drive-in campsites
Electric: 28 electric campsites
Bike or carry-in: 13 walk-in campsites
Canoe campsites: no
Dump station: yes
Toilets: flush toilets
Showers: yes
Group Campground: primitive group campground

TRAILS

Hiking Trails: 13 miles
Hiking Club Trail: 2 miles, starting at the main parking lot
Biking Trails: no
Cross-country Ski: 8 miles
Warming house: yes
Snowmobile Trails: 5 miles
Horse Trails: no
Horse Campsites: no

INTERPRETIVE PROGRAMS

There are seasonal interpretive programs available in the park. Check with the park headquarters or bulletin boards for schedules.

NERSTRAND BIG WOODS STATE PARK

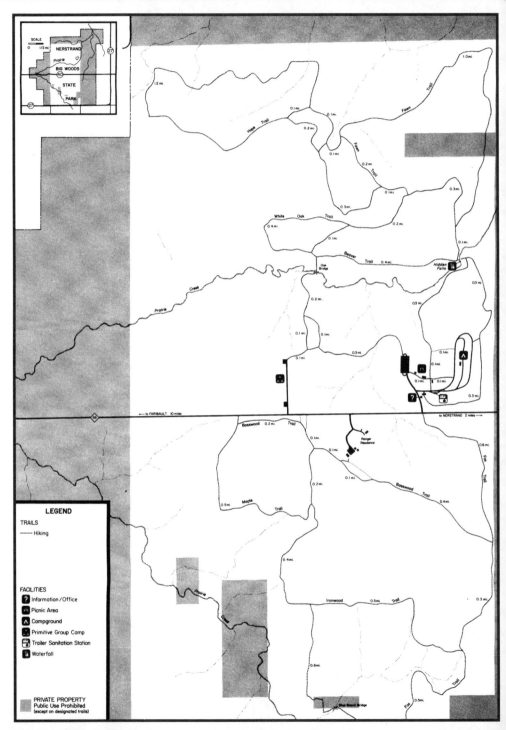

SCALE
0   1/2 mi.

NERSTRAND
Prairie Cr.
BIG WOODS
STATE
PARK

1.2 mi.

Hope   Trail
0.1 mi.
0.2 mi.
0.1 mi.

Fawn   Trail
1.0 mi.
0.1 mi.
0.2 mi.
Trail
0.1 mi.
0.3 mi.

White   Oak   Trail
0.4 mi.
0.1 mi.
0.3 mi.
0.2 mi.
0.1 mi.

Beaver   Trail   0.4 mi.
Oak
Bridge
Hidden
Falls

Prairie   Creek
0.3 mi.
0.2 mi.
0.3 mi.
0.1 mi.
0.1 mi.
0.3 mi.
0.1 mi.
0.1 mi.
0.1 mi.
0.1 mi.
0.1 mi.
0.1 mi.
0.1 mi.
0.3 mi.

← to FARIBAULT   10 miles
to NERSTRAND   2 miles →

Basswood   0.2 mi.   Trail
0.1 mi.
Ranger
Residence
0.6 mi.
Fox
Trail
0.1 mi.
0.2 mi.
0.1 mi.
Basswood   Trail
0.4 mi.
0.5 mi.   Maple   Trail

0.4 mi.
Prairie
Creek
Ironwood   0.5 mi.   Trail
0.3 mi.

0.6 mi.
Blue Beech Bridge
Fox   0.5 mi.
Trail

LEGEND

TRAILS

------- Hiking

FACILITIES

? Information/Office

Picnic Area

Campground

Primitive Group Camp

Trailer Sanitation Station

Waterfall

PRIVATE PROPERTY
Public Use Prohibited
(except on designated trails)

Photo by Dudley Edmondson

NEARBY PLACES TO VISIT

Alexander Faribault House - Faribault, 507-334-7913, 507-332-2121
Gunderson House - Kenyon, 507-789-6329, 507-789-6123
Northfield Area Chamber - Northfield, 800-658-2548, 507-645-5604
Northfield Historical Museum - Northfield, 507-645-9268
Rice County Historical Society Museum - Faribault, 507-332-2121
Zumbrota Covered Bridge - Zumbrota, 507-732-7318

OUR NOTES

Date visited   What we liked

_____

_____

_____

_____

The Dwarf Trout Lily is only found in Nerstrand Big Woods.

Rice Lake State Park
RR 3 Box 45
Owatonna, MN 55050
507-451-7406

DIRECTIONS

The park is located 7 miles east of Owatonna on County Road 19.

ABOUT THE PARK

Rice Lake State Park was created in 1963 and contains about 1,060 acres. There were well used trails in the area when the first settlers arrived, so it is thought that prehistoric people frequented the lake for the wild rice growing in it. In the 1870s a water-powered mill was constructed here, but even with dams to enhance the water level the mill would periodically have to be shut down. In the late 1850s the town of Rice Lake was established, but it disappeared when the railroads bypassed the town. All that remains of the town is the Rice Lake Church, built in 1857, located on the northern border of the park.

Rice Lake, the headwaters of the Zumbro River, is very shallow with marshy shores, making for great wildflowers and bird watching.

IF YOU GO . . .

Bring your binoculars! Rice Lake State Park is an excellent place to watch the spring and fall bird migrations. This is the only sizable lake in the vicinity, making it an attractive place for birds to stop and rest.

RICE LAKE STATE PARK

FACILITIES

Visitor Center: no
Picnic Area: picnic area on Rice Lake

RECREATION

Children's play area: available in the picnic area
Horseshoe pits: yes
Volleyball courts: no
Swimming: swimming beach on Rice Lake
Fishing: no
Boating: drive-in boat access to Rice Lake

CAMPGROUND

Campsites: 42 drive-in campsites
Electric: 16 campsites
Hike or carry-in: 5 walk-in campsites
Canoe campsites: 5 canoe in campsites
Dump station: yes
Toilets: flush toilets
Showers: yes
Group Campground: primitive group campground

TRAILS

Hiking Trails: 4 miles
Hiking Club Trail: 2.4 miles, starting at the picnic shelter
Biking Trails: no
Cross-country Ski: 4 miles
Warming house: yes
Snowmobile Trails: 2.5 miles
Horse Trails: no
Horse Campsites: no

INTERPRETIVE PROGRAMS

There are seasonal interpretive programs available in the park. Check with the park headquarters or bulletin boards for schedules.

RICE LAKE STATE PARK

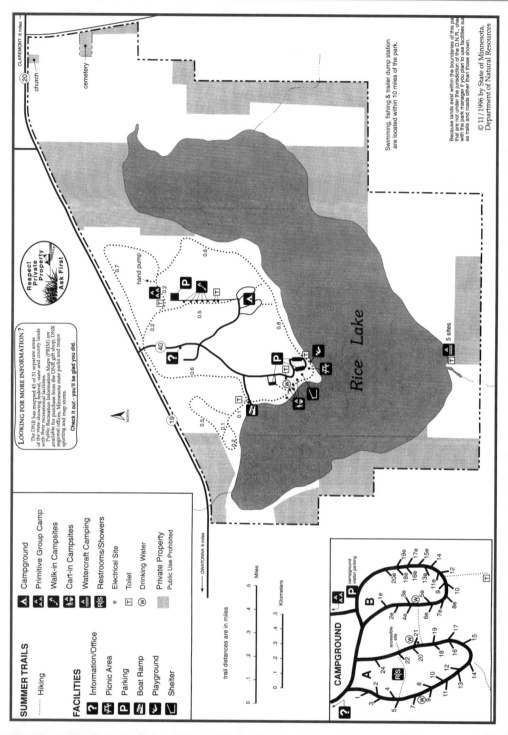

Respect Private Property — Ask First

NORTH

CLAREMONT 8 miles

20

church

cemetery

hand pump

Rice Lake

40

19

?

5 sites

OWATONNA 8 miles

Swimming, fishing & trailer dump station are located within 10 miles of the park.

Because lands exist within the boundaries of this park that are not under the jurisdiction of the D.N.R., check with the park manager if you plan to use facilities such as trails and roads other than those shown.

© 11/1996 by State of Minnesota, Department of Natural Resources

LOOKING FOR MORE INFORMATION?

The DNR has mapped 45 of 51 separate areas of the state showing federal, state and county lands with their recreational facilities.

Public Recreation Information Maps (PRIM) are available for purchase from the DNR gift shop, DNR regional offices, Minnesota state parks and major sporting and map stores.

Check it out - you'll be glad you did.

SUMMER TRAILS

...... Hiking

FACILITIES

- ? Information/Office
- 🏕 Picnic Area
- P Parking
- Boat Ramp
- Playground
- Shelter

Campground

Primitive Group Camp

Walk-in Campsites

Cart-in Campsites

Watercraft Camping

R/S Restrooms/Showers

e Electrical Site

T Toilet

W Drinking Water

Private Property
Public Use Prohibited

trail distances are in miles

0 .1 .2 .3 .4 .5 Miles

0 .1 .2 .3 .4 .5 Kilometers

CAMPGROUND

P campground visitor parking

accessible site

A

B

1 3 5 7 9 11 13 14 16 18 20 22 24
4 8 10 12 15 17 19
2e 4e 6e 8e 10 12 14 15e 17e 19e
1e 3e 5e 7e 9 11e 13e 16e 18e 20e

?

R/S

W

T

Ring-billed Gull   Photo by Dudley Edmondson

NEARBY PLACES TO VISIT

Alexander Faribault House - Faribault, 507-334-7913, 507-332-2121
Dodge County Historical Society Museum - Mantorville, 507-635-5508
Gunderson House - Kenyon, 507-789-6329, 507-789-6123
Kaplan Woods Parkway - Owatonna, 507-455-0800
Nerstrand Big Woods State Park - Nerstrand, 507-334-8848
Owatonna Convention/Visitor's Bureau
    Owatonna, 800-423-6466, 507-451-7970
Rice County Historical Society Museum - Faribault, 507-332-2121
Village of Yesteryear - Owatonna, 507-451-1420

OUR NOTES

Date visited   What we liked

T R I V I A

In Minnesota there are 65 Rice Lakes, 118 Long Lakes, and 201 Mud Lakes.

Sakatah Lake State Park
RR 2 Box 19
Waterville, MN 56096
507-362-4438

DIRECTIONS

The park is located 14 miles west of Faribault on Highway 60.

ABOUT THE PARK

Sakatah Lakes State Park was established in 1963, and contains 842 acres. The park is located where the prairie and woods meet, and offers a remnant of Minnesota's "big woods."

Adjacent to the park is an abandoned railroad bed that has become park of the Sakatah Singing Hills Trail, which is great for biking, hiking, and snowmobiling.

IF YOU GO . . .

Bring your bike! The Sakatah Singing Hills Trail goes through the park. The trail is 39 miles long, running between Mankato and Faribault.

SAKATAH LAKE STATE PARK

FACILITIES

Visitor Center:	seasonal interpretive/Visitor Center
Picnic Area:	yes

RECREATION

Children's play area:	yes
Horseshoe pit:	no
Volleyball courts:	yes
Swimming:	swimming beach on Sakatah Lake
Fishing:	fishing on Lake Sakatah
Boating:	drive boat access to Lake Sakatah

CAMPGROUND

Campsites:	63 drive-in campsites
Electric:	14 electric campsites
Hike or carry-in:	no
Canoe campsites:	no
Dump station:	yes
Toilets:	flush toilets
Showers:	yes
Group Campground:	primitive group campsite

TRAILS

Hiking Trails:	5 miles
Hiking Club Trail:	2.2 miles, starting just south of the Trail Center
Biking Trails:	42 miles
Cross-country Ski:	5 miles
Snowmobile Trails:	42 miles
Horse Trails:	no
Horse Campsites:	no

INTERPRETIVE PROGRAMS

There are seasonal interpretive programs available at the nature center.

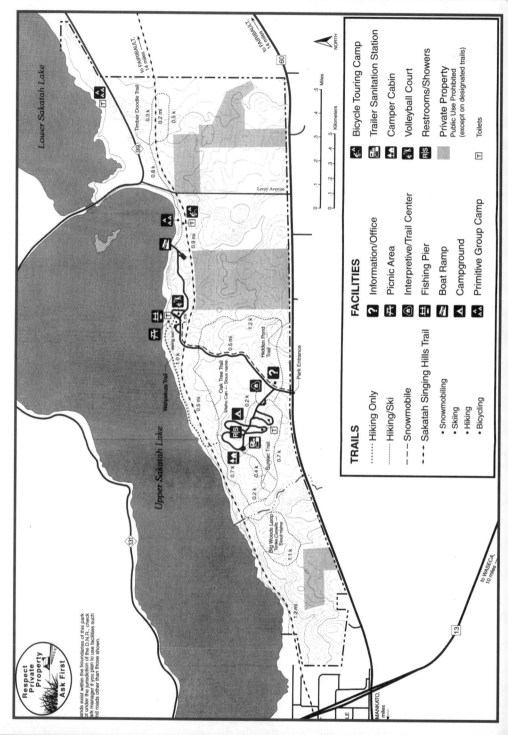

Sakatah Lake State Park
Photo by author

NEARBY PLACES TO VISIT

African Sports and Museum - Mankato, 507-386-1548
Alexander Faribault House - Faribault, 507-334-7913, 507-332-2121
Blue Earth County Historical Society - Mankato, 507-345-5566
Kaplan Woods Parkway - Owatonna, 507-455-0800
Le Sueur Cty History Society Museum - Elysian, 507-267-4620, 507-362-8350
Mankato Convention/Visitor's Bureau - Mankato, 800-657-4733, 507-345-4519
MN Valley Regional Library-Maud Hart Lovelace Collection - Mankato, 507-387-1856
Nerstrand Big Woods State Park - Nerstrand, 507-334-8848
Owatonna Convention/Visitor's Bureau - Owatonna, 800-423-6466, 507-451-7970
R. D. Hubbard House - Mankato, 507-345-5566
Red Jacket Trail - Mankato, 507-387-8627
Rice County Historical Society Museum - Faribault, 507-332-2121
Sakatah Singing Hills State Trail - Mankato, 612-296-6699
Village of Yesteryear - Owatonna, 507-451-1420

OUR NOTES

Date visited   What we liked

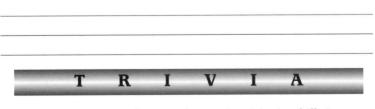

T R I V I A

Sakatah is a Dakota work meaning "singing hills."

Whitewater State Park
RR 1 Box 256
Altura, MN 55910
507-932-3007

DIRECTIONS

The park is located 3 miles south of Elba on Highway 74.

ABOUT THE PARK

Whitewater State Park was created in 1919 to protect 1,656 acres of beautiful wooded land. The park is situated in a deep valley with limestone bluffs that rise above the valley floor.

This area was inhabited by a branch of the Dakota long before settlers ever came to the area. The Dakota named the Whitewater River for the milky white color of the water in the spring

Poor farming and soil conservation practices led to the erosion and flooding of the area, until new conservation measures were implemented in the 1940s. Despite these efforts, occasional flooding still occurs. The park benefited from the Civilian Conservation Corps (CCC), and offers some fine examples of their building skills. During World War II, the park was home to a prisoner of war camp

Today, visitors can hike along the bluffs to scenic overlooks and enjoy the wildlife.

IF YOU GO . . .

Come for the scenery! Whitewater River flows through a beautiful valley. From the campground, head across the river along Coyote Point Trail for some spectacular views. Be sure to check out Coyote Point, and then follow the Dakota Trail back down to the road to enjoy the swimming beach. After a swim, head back to the campground.

WHITEWATER STATE PARK

FACILITIES

Visitor Center: yes
Picnic Area: 2 picnic areas with an open shelter

RECREATION

Children's play area: yes
Volleyball courts: yes
Horseshoe pits: yes
Swimming: swimming beach with changing rooms
Fishing: fishing on the Whitewater River
Boating: no

CAMPGROUND

Campsites: 2 campgrounds
                         total of 106 drive-in campsites
Electric: no
Hike or carry-in: 4 hike-in campsites
Canoe campsites: no
Dump station: yes
Toilets: flush toilets
Showers: yes
Group Campground: primitive group campsite
Modern Group Center: group center at Whitewater
                         7 barracks that sleep 18 people
                         staff quarters for 6 people
                         central sanitation building, dining hall and
                         kitchen, and athletic fields
                         maximum capacity in the summer is 132
                         three of the barracks are winterized with a
                         winter capacity of 60
                         minimum of 50 people required

TRAILS

Hiking Trails: 10 miles
Hiking Club Trail: 2.2 miles, starting at the Visitor Center
Biking Trails: no
Cross-country Ski: 5 miles
Snowmobile Trails: no
Horse Trails: no
Horse Campsites: no

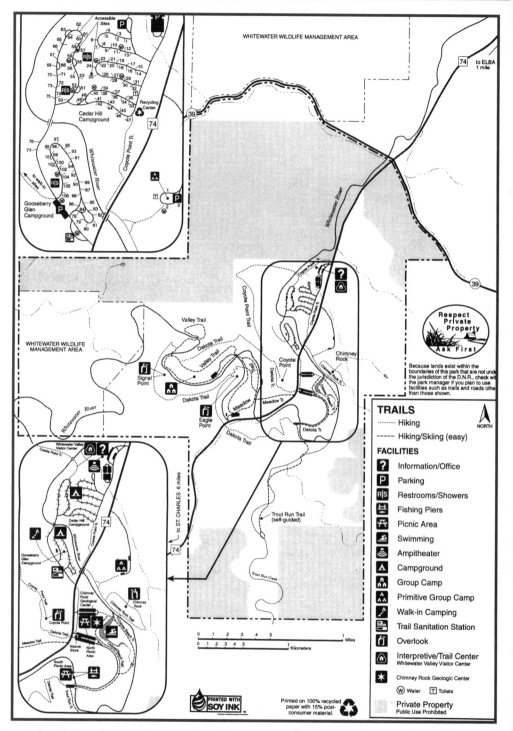

TRAILS
- .... Hiking
- - - - - Hiking/Skiing (easy)

FACILITIES
- **?** Information/Office
- **P** Parking
- **R|S** Restrooms/Showers
- Fishing Piers
- Picnic Area
- Swimming
- Ampitheater
- **A** Campground
- Group Camp
- Primitive Group Camp
- Walk-in Camping
- Trail Sanitation Station
- Overlook
- Interpretive/Trail Center
  Whitewater Valley Visitor Center
- **✶** Chimney Rock Geologic Center
- **W** Water **T** Toilets
- Private Property
  Public Use Prohibited

Respect Private Property Ask First

Because lands exist within the boundaries of this park that are not under the jurisdiction of the D.N.R., check with the park manager if you plan to use facilities such as trails and roads other than those shown.

PRINTED WITH SOY INK

Printed on 100% recycled paper with 15% post-consumer material.

Whitewater State Park — Photo by author

NEARBY PLACES TO VISIT

Arches Museum of Pioneer Life - Lewiston, 507-523-2111
Bluffside Park - Winona, 507-452-8550
Bunnell House Museum - Winona, 507-454-2723, 507-454-2723
Douglas State Trail - Rochester, 507-285-7176
Great River Bluffs State Park - Winona, 507-643-6849
Heritage House of Rochester - Rochester, 507-286-9208, 507-282-2682
Olmsted County History Center - Rochester, 507-282-9447
Oxbow Park and Zollman Zoo - Byron, 507-775-2451
Polish Cultural Institute - Winona, 507-454-3431
Rochester Art Center - Rochester, 507-282-8629
Rochester Civic Music - Rochester, 507-285-8076, 507-281-6005
Rochester Convention/Visitor's Bureau - Rochester, 800-634-8277, 507-288-4331
Rochester Repertory Theatre - Rochester, 507-289-1737, 507-289-7800
Whitewater State Park - Altura, 507-932-3007
Winona Convention and Visitor's Bureau - Winona, 800-657-4972, 507-452-2272
Winona County Historical Museum - Winona, 507-454-2723

OUR NOTES

Date visited   What we liked

T R I V I A

Whitewater State Park was once the site of a prisoner of war camp.

PARK	ACREAGE
Afton State Park	1,702 acres
Fort Snelling State Park	3,300 acres
Minnesota Valley Trail State Park	5,490 acres
William O'Brien State Park	1,403 acres

METRO REGION

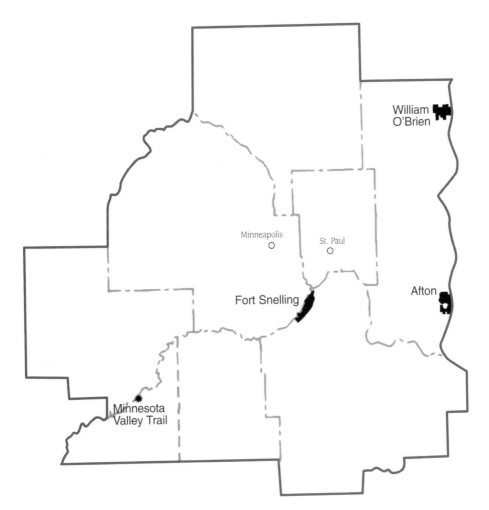

William
O'Brien

Minneapolis
○

St. Paul
○

Afton

Fort Snelling

✹ Minnesota
Valley Trail

✹ Boundries not available

Afton State Park
6959 Peller Ave So
Hastings, MN 55033
612-436-5391

DIRECTIONS

To get to the park entrance, head 9 miles east of St. Paul on Interstate 94 to County Road 15. Take County Road 15 south for 7 miles to County Road 20, then go east for 3 miles.

ABOUT THE PARK

Afton State Park was established in 1969. The park, located just east of the Twin Cities, encompasses 1,702 acres of land along the St. Croix River. The park's many trails cover miles of prairie and forested ravines. Some of these trails are quite rugged, offering a challenging hike or cross-country ski. The swimming beach and lower picnic area are handicap accessible. The park is located next to the Afton Alps ski area, which operates a golf course during the summer. In the fall, the leaves are spectacular and the St. Croix River is a migrating route for hawks and eagles.

IF YOU GO . . .

Come for a hike! There are several areas in the park where the native prairie is being restored. For a fun hike, start at the Interpretive Center, and head south along the short, self-guided interpretive trail. Once you've taken the loop back to the center, head towards the swimming beach, but continue northwest up the bluff. This will lead you to several scenic overlooks and an additional prairie restoration area. The trail eventually circles back to the swimming beach and picnic area.

AFTON STATE PARK

FACILITIES

Visitor Center:
open year round with interpretive displays
and information
serves as a warming house in the winter
can be reserved for group use

Picnic areas:
two, near the river and the Visitor Center

RECREATION

Children's play area:
no

Volleyball court:
at the upper picnic area near the Visitor Center

Horseshoe pit:
yes

Swimming:
swimming beach on the St. Croix River

Fishing:
fishing on the St. Croix River

Boating:
boating on the St. Croix River
no boat access

CAMPGROUND

Campsites:
no

Electric:
no

Hike or carry-in:
24 backpack campsites

Canoe campsites:
1 canoe campsite on the St. Croix River

Dump station:
no

Toilets:
flush toilets

Showers:
no

Group Campground:
2 rustic group campsites

TRAILS

Hiking Trails:
18 miles

Hiking Club trail:
2.5 miles, starting at the Visitor Center

Biking Trails:
4 miles

Cross-country Ski:
18 miles

Snowmobile Trails:
no

Horse Trails:
5 miles

Horse Campsites:
no

INTERPRETIVE PROGRAMS

Interpretive programs are offered in this park, including a self-guided interpretive trail. For more information on program offerings, check at the Visitor Center.

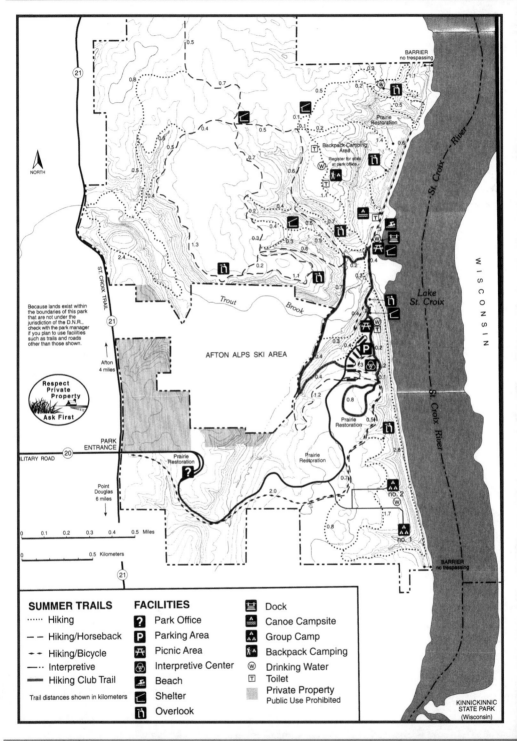

Because lands exist within the boundaries of this park that are not under the jurisdiction of the D.N.R., check with the park manager if you plan to use facilities such as trails and roads other than those shown.

Respect Private Property Ask First

NORTH

Afton 4 miles

PARK ENTRANCE

Point Douglas 6 miles

MILITARY ROAD

AFTON ALPS SKI AREA

Prairie Restoration

Prairie Restoration

Prairie Restoration

Backpack Camping Area
Register for sites at park office

Trout Brook

ST CROIX TRAIL

Lake St. Croix

St. Croix River

WISCONSIN

BARRIER no trespassing

BARRIER no trespassing

St. Croix River

KINNICKINNIC STATE PARK (Wisconsin)

no. 2

no. 1

| 0 | 0.1 | 0.2 | 0.3 | 0.4 | 0.5 | Miles |

| 0 | | | | 0.5 | Kilometers |

SUMMER TRAILS

⋯⋯ Hiking

– – Hiking/Horseback

-•- Hiking/Bicycle

-•-• Interpretive

—— Hiking Club Trail

Trail distances shown in kilometers

FACILITIES

? Park Office

P Parking Area

Picnic Area

Interpretive Center

Beach

Shelter

Overlook

Dock

Canoe Campsite

Group Camp

Backpack Camping

W Drinking Water

T Toilet

Private Property
Public Use Prohibited

Afton State Park   Photo by author

NEARBY PLACES TO VISIT

Hastings Area Chamber of Commerce - Hastings, 612-437-6775, 888-612-6122
Stillwater Depot/Logging & Rail Museum - Stillwater, 612-430-3000
Washington County Historic Courthouse - Stillwater, 612-430-6233
Washington County Historical Museum/Warden's House Museum
    Stillwater, 612-439-5956

OUR NOTES

Date visited   What we liked

First church for white settlers was built in 1841.

FORT SNELLING STATE PARK

Fort Snelling State Park
Highway 5 and Post Road
St. Paul, MN 55111
612-725-2390

DIRECTIONS

The park is located off Highway 5, just below the Minneapolis/St. Paul airport.

ABOUT THE PARK

Fort Snelling State Park is located on the land below historic Fort Snelling. Its location within the Twin Cities metropolitan area makes this park the second most visited in the state. The park now encompasses the lands where the traders and the Indians camped and made their homes. It also includes Pike Island, named for Zebulon Pike, who visited this area in 1805 and negotiated a treaty with the Dakota for a tract of land along the confluence.

Fort Snelling is adjacent to, but not part of the park. Josiah Snelling arrived in 1819 with troops to build a fort. Construction was completed in 1825, and the fort soon became a social and economic hub. As the frontier progressed west, Fort Snelling became a supply depot and training center. The fort was used during World War II to process inductees, and it was given to the Veterans Administration following the war. The Federal Government eventually declared the fort surplus property, and gave it to the State of Minnesota. In 1960 the fort was declared a National Historic Landmark, and turned over to the Minnesota Historical Society in 1969. Since then, the fort has been restored and filled with many worthwhile exhibits.

The Fort is open to the public during the summer, and used for special events during the winter. The picnic area is extremely popular, and is located near the fort's old steamboat landing. There are also some bike trails in the park, which connect to other bike trails along the Mississippi River.

IF YOU GO . . .

Bring your bike! Start at the swimming beach parking lot, and follow the bike trail as it follows the Minnesota River to the Mississippi beneath Fort Snelling. Continue on this trail to Minnehaha Falls, then double back to Pike Island. Bikes are not allowed on Pike Island, but there are bike racks available. Be sure to bike to the Interpretive Center and check out their displays. There is a trail which circles the island, one side along the Mississippi River, and another along the Minnesota River. When you're finished, bike back to the parking lot for a quick swim in Snelling Lake.

FORT SNELLING STATE PARK

FACILITIES

Visitor Center:	Pike Island Interpretive Center, open weekends
Picnic Area:	large picnic area on "Picnic Island"

RECREATION

Children's play area:	yes
Horseshoe pit:	no
Volleyball courts:	yes
Swimming:	swimming and changing areas at Snelling Lake
Fishing:	fishing in Snelling Lake, Minnesota and Mississippi Rivers
	fishing pier on Snelling Lake
Boating:	boat launches into Snelling Lake (electric motors only) and Minnesota River
	portage to Gun Club Lake
	boat rentals

CAMPGROUND

Campsites:	no
Electric:	no
Hike or carry-in:	no
Canoe campsites:	no
Dump station:	no
Toilets:	flush toilets
Showers:	no
Group Campground:	no

TRAILS

Hiking Trails:	18 miles
Hiking Club Trail:	3 miles, starting on Pike Island
Biking Trails:	5 miles
Cross-country Ski:	18 miles
	9 skate/ski trail miles
Snowmobile Trails:	no
Snowshoeing:	snowshoes are available for rental
Horse Trails:	no
Horse Campsites:	no

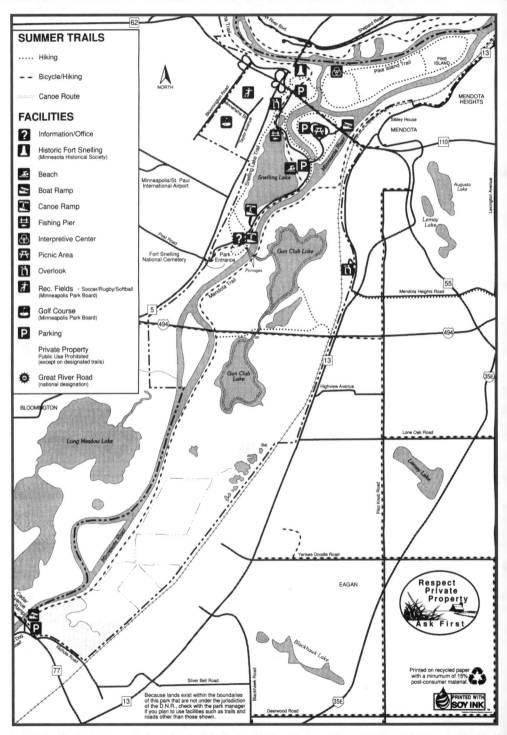

NEARBY PLACES TO VISIT

Alexander Ramsey House - St Paul, 612-296-0100, 612-296-8760
Cathedral of Saint Paul - St Paul, 612-228-1766
Confederate Air Force - South St Paul, 612-455-6942
Dakota County Historical Museum - South St Paul, 612-451-6260
Historic Fort Snelling - St Paul, 612-726-1171
James J. Hill House -St Paul, 612-297-2555, 612-296-8205
Minnesota Air Guard Museum - St Paul, 612-725-5609
Minnesota History Center - St Paul, 612-296-6126, 800-657-3773
Minnesota State Capitol-St Paul, 612-297-3521, 612-296-2881
Pioneer Telephone Museum - St Paul, 612-344-5994, 612-774-5260
St Paul Response Center, Office of Tourism
    St Paul, 612-296-5029, 800-657-3700
Trains at Bandana,Twin City Model Railroad Club - St Paul, 612-647-9628
World Trade Center - St Paul, 612-291-5900

OUR NOTES

Date visited   What we liked

_____

_____

_____

_____

_____

T R I V I A

The first school in Minnesota opened its doors within Fort Snelling in 1823.
Fort Snelling also housed the first hospital and first circulating library.

Minnesota Valley Trail State Park
19825 Park Blvd.
Jordan, MN 55352
612-492-6400

DIRECTIONS

The park is located along the Minnesota River Valley, with its headquarters near Jordan on County Road 57.

ABOUT THE PARK

The Minnesota Valley Recreation Area was created in 1969, with plans for an area that would contain 24,000 acres, including the Minnesota Valley National Wildlife Refuge, and 75 miles of trails. The area currently contains 8,000 acres of land along the lower Minnesota River Valley with approximately 35 miles of trails designated for snowmobiling, hiking, horseback riding, and mountain biking.

The park protects an area rich in history and natural resources. Known to have been home to prehistoric peoples and, more recently, the Dakota, European explorers first came into the area during the latter portion of the 17th century. The area was settled in the 1860s, when the Minnesota River was important to the commerce of the region. But river use dwindled when the railroads came through, and many of the river settlements faded away.

The recreation area is presently comprised of six different areas:

- Lawrence Area: this is where the headquarters and campgrounds are located. Access is from Jordan or Belle Plaine on County Road 57. Visitors can see the only remaining building from the 1850s town of St. Lawrence. Access to the trail systems can be found at the parking lot in the campground. There is an old gravestone along a hiking trail.

- Rush River Area: this is a 300 acre of wooded land along the Rush River. It has a picnic area and some hiking.

- Carver Rapids/Louisville: this portion is located on Highway 169 2 miles south of Highway 41. There are 7 miles of hiking trails. Access to the main trail system is from the north end of the parking lot. There are two canoe campsites located along this portion of the river.

- Gifford Lake: this portion is located just south of Chaska on Highway 41. Fishing at Gifford Lake is only activity here.

- Nyssen's Lake: this portion is also located just south of Chaska on Highway 41. From here access to the main trail system is available.

- Chaska/Shakopee Bike Trail: access to this portion is either from Chaska at the Courthouse Lake (near the Courthouse) or from Shakopee at Memorial Park or Huber Park. The bike trail is paved and 4 miles long. It crosses the Minnesota River on the original railroad swing bridge.

IF YOU GO . . .

Bring your mountain bike, hiking boots, or horse! This trail system provides several places to explore the Minnesota River Valley within a close proximity to the Twin Cities. There are even canoe campsites along the river. Put your canoe in the river just west of Le Sueur and paddle down to Fort Snelling State Park. This way, you can explore the river as the explorers did 150 years ago.

FACILITIES

Visitor Center:	no
Picnic Area:	yes, available for group use

RECREATION

Children's play area:	no
Volleyball courts:	no
Horseshoe pits:	no
Swimming:	no
Fishing:	fishing on Beason Lake or the Minnesota River
Boating:	boating and canoeing on the Minnesota River
	drive-in and carry-in access to the river

CAMPGROUND

Campsites:	25 drive-in campsites at the Lawrence area
Electric:	no
Hike or carry-in:	8 walk-in campsites
Canoe campsites:	1 canoe campsite
	5 canoe or hike-in campsites
Dump station:	no
Toilets:	pit toilets
Showers:	no
Group Campground:	primitive group campground

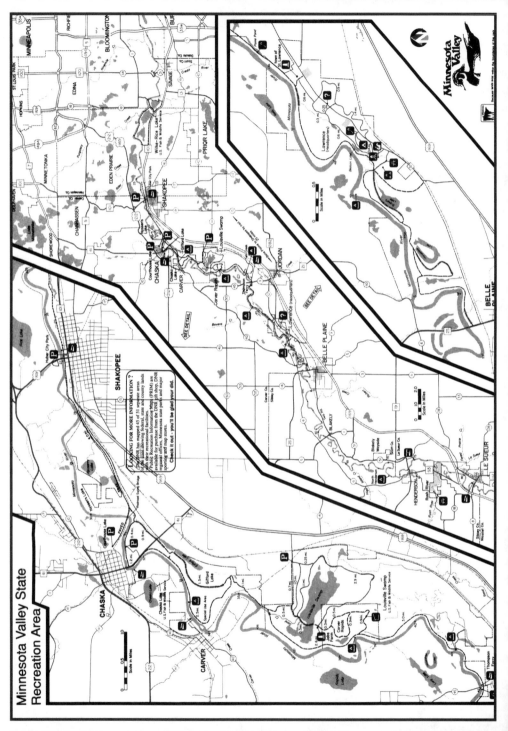

TRAILS

Hiking Trails:	4 miles
	access to 35 miles of hiking
Hiking Club Trail:	4 miles, starting at the Trail Center
Biking Trails:	6 paved miles at the Chaska/Shakopee area
	35 miles of mountain bike trails
Cross-country Ski:	4 miles
Warming house:	yes
Snowmobile Trails:	access to 34 miles
Horse Trails:	access to 31 miles
Horse Campsites:	can make use of group campground

INTERPRETIVE PROGRAMS

There is not an interpretive program available at the park.

NEARBY PLACES TO VISIT

Historic House with 2 Story Outhouse - Belle Plaine, 612-873-6109
Historic Murphy's Landing - Shakopee, 612-445-6900, 612-445-6901
Historical Episcopal Church - Belle Plaine, 612-445-0378
Scott County Historical Society/Stans Historical Center - Shakopee, 612-445-0378
Shakopee Minnesota Valley Nat'l Wildlife Refuge - Bloomington, 612-335-2323

OUR NOTES

Date visited   What we liked

T R I V I A

The Minnesota River Valley at some places is
five miles wide and 300 feet deep.

William O'Brien State Park
16821 O'Brien Trail N
Marine on St. Croix, MN 55042
612-433-0500

DIRECTIONS

The park is located 2 miles north of Marine on St. Croix on Highway 95.

ABOUT THE PARK

William O'Brien State Park was established in 1945, with the gift of 180 acres to the state by Alice O'Brien. Her father, William O'Brien, was a logger who bought up much of the St Croix River front land after it was logged during the mid 19th century. Before the loggers, the Dakota and, later, the Ojibway Indians inhabited the St. Croix River Valley.

Its proximity to the Twin Cities makes this a popular park. So popular, in fact, that it is current rently experiencing overuse. Highway 95 intersects the park, and land has been added west of the highway. The park is now a haven for wildlife and a variety of vegetation.

IF YOU GO . . .

Plan for fun! Head down to the park on the east side of Highway 95, and park at the picni area, which offers a fine swimming beach on Lake Alice. Canoe rental is available for you to paddle out onto the St. Croix River and circumnavigate Greenberg Island.

WILLIAM O'BRIEN STATE PARK

FACILITIES

Visitor Center: year round Interpretive Center
Picnic Area: picnic area along the St. Croix River

RECREATION

Children's play area: yes
Volleyball courts: yes
Horseshoe pits: yes
Baseball field: yes
Swimming: swimming beach on Lake Alice
Fishing: both lake and river fishing
Boating: drive-in boat access to the St. Croix River
     canoe rental and shuttle service

CAMPGROUND

Campsites: 125 drive-in campsites
Electric: 62 electric campsites
Bike or carry-in: no
Canoe campsites: 1 campsite
Dump station: yes
Toilets: flush toilets
Showers: yes
Group Campground: primitive group campsite

TRAILS

Hiking Trails: 12 miles
Hiking Club Trail: 6 miles, starting at the Interpretive Center
Biking Trails: 2 miles
Cross-country Ski: 11.5 miles
Warming house: yes
Snowmobile Trails: 1 mile
Horse Trails: no
Horse Campsites: no

INTERPRETIVE PROGRAMS

The Interpretive Center and trail center are open year round, offering naturalist programs and activities. Visitors should check the bulletin boards for schedules. The center also has exhibits and displays regarding the cultural and natural history of the park.

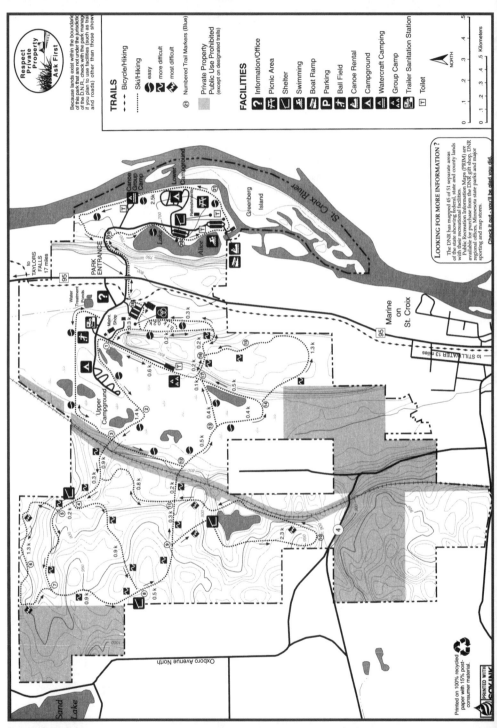

Respect Private Property — Ask First

Because lands exist within the boundaries of the park which are not under the jurisdiction of the D.N.R., check with the park management if you plan to use facilities (such as trails and roads) other than those shown.

TRAILS

- - - Bicycle/Hiking
▪▪▪ Ski/Hiking
easy ● / more difficult ■ / most difficult ◆

㉗ Numbered Trail Markers (Blue)

Private Property
Public Use Prohibited
(except on designated trails)

FACILITIES

- ? Information/Office
- Picnic Area
- Shelter
- Swimming
- Boat Ramp
- P Parking
- Ball Field
- Canoe Rental
- Campground
- Watercraft Camping
- Group Camp
- Trailer Sanitation Station
- T Toilet

NORTH

0 .1 .2 .3 .4 .5 Kilometers

LOOKING FOR MORE INFORMATION?

The DNR has mapped 45 of 51 separate areas of the state showing federal, state and county lands with their recreational facilities.

Public Recreation Information Maps (PRIM) are available for purchase from the DNR gift shop, DNR regional offices, Minnesota state parks and major sporting and map stores.

Check it out — you'll be glad you did.

St. Croix River

Greenberg Island

Canoe Group Camp

Lower Campground

Lake Alice

2.5k

PARK ENTRANCE

to TAYLORS FALLS 17 miles

95

Water Treatment Ponds

Maint. Shop

Upper Campground

Marine on St. Croix

95

to STILLWATER 13 miles

Oxboro Avenue North

Sand Lake

Bald Eagles   Photo by Dudley Edmondson

NEARBY PLACES TO VISIT

Fillebrown House - White Bear Lake, 612-426-0479
Hay Lake Museum - Scandia, 612-433-5972
Historic Corners Museums - Scandia, 612-433-5972
Interstate State Park - Taylors Falls, 612-465-5711
Stillwater Depot/Logging & Rail Museum - Stillwater, 612-430-3000
Stone House Museum - Marine on St Croix, 612-433-2061
W H C Folsom House - Taylors Falls, 612-465-3125
Washington County Historic Courthouse - Stillwater, 612-430-6233
Washington County Historical Museum/Warden's House Museum
    Stillwater, 612-439-5956

OUR NOTES

Date visited   What we liked

*The Minnesota state park sticker was introduced
in 1958 as a way to provide revenue for the parks.*

INDEX